The Endangered Sector

THE
ENDANGERED
SECTOR. ▶▶▶▶▶▶▶

WALDEMAR A. NIELSEN

COLUMBIA UNIVERSITY PRESS
New York   1979

COLUMBIA UNIVERSITY PRESS
NEW YORK   GUILDFORD, SURREY
COPYRIGHT © 1979 BY COLUMBIA UNIVERSITY PRESS
ALL RIGHTS RESERVED
PRINTED IN THE UNITED STATES OF AMERICA

LIBRARY OF CONGRESS CATALOGING IN PUBLICATION DATA

NIELSEN, WALDEMAR A
  THE ENDANGERED SECTOR.

  INCLUDES BIBLIOGRAPHICAL REFERENCES AND INDEX.
  1. ENDOWMENT—ECONOMIC ASPECTS—UNITED STATES.
2. CORPORATIONS, NONPROFIT—UNITED STATES.
3. PLURALISM (SOCIAL SCIENCES)   I. TITLE.
HV95.N46   338.4'7'001440973   79–15772
ISBN 0–231–04688–X

Contents

Preface

THE PRESENT STUDY is a continuation of my work on nonprofit institutions in American life. In an earlier volume, *The Big Foundations* (New York: Columbia University Press, 1972), I concentrated on one small but significant subspecies, the private philanthropic bankers of the business. But because the interactions between foundations and other institutions in our society are so many and so important, I was led to extend my research to the entire nonprofit field and, beyond that, to the interrelationships between the nonprofit sector and the other major elements of the American pluralistic system. This volume is the result.

Nonprofit institutions are extraordinarily numerous and diverse and they play a particularly important role in our democracy. Yet for all that, they remain to a remarkable degree unfamiliar and unstudied. Anything resembling comprehensive and reliable information about them is simply unavailable. One can readily find ample data about the structure and economics of the chemical fertilizer industry, for example, but that concerning cultural institutions, churches, and charitable organizations is both flimsy and fragmentary. Even more lacking is any set of analytical concepts by which to try to understand and evaluate these curious but crucial institutions.

It has therefore been necessary to piece together such information as could be found, to strip some of it of a self-serving and romanticized overlay, to fill certain gaps with my own impressionistic judgments, and to construct as I went along aome tentative theories by which to interpret this patchwork of evidence. My hope is that this crude first effort to break the ground may at least encourage others to plow it more deeply and thoroughly.

My object in writing about the nonprofit sector at this time, however, has not been purely scholarly. It is visibly in decline and in serious difficulty, and my primary purpose has been to identify the most threatening of the problems confronting it, to trace their underlying causes, and to suggest some remedies.

I shall give detailed attention to five of its major subsectors —higher education, basic science, health, culture, and social action—because they span and illuminate most of the major and often contrasting afflictions besetting subparts of the nonprofit sector as a whole. This short list necessarily omits some important institutional categories, most obviously the churches and private social welfare agencies. A word of explanation in this regard may be in order.

The churches still form the largest single body of voluntary associations in American society, though there remains much dispute as to whether or not their membership is slipping. To the extent they are suffering from the effects of inflation, lessened giving, and demographic shifts, their problems are similar to those of most other nonprofit institutions. To the extent, however, that they are suffering from the effects of the secularization of American life, and from turmoil among their membership over ethical and doctrinal issues—ranging from abortion to egalitarianism—these are matters well beyond the scope of the present study.

Private social welfare agencies represent the strong and still vigorous base of the tradition of voluntarism and private charity in the United States. They number in the tens of thousands, from neighborhood day care centers to the United Ways to the Red Cross. They are in fact so numerous and diverse that they cannot be dealt with in a summary chapter as if they constituted a reasonably homogeneous subsector. Or so at least it has seemed to me.

One other apparent omission calls for comment. In the recommendations for action presented in the latter chapters, I have made only brief reference to the inefficient and incompetent management of many nonprofit institutions and to their frequently antiquated procedures and outdated priorities. These are indeed important deficiencies which must be addressed more forthrightly and energetically than their governing boards have generally been inclined to do. But for purposes of the present analysis, the main emphasis in the proposals for action had to be given to an even more serious range of problems, namely those of assuring an adequate flow of financial resources to the nonprofit sector generally and of protecting its autonomy and diversity in the face of an increasingly complicated and dependent relationship with government.

I would like to express my appreciation to Dr. Reynold Levy and Dr. Martin Kaplan, who were of great help both in the design of the study and in the research involved, and to the Rockefeller Brothers Fund which generously provided funding. The Center for Policy Research at Columbia University efficiently and responsibly administered the grant and provided various supporting services.

To the Aspen Institute for Humanistic Studies, of which I am a Fellow, I owe a very special debt. Its various programs have as their common theme the more just and effective governance of democratic societies. Joseph Slater, the president of the Institute, and the dozens of outstanding individuals from many countries and areas of experience who are brought together in its seminars, have greatly enriched my understanding of the role of nonprofit institutions in broad historical, comparative, and philosophical terms.

Finally, there are two individuals who have deeply affected my ideas about what will here be called the Third Sector and whose indirect contribution to the substance of this study I must acknowledge. The first is John Gardner, former Secretary of the Department of Health, Education and Welfare and founder of Common Cause, who is surely the most original and constructive thinker, and the most eloquent and persuasive writer, on this fundamental aspect of our pluralistic system. The second is the late John D. Rockefeller 3d, whose entire life, until his untimely death in mid 1978, was dedicated to philanthropy and the general advancement of educational, scientific, cultural, and voluntary organizations. He was unique in the scope and the consistency of his concern for these institutional embodiments of private initiative and of individual responsibility for the general welfare. His example and encouragement have been most important to me during what otherwise would have been a rather lonely quest.

WALDEMAR A. NIELSEN

New York
May 30, 1979

The Endangered Sector

I
THE DISLOCATION
OF THE AMERICAN SYSTEM

1 ▶▶▶▶

The Sector Nobody Knows

LIKE CAESAR'S GAUL and most other things, the structure of the American pluralistic system can be divided into three parts: There is government. There is the economy. And there is something else, whose boundaries are ambiguous, whose substance is amorphous, whose nature is elusive, and which may be the most distinctively American element of all.

It consists of that vast array of institutions and associations—colleges, the churches, voluntary hospitals, philanthropic foundations, symphony societies, scientific research centers, and multitudes of other entities, both permanent and transitory—whose common characteristics are that they are private, do not operate for profit, and are devoted to serving the general welfare—not simply the welfare of their members or supporters. For this huge element in our national life, there is not even an accepted name. It is an anonymous realm. For want of some better term I shall call it the Third Sector.[1]

To the extent that it functions well, the Third Sector adds important qualities of diversity, creativity, and responsiveness to the American system. To the extent that it functions badly, or eccentrically, the Third Sector throws another powerful, destabilizing force into the social machinery. Currently it is functioning badly and is in serious and growing difficulty, the result of a sweeping process of transformation and erosion. But word of what is happening to it rarely breaks into the media or enters the mainstream of political discussion. So this great calamity proceeds, so far at least, unrecognized and in silence.

The Unseen, but Considerable, Presence

That something of the scale of the Third Sector could continue to pass almost unnoticed is extremely curious, for in fact it constitutes even in quantitative terms a considerable part of what James Madison called our "compound Republic." Private nonprofit institutions eligible to receive tax deductible gifts have annual outlays of more than $80 billion. They own some 10 percent of all property in the United States and by some estimates employ about that same proportion of the working population. Perhaps more significant, some 40 million Americans make substantial contributions of time or money, or both, to them every year.[2] These are not inconsiderable numbers, but they are only crude and incomplete indications because so little is known about this sprawling territory, and so little has it been studied, that there does not exist even a reasonably accurate count of the number of entities involved. Some 400,000 of them are registered with and accorded tax privileges .by the Treasury Department. In addition it is estimated that there are two to three million functioning private nonprofit groups and associations (some guess the total is closer to seven million!) of a less formal nature.[3]

Size, however, is the least measure of the Third Sector: the more important is what it does and what it represents. The direct functions which the component institutions and associations perform are plain and familiar; they teach, they cure, they engage in the search for new knowledge, they entertain, they preach, they agitate for reforms. They operate in that large sphere of life which does not center on power and authority or on the production and acquisition of material goods and money. They embody the countervalues and complementary beliefs of our competitive, capitalistic, materialistic, egalitarian culture.[4]

In providing outlet and expression for the human needs that government, the army, the office, the store, the factory, and the farm cannot satisfy, the institutions and voluntary associations of the Third Sector perform a still deeper, and less readily understood, range of functions: They are instrumentalities of cultural continuity (historical societies, Ukrainian Saturday schools, and ethnic social clubs) seeking to preserve and transmit traditional values. They are a primary means by which many people escape the barriers and compartments limiting their personal fulfillment (the NAACP, the National Organization of Women). They are a major vehicle of social integration (the numerous immigrant associations that have sprung up successively among the Germans, the Irish, the Jews, the Italians, the Slavs, the Puerto Ricans, helping to satisfy their craving for affiliation).

They are a seed-bed for new social forms and modes of human relations exemplified by the avant garde and the "counter culture." They are the source from which new ethical standards by which to measure institutional performance arise and from which the periodic outbursts of reformism in public life spring. They are the living laboratory of esthetic, spiritual, and intellectual innovation. They represent the sense of mystery, wonder, and the sacred; they offer the old forms of worship as well as new forms of consciousness-raising and spirituality. They provide means for countervailing definitions of reality and morality. They channel and encourage the impulse to altruism.

They therefore exist in a sense in the interstices of the structures of authority and materiality, and most of their products are essentially intangible, as unmeasurable as compassion, inspiration, or dissent. Which may help to explain why the Third Sector has remained an invisible presence, a kind of Holy Ghost of the American Trinity.

Attitudes toward it, or toward specific parts of it, vary in the extreme. Some social planners see it as simply anachronistic and inadequate to cope with the needs of the times; some conservatives venerate the traditional elements—the churches and the museums, for example—but see the growing number of new activist groups as dangerous and disruptive to the stability of the society; some young activists consider most nonprofit institutions as elitist and old hat but are passionately committed to their own newer groupings. Yet tens of millions of Americans, to judge by their actual patterns of behavior, are directly involved with one or more nonprofit institutions, as donors, volunteers, or members. For some, such involvement may be casual. But for most, their church or alma mater or scientific society embodies social or cultural or spiritual values that are personally precious. For not a few they even represent what makes life worth living, death worth facing, and the country worth defending.

Articulation, Interaction, and Complementarity

If the Third Sector is vitally important to individuals, it is not less so, though for different reasons, to the proper functioning of the other components of the entire American pluralistic system. Though it is convenient to discuss them as discrete elements, its major sectors are not sharply separated but blend into each other and overlap. Where the Third Sector overlaps the profit-making sector are such hybrids as proprietary hospitals; the many training centers and research institutes financed and operated by business corporations; and cooperatives and mutual insurance companies, which are nonprofit in legal form but which serve primarily the interests of their own members or policy holders.

Where the Third Sector overlaps government are those many undertakings which are private and nonprofit in form—such as the Rand Corporation, the Corporation for Public Broadcasting, and the network of "federally funded research and development centers"—but which have been created by government and are controlled by it. The flexibility, adaptability, and complexity of American pluralism is nowhere more clearly manifested than in this luxuriant profusion of institutional creations, all categories of which interact with the others.

The economy, as Eli Ginzberg and others have demonstrated, depends heavily on the other sectors to produce the goods and services demanded by the market. The prosperity of the automotive industry has long depended on an expanding national highway system, which is to say government. The advanced technology and service industries that are the "growing edge" of the economy depend heavily on the manpower trained in and the research done in the colleges and universities of the nonprofit sector.[5] They also depend, in some cases, on a high and predictable level of government contracts.

The interaction of the economy with the other sectors is in fact essential to the continued existence of a market system. Adam Smith argued that the unfettered operation of the market and unrestrained pursuit of individual self-interest would not only maximize wealth but would produce as byproducts social justice, benevolence, and stability. But most contemporary economists would call Smith's "invisible hand"—if unrestrained by ameliorating social and political influences—an "invisible fist" that would ultimately smash a pure market economy to bits. In the words of Arthur Okun, "Capitalism and democracy are really a most improbable mixture. Maybe that is why they need each other—to put some rationality into equality and some humanity into efficiency."[6]

The way this is accomplished, in the view of economic theorist Kenneth Boulding, is in large part via the nonprofit sector. According to him, in the United States as in all advanced capitalistic nations, a vast "grants economy" encompassing 20 percent to 50 percent of all transactions operates parallel to the venerated "exchange economy." Without this symbiotic and indispensable element, the economy would quickly develop "conditions which would be widely recognized as pathological. It would be deficient in public goods, it might easily produce distributions of income which will be regarded as unacceptable, and if carried to extreme, it might destroy . . . that minimum sense of community and maintenance of order which is necessary to sustain exchange."[7]

For the political system as well, the existence of a vigorous Third Sector is an essential mediating and corrective mechanism. The civil rights movement, the student rebellion and the anti-Vietnam-war movement, consumerism, environmentalism, women's liberation, the public interest law movement, and many others provide dramatic examples. Born in recent decades they have by now profoundly affected government policy and the structure and processes of government as well. Indeed, in this interplay between Third Sector initiatives and the political and governmental establishment much of the history of the post-World War II period has been written. John Gardner, former Secretary of HEW and the founder of Common Cause, describes the relationship in these words:

Very few—almost no—major policy innovations are enacted at the federal level that are not preceded by years (say 3 to 10 years) of national discussion and debate. The national dialogue is an untidy but impressive process. Ideas that will eventually become the basis for some major innovation in federal policy are first put into circulation by individuals and small groups. . . . They provide the first formulations of the problem and are the first to sound the alarm. In short, they're "the first birds off the telephone wire". . . . Their job is to put their issue (abolition of slavery, child labor, the vote for women, the environment, fiscal responsibility, etc.) on the national discussion agenda and move it as far up the list of priorities as possible. . . . The national dialogue that precedes action is *primarily a private sector responsibility*, particularly in its early stages. The private sector has the pluralism, looseness, and free-market characteristics necessary to let a hundred ideas bubble up, sift the ones that speak to the condition of the times and let the rest evaporate.[8]

Without the opportunity for such manifestations of citizen initiative—outside the usual channels of parties and politics when those become blocked—the American political system would progressively lose its resilience and ultimately destroy its own legitimacy.

None of which is to contend that the Third Sector is more important or more indispensable than the other major sectors. But it is to assert that it is an important and necessary element in the arch and architecture of the American system. The various elements together help provide for constitutional order and authority, material well being, freedom, and the diversity and quality of national life. No part can stand alone; the collapse of any major sector has to radically affect the whole. And one part of that complex, delicately balanced structure, the Third Sector, is now unmistakably beginning to weaken.

The Eroding Financial Foundations

The most apparent and immediate problem private nonprofit organizations confront is financial insolvency. It is a complicated one because of short-term fluctuations and longer-term trends in the American economy, and because of still more fundamental shifts in social attitudes and in the relationship of government to all private institutions, profit and nonprofit alike.

The latter, in their objectives and principles of operation, are noneconomic—even anti-economic—institutions. But they must nonetheless struggle to exist in the real economic world, somehow obtaining the resources they require and balancing their budgets. Their ability to do this and to continue to operate as private, independent entities has always rested on a rather fragile combination of factors—traditions (of charitable giving and religious practice), intangibles (from sentimentality to civic spirit), privileges (principally fiscal), and the general state of the nation (especially a vigorously growing national economy). All these underpinnings are now weakening, and the remaining years of the century are going to be a cruel test of survival.

Nonprofit institutions are going into that difficult period in wobbly condition, having just been on quite a roller coaster ride. The 1950s and 1960s were a boom period, a time of increasing college enrollments and of increasing government outlays for scientific, educational, and social programs. The securities markets were buoyant, lifting the value of endowments. Giving by individuals and corporations as well as the level of foundation grants steadily increased. New facilities were built, staffs expanded, salaries rose, and the nonprofits were flushed with prosperity.

By the early 1970s, the bust had come. Double-digit inflation, falling security markets, and cutbacks of government spending struck Third Sector agencies with damaging force, both in their expenses and their income. By the mid 1970s, such examples as the following were regularly reported by the press:

The Ford Foundation, the largest in the field, announced plans to cut its outlays, which had reached the rate of $300,000,000 per year in the late 1960s, to a sustained level of $100 million by the late 1970s.

"The financial situation of Princeton University has changed suddenly and dramatically," stated a 1975 report to the trustees. Even with a $625 increase in tuition, room, and board, there is "no hope of a balanced budget for 1975–76." Although Princeton has the resources to absorb deficits in the *short* run, it has reached "the point where we must consider sharply curtailing, or even dropping, entire activities in the academic and supporting areas."

The American Historical Society, after a survey of prospects in the academic job market, concluded that only one of ten new PhD's in history could expect to find regular employment in that profession.

The labor costs of many, particularly those in the health field, will probably continue to rise, particularly as unionization of previously low paid employees becomes more pervasive. The massive and continuing movement of women into the work force, and the consequent decline in the availability of volunteers for many social-service institutions, further intensifies this pressure on their payrolls. Their tax bills, too, will grow as government increasingly funds social services and human resources programs through levies on employment; in effect private nonprofit institutions will pay an increasing portion of their income into social security and other government trust funds for the benefit of their employees. Their costs of compliance with proliferating government regulations—such as providing special facilities for the handicapped—will continue to rise. Their energy costs, already heavy, will also progressively increase.

More basically, a number of economists now believe that labor-intensive nonprofit institutions functioning in the context of an industrialized economy with steadily increasing productivity are bound to fall further and further behind in their financial position. Industrial enterprises can offset increasing labor costs by mechanization and technological innovation; but it will always take four musicians to play a quartet.[9]

On the income side, there has been a persistent decline in the propensity of Americans to make charitable gifts. The United States Treasury found that charitable giving by taxpayers dropped from 3.47 percent of adjusted gross income in 1956 to 2.10 percent in 1970—a decline of some 40 percent. Dr. Ralph Nelson, using a somewhat different measure, found that in the twelve-year period from 1960 to 1972, giving by individuals, as a proportion of personal income, dropped by about 15 percent—from 1.97 percent to 1.67 percent. The American Association of Fund Raising Counsel, in the most recent data available, reports that total private giving as a percent of Gross National Product fell from 1.98 percent in 1969 to 1.80 percent in 1974.

Within these broad trends it appears that religious giving has slumped more than contributions in general. Also, gifts by individuals in the $10,000 to $25,000 income range have fallen more sharply than those by wealthier persons.[10] Since religious institutions receive almost half of all private gifts, and since middle-income families provide more than half the total private giving, these particular declines are especially significant. Indeed, the whole relationship of religious belief and organized religion to the American tradition of voluntarism, social service, and support for the Third Sector has been little studied but is obviously of great importance. The United States for most of its history has been an intensely religious nation and many of its nonprofit institutions are religious in origin—not only churches but also colleges, welfare agencies, hospitals, and reformist groups. Whether the tradition and the Sector it helped produce can survive in an increasingly secular age remains to be seen.

To some extent the decline of private giving may also be the result of changes in the tax law detrimental to charity—some deliberate and some inadvertent. In the hearings on the 1969 Tax Reform Act for example it became clear that as part of a gathering "taxpayers' revolt' increasing public antagonism had begun to develop toward incentives for charitable giving because of a belief that they provided an inequitable loophole of benefit primarily to the wealthy. In the legislation which resulted, the tax benefits accorded to certain kinds of charitable gifts, particularly gifts of appreciated property, were reduced, as they were to gifts to particular kinds of institutions, notably private foundations.

But the greatest damage to the flow of charitable gifts from tax law changes has been an unintended side effect of measures designed for other purposes. The so-called "standard deduction" in the income tax (an automatic lump sum deduction in lieu of itemized evidence of charitable gifts and certain other deductible expenditures) was introduced in order to simplify the tax forms and to ease the administrative burdens on the Internal Revenue Service. But its impact on the Third Sector has been very costly because, in effect, the full deduction is available to nonitemizers whether or not they have given anything to charity. Five extensions in the scope of the deduction in the last decade have decreased the proportion of taxpayers itemizing their deductions from almost 50 percent in 1970 to less than 25 percent today. Because of these increases in the use of the standard deduction, various studies estimate that charities have lost about $5 billion in contributions. In 1977 alone the loss was more than $1.3 billion. The Carter Administration's 1979 tax reform proposals, if passed, will further reduce the proportion of taxpayers itemizing their deductions to an estimated 16 percent, adding further to the attrition of charitable giving.[11]

The problems facing the Third Sector of balancing heavier expenses and shrinking income in the years ahead will be greatly aggravated by still another factor—the necessity to adjust to major demographic and geographical shifts now underway. Because of a steep decline in the birth rate, which began in the 1960s, the number of college age students from now until the end of the century will decrease, which in turn will require great program and financial adjustments by institutions of higher education. The increasing proportion of the population which is elderly will impose costly new demands on health-related institutions. Most important of all perhaps in terms of the future capital requirements of the private nonprofit sector is the huge population movement out of the central cities to the suburbs, and regionally from the Northeast to the so-called Sunbelt.[12] These shifts mean a drain of higher-income families away from locations where the bulk of private cultural, educational, religious and welfare institutions have historically been located into areas in which they are relatively lacking.

The American landscape is now strewn with the physical evidence of this evolution: churches in central cities much of whose membership (and traditional base of support) has now moved away; private voluntary hospitals whose traditional clientele (and source of support) has now departed, to be replaced by a new clientele made up largely of the poor and racial minorities; and private universities like Chicago, Columbia, and Yale which once existed in stable and affluent neighborhoods but which now find themselves surrounded by urban decay. Numerous comparable examples can be found of private secondary schools, symphony halls, and art museums which have been stranded, financially and otherwise, as a result of these patterns of migration.

For these private nonprofit institutions "left behind," so to speak, in central cities and in the Northeast, there is the prospect not only of growing operating deficits in the future but also the need for huge new amounts of capital in order to make possible the adaptation of their old facilities to the needs of their new clientele. For the suburbs and the Sunbelt, there is the need to build a new set of facilities at massive cost, which will absorb much of the private energies and resources which formerly were devoted to the support of the old infrastructure.

Among other consequences, the geographical redistribution of the American population now taking place imposes serious strains on the ties between older private nonprofit institutions and their constituents and contributors. Although Harvard, Princeton, and Stanford will continue to receive the financial support of their alumni, wherever those alumni are eventually located, the same is not true for most private colleges, nor for cultural institutions, hospitals, and other welfare agencies.

The diversity within the private nonprofit sector is so great that some categories of institutions may be in far less difficulty than others. Nevertheless the overall economic, physical, and legislative evidence is consistently disquieting; nonprofit institutions go into the last two decades of the century with mostly aging and often mislocated facilities, their financial reserves are seriously depleted, their costs are rapidly going up, and their income from private sources is declining. Even the privileges and encouragement they have traditionally received from government seem to be eroding. Inflation has had ruinous effects upon them already, and in the slow growth and inflationary economy of the future, which is now generally anticipated, and with the heavy new demands likely to be made upon them, nonprofit institutions are on the whole facing a grim and relentless financial struggle to survive. Or, more precisely, to survive as reasonably autonomous private factors.

The Onset of Government

Through most of American history government has been an active partner and financier of the Third Sector to a much greater extent than is commonly recognized. But in the last decades of the nineteenth century and the first decades of the twentieth, many Third Sector institutions—in addition to the churches—developed private sources of support and simultaneously an ideology of separateness which affected the policies of both private agencies and government. In sharp contrast to their previous attitudes the private agencies became disdainful of public funding, and the government came to consider grants of public money to private institutions improper if not unconstitutional. But increasingly over the past 40 years the older pattern of collaboration and public funding has been resumed. Private organizations have dropped their inhibitions and have eagerly, sometimes desperately, turned to government for support. And government, faced with urgent new responsibilities, has been willing, sometimes eager, to provide that funding in order to make use of their capabilities. The result is that the interdependence of the two sectors is now more extensive than ever before, and this interdependence can be, and has been, interpreted in various ways—as a means of financial salvation for many private agencies; as a great boon to government; as a pathway by which educators, scientists, and others can penetrate and exercise influence upon the policies of government; or as a dangerous process that will destroy the autonomy of the Third Sector by converting it into a hired agent, an appendage of the apparatus of government. But there is unanimity on at least one point: the trend is part of a historic expansion in the role of government which has been powerfully underway for much of the twentieth century. The thrust of that evolution is far from spent. Indeed, its pace in many fields is accelerating. In 1940, the Federal budget was $9.5 billion; by 1960 it was $92 billion; President Carter's proposed budget for 1979 was over $500 billion.

At certain periods during World War II, for example, or in the Cold War years, a sharp rise in military costs was the principal cause of the increases. More important overall, however, has been the sustained growth of expenditures for social programs: mainly education, social welfare, and health. The bulk of the increases in social expenditures has been used to enlarge and extend the direct operations, staffs, and facilities of government itself—Federal, state, and local. This growth, institutionally speaking, has not taken place in empty territory. Rather, it has typically occurred in fields already populated more or less densely with private agencies. They have as a result either been displaced or run over, or they have had to adapt themselves to the presence of a huge and sometimes highly aggressive new neighbor. Thus the creation of the Peace Corps in the first months of the Kennedy Administration brought into being a valuable new program, and at the same time extinguished a number of smaller private efforts of the same character which were its predecessors.

More often, the result of the advent of new or enlarged government operations has not been the sudden demise of adjacent private institutions but rather a gradual undercutting of their viability. The most conspicuous example of this has occurred in higher education. During the 1950s and 1960s, a rapid expansion of state-supported colleges and universities took place. So long as the total number of students entering college continued to rise, the viability of private institutions was not seriously affected, especially since they were also benefiting from increased government funding of various kinds. But with the more recent levelling off in the growth of the student population, with reductions in government grants and contracts, and with the general economic downturn, many private schools with fees of $3000 to $7000 per year have found themselves competing at a heavy disadvantage for their share of the available supply of students. The competition comes from state institutions charging tuition of only a few hundred dollars and offering newer and better facilities. Spokesmen for the private schools now contend that for many it will be impossible to continue in that unequal contest for very long. So far, very few four-year institutions have actually been forced out of existence, but in a sample of 90 private institutions studied in 1975–76, about one-third were judged to be losing ground in the financial struggle.[13]

Although the bulk of the increased resources of government has been used to create its own facilities and to support its own direct operations, a considerable part has been used to fund and obtain goods and services from private agencies. To gauge the full effects of this upon the beneficiaries—or victims—is exceptionally difficult because of the organizational complexities and the financial magnitudes involved. At the Federal level alone, dozens of agencies and hundreds of pieces of legislation come into play—the Departments of HEW, Defense, Labor, Agriculture, Energy, and others; the National Science Foundation, NASA, the Veterans Administration, the National Endowments for the Arts and the Humanities, and others. Many operate in the same fields; some 14 agencies are major funders of research and development. Many deal with the same clientele; at least 12, for example, provide substantial assistance to minorities. Sixty different agencies administer some 375 separate programs supporting some activity in higher education.

Moreover, the means by which governmental funds are distributed are many. The Federal government in 1979 transferred some $85 billion in grants to state and local governments, which in turn used a part of the money for grants and to purchase goods and services from private organizations, both profit-making and nonprofit.[14] The extravagant variety of such transfers is suggested by the case of John Wood Community College in Quincy, Illinois. It is a publicly supported phantom institution, with no buildings and no faculty. Its students pay their tuition to it but then attend classes at one or more of the five private colleges in the area which have contracts with John Wood for teaching them. In addition, the Federal government uses a sizable portion of the funds it spends directly in the same way. Its purchases of goods and services from private suppliers, profit and nonprofit, totalled some $81 billion in 1977 ($57 billion for defense purposes, $24 billion for nondefense).[15]

Because the flow of Federal, state, and local government funds into the private sector—and more specifically into the private nonprofit sector—derives from so many sources and is channeled via so many meandering streams and rivulets—and even some underground springs—no complete data are available. But the crude numbers which have so far been assembled suggest that, overall, government now provides at least one third, and more likely about one half, of all the funds used by the institutions of the Third Sector other than the churches (whose religious functions government is, of course, constitutionally barred from supporting).

In the mid-1970s, the total outlays of private nonprofit organizations, excluding churches, were on the order of $80 billion. Of this total, $25 billion came from private gifts and philanthropy; $23 billion came from government grants, contracts, and purchases of goods and services; and $32 billion from fees, service charges and endowment income. But of the latter, a considerable part of the "earned income" came indirectly from government, as in the case of indigent hospital patients whose fees are reimbursed under Medicaid and of those college students whose tuition is provided under one government scholarship program or another.[16]

Because of the pattern of concentration, government funding is of decisive importance in several major fields. Private centers of basic scientific research are the most heavily dependent, receiving 80 to 90 percent of their resources from government. In the health field, voluntary hospitals receive 40 percent or more of their income directly or indirectly from government; private medical schools receive a still-higher proportion. Private welfare agencies vary greatly in this regard, some receiving the bulk of their funding in the form of government grants and contracts while others are largely supported by private gifts. Private colleges and universities rely on government overall for about one-third of their income, although some of the largest research-oriented institutions greatly exceed this proportion. Cultural institutions now receive 15 to 20 percent of their resources from government. Least dependent are the social-action movements, which in most cases receive no official funding.*

Despite the inadequacies of available data, at least two major

---

* The limitations of these estimates must be emphasized. They are principally based on information about the flow of Federal funds; much less is known about state and local distributions. Also, they do not include the assistance provided to nonprofit organizations in the form of exemptions from income, property, or other taxes.

facts are clear: First, the persistent idea that the United States has parallel and largely independent structures of private and public institutions in higher education, scientific research, health care, and welfare services is a myth. Instead, it has a publicly financed and operated system in each field, and an intimately intertwined, privately governed sector which is heavily dependent on government funding. Thus, leading liberal arts institutions like Stanford, Harvard, Columbia, Chicago, and Yale are now from one-third to one-half financed by national government. In technically oriented institutions like MIT and Cal Tech, this degree of dependence is well over half. Woods Hole, the great private center of research in marine biology, receives 90 percent of its income from government. The Federation of Jewish Philanthropies in New York City raises some $25 million a year in private contributions but it spends more than $700 million annually on its programs, the difference—consisting of more than 95 percent of its income—derives from government. Nor are these unusual examples. The churches, many cultural institutions, and the social action movements remain largely independent. But it is the interrelationship and interdependence of government and the rest of the Third Sector—not their separate existence—which is the dominant reality.*

Second, as a direct consequence of their financial dependence, Third Sector institutions have become entangled in an increasingly dense web of government rules and requirements and have lost a large degree of control over their own policies, procedures, and programs. This is an obvious development, logically to have been expected. Yet the process of many small, incremental steps by which it has occurred and the extent to which it has now advanced are not commonly appreciated.

The instruments by which the relationship between government and a private agency is defined are formal grant agreements

---

* Alan Pifer, head of the Carnegie Corporation, in the late 1960s discovered and described a subspecies of the Third Sector which he called "Quasi non-governmental organizations." These were, by his definition, legally private but created and financed largely by government to serve public purposes as instruments of government. He predicted that other private organizations, by their growing dependence on government funds, might be moving toward this halfway position between privateness and publicness. His perception was right but his timing was wrong. Even when he wrote, a very large part of the Third Sector was already at that point.[17]

or contracts.* These pieces of paper are typically long and detailed, indicating not only the tasks to be performed and the payments to be made—but also the reports to be prepared, the financial and "performance" audits to which the contractor must submit, and the various personnel, clearance, and arbitration procedures to be followed.

These seemingly reasonable and necessary provisions have led to a profusion of petty but altogether burdensome difficulties. Many medium and larger size nonprofits have grants or contracts with a number of official agencies, each with its particular reporting requirements and with its own voluminous rules and regulations. The result for the private institution can be an endless drudgery of paperwork and administrative disputes.

Even more objectionable, however, than the direct operational requirements placed on the private institutions in connection with the project or activity being supported are the broader, less defined requirements imposed by the numerous pieces of social legislation with which a recipient of government funds must comply—legislation relating to the elimination against women, minorities, and the aged; to the protection of the environment; to raising standards of occupational health and safety; and to many other purposes including the suppression of child labor and of inhumane methods of animal slaughter. The sheer expense of complying with such regulations is considerable. A recent study of the American Council on Education concluded that institutional costs for implementing federally mandated social programs had increased ten to twenty times in the past decade and now total hundreds of millions of dollars annually.

A still more serious complaint against these sweeping mandates is the threat they pose to what is seen as institutional autonomy and integrity, because they apply official strictures to an entire institution if *any* project or program receives Federal support. In the words of Kingman Brewster, former president of Yale, the government, "having bought the button, now feels it has the right to design the coat." Under legislation banning sex discrimination,

---

* At one time there was a difference between "grants" and "contracts"—the former being less restrictive and specific in the obligations imposed on the private recipient. But in practice these distinctions have become obliterated and the terms can now be used interchangeably.

for example, schools with government contracts or grants are now subject to government scrutiny and supervision over all their athletic programs and facilities, placement programs, student financial assistance, and housing arrangements both on and off campus, in addition to their policies regarding the hiring of professional and other staff.

This "dangerously fashionable" tendency to "use the leverage of the government dollar to accomplish purposes which have nothing to do with the purposes for which the dollar is given" has led, in Brewster's view, to raw, "smoking gun" political abuses: the effort of the Nixon Administration to withhold funds from MIT for vindictive political motives, for example, and the attempt by the Armed Services Committee of the House of Representatives a few years ago to divert contracts from colleges and universities which had terminated their ROTC programs.[18] Beyond that, according to Derek Bok, president of Harvard, this new pattern of government actions strikes directly "at the central academic functions of colleges and universities," diminishing initiative and experimentation, threatening the diversity of the system, and undermining the authority and responsibility of faculty and trustees.[19]

There is of course a government side, and a strong one, to this argument. Given the great and growing scale of government funding of the private sector, officials of the executive branch are under strong Congressional pressure to negotiate and police their contracts with care. Much past experience has taught some painful lessons; private agencies can be extravagant and wasteful almost without limit, as many examples have shown, and they have repeatedly demonstrated not only their willingness but their extraordinary ingenuity in taking advantage of government in their financial dealings. Nor have defense contractors and profit-making corporations necessarily been the worst offenders. Universities, hospitals, scientific laboratories, and welfare agencies consistently attempt to cover not only their direct costs but also to ease the general financial strains upon them through their contract revenues; and now that those strains are increasing, government contract officers and auditors feel they must be more alert than ever in controlling abuses.

As to the costs and inconveniences imposed by the general requirements of new social legislation, the government view is that nonprofit institutions, like all others, should be required to obey the law. Their financial difficulties should not excuse them from compliance with environmental requirements, for example, nor their old institutional habits from complying with equal employment opportunity standards.

What is indisputable, however, is that the influence of government upon private nonprofit institutions has become immeasurably greater than ever before. It now sets the priorities for the nation's scientific laboratories, as it determines the extent of access to medical care, as it controls, through the power of its purse, that part of the income of educational and welfare institutions which decisively shapes their growth and character.

The Old Liberal Consensus

The expansion everywhere of state-managed or state-directed societies was the most crucial and obvious political fact about the third quarter of the twentieth century. In the United States, for at least the past 40 years, a broad liberal consensus has existed in favor of greater government responsibility for welfare, education, scientific research, higher education—and now culture—and also for greater governmental influence over the policies and performance of private nonprofit institutions.

That consensus has been the sum of three converging lines of thinking: the realistic, the managerial, and the ideological. The realistic view looks at basic facts. The major episodes of recent history—the New Deal, World War II, the Cold War, and the so-called Revolution of Rising Expectations—have, according to this perspective, simply made the decline of the private nonprofit sector and the increase of government power and responsibility inevitable. In purely practical terms, during the Depression there was no way for private welfare agencies alone to meet the social needs of the time; there was no way that the scientific and technological requirements of modern warfare could have been met by privately financed institutions; and, in more recent years, there was no way for the surge of demand for educational opportunity and health care to have been met by charity.

For private resources to be generated in the volume needed for such vast national undertakings would assume a concentration of wealth in the upper classes which would be intolerable, as well as a degree of philanthropic and patriotic impulse on their part which would be unimaginable.

The managerial view provides the justification of rationality for what has occurred. From this perspective, the costs of meeting the military and social requirements imposed on the American government both by external circumstances and internal political pressures require large, comprehensive, administrative structures, planned and coordinated programs, and effective allocation of available resources on the basis of some coherent system of priorities. Without this, defense budgets, or welfare budgets, or health budgets, would quickly become insupportable. Thus, small, duplicative, and badly distributed private agencies and programs operating independently are both inadequate to the needs and intolerably wasteful. As sentimental relics they may remain in existence for a time longer, but in fact, according to this view, they have been overtaken and bypassed in the onrush of events.

The third line of justification, and the most widely influential of all, is ideological. It is the case for the modern welfare state— that in a developed western society like the United States it is no longer acceptable for most of the population to have to depend for their vital needs in education, health, scientific research, and social assistance on the benevolence of a wealthy few. Rather, those needs are best provided through government as the accountable and responsible instrument of the citizenry. It is the dignified, participatory, equitable, democratic way. Charity, for all its sweetness, is a hangover of another time and other values.

These are not just hypothetical positions. Some or all are rooted in the attitudes of many, possibly most, Americans and confirmed by their own experience. Large and powerful segments of American society have effectively pressed their claims for civil rights, jobs, educational opportunity, social insurance, and health services through the political process and the structures of government. And they continue to believe that it is their best available avenue for achieving their social and economic objectives. By comparison, the private nonprofit sector seems both inconsequential and inaccessible. To many millions of people—not only the poor and disadvantaged but organized labor and much of rural America—the Metropolitan Opera, the Ivy League colleges, and quite often the local private hospitals are not symbols of freedom and diversity but of elitism and discrimination. Institutions far more relevant to their lives and responsive to their needs are the public schools, Social Security, and the state land-grant colleges.

The Emerging Confrontation

But now, that consensus has begun to crumble. Among many who are still inclined to believe that government should be the great vehicle of social progress, there is spreading doubt whether it is up to the task. Doubts even more profound than those about the competence of government have been generated by the War on Poverty, Vietnam, and Watergate. Although some of the passion aroused by those disasters is now dissipating, they have nevertheless shattered traditional assumptions about the accountability of government and even of its integrity. Some two-thirds of the American public, according to polling data, now classify "big government" as one of the principal threats facing the country.

Such distrust of unrestrained governmental growth and power was once confined largely to the conservative minority. But no more. Ralph Nader and Common Cause, for example, have made government, even more than the large corporation, the target for their demands for openness and responsiveness and for higher ethical standards. The new coalitions forming around these issues are very broad, and they cut through so many familiar political demarcations that the old labels of liberal and conservative are of little application.

These changes are reinforced by others which have taken hold in the realm of social and personal values—an upsurge of concern about the dehumanizing effects of the gargantuan scale of modern institutions; an increased assertiveness on behalf of ethnic, linguistic, sexual, and other kinds of diversity; and increased preoccupation with self-expression and self-realization, accompanied by demands for fewer restraints on individual freedom.

Recent governmental scandals and fiascoes have undoubtedly helped bring these new demands to the surface, but their ultimate causes run far deeper. Rather than being superficial changes in intellectual fashion and public mood, they appear to be responses to profoundly felt problems of alienation, powerlessness, and spiritual hunger resulting from the circumstances of modern urbanized, industrialized, secularized existence. They constitute the ingredients of a new, evolving social and personal ethic widely shared among young and old, rich and poor, college educated and blue collar.[20]

There are of course many paradoxes and obscurities: a new individualism has grown up alongside the continuing thrust of the old collectivism; growing demands upon government have combined with growing doubt and distrust of it. But there is more than a little reason to believe that the era of the untrammeled extension of government has now about run its course and that new forces are arising to check its onrush.

Fortunately or unfortunately, the Third Sector lies directly at the intersection of these great conflicting tendencies. Its destiny depends directly on the outcome of the struggle between those forces which would further centralize and governmentalize the affairs of the nation, and those which seek to maintain decentralization, diversity, and a strong element of private activity, both profit making and nonprofit, as a check on and counterbalance to government.

In this kind of dialectical and political confrontation, however, there cannot in the end be winner or loser, but only accommodation. There is too much validity in the concepts and values represented by both sides, and too many large segments of the population are ranged on each (and in many respects on both) for the outcome to be other than some new synthesis, the shaping of some new balance of policy and practice, some creative adaptation—perhaps in largely new and now barely discernible patterns—of the American system of pluralism to the needs of a new era. If that happens, it will not be the first time, as a review of the experience of the first two centuries of the New Republic will show.

2 ▶▶▶▶

The Folklore of American Pluralism

THE HISTORICAL ROLES and shifting relationships of the parts of the American pluralistic system, difficult enough to comprehend in their natural complexity, are now thickly enshrouded in a retroactively fabricated mythology. Regrettably, this obscures important aspects of the American experience and the American genius. The beclouding myth is essentially this: the sectors of American society are neatly separated and exist in a static, ideologically partitioned relationship to each other, always have been, and ideally always should be. It was the late nineteenth century which gave rise to this piece of simplistic folklore which has ever since confused our vision both of the Third Sector's past and its potential future. The actual story of the convergence, separation, and reconvergence of the public and private sectors, of the shifting balances within the total structure, and of the interplay of intellectual, religious, economic, and social forces upon it is a great deal more dynamic, dramatic, and instructive than the mythology which has been substituted for it. The present extension of government influence upon the Third Sector, seen against the patterns of two centuries of history, is thus a recurrence—an exaggerated recurrence, but not an unprecedented departure. Which makes it more comprehensible but not necessarily less threatening.

The Colonial Coalescence

From our present perspective, the most striking feature about Colonial America was its thorough integration and intermingling of church, state, the economy, and the private voluntary sector. The settlers included an exceptional proportion of religious and political zealots, and their intellectual disputes were suffused with the spirit of the Enlightenment. But their primordial problem was to survive in an alien and dangerous place and, once that had been assured, to build from bare ground the infrastructure of a new society. Their approach to these necessities was in the highest degree pragmatic, and they brought to every task whatever resources were at hand and in whatever combination promised to be helpful.

The Compact made on the Mayflower in 1620 by the devoutly religious Puritans was only the first of many demonstrations. In a single undifferentiated package, it affirmed their faith in God, specified the rules and sanctions by which they would govern themselves, and set forth the framework of a communal economy: land owned in common, work done according to ability, goods distributed according to need.

The experiment soon proved to be a disaster. In the winter of 1622 one-third of the colony starved to death, and Governor Bradford with his chief advisers tried to analyze the reasons. The elimination of property rights and incentives for gain "was found to breed much confusion and discontent and retard much employment that would have been to their benefit and comfort." At length, after much debate, "the Governor gave way that they should set corn every man for his own particular, and in that regard to trust to themselves." The change, they found, "had very good success, for it made all hands very industrious."[1]

Throughout the seventeenth and eighteenth centuries, local governments in the colonies readily "interfered" in the economy by granting monopolistic charters to ferry companies and rights to dam rivers and streams to the builders of saw- and gristmills. They regulated the use of seines as a means of catching fish, determined the "just" value of labor, and frequently fined merchants or craftsmen who overcharged their customers and lenders who extracted more than a "fair" rate of interest from borrowers.

A similar indifference to sectoral boundaries was evident in the methods used to care for the sick, to encourage science, and to create colleges to educate clergymen and others. The private Pennsylvania Hospital, founded in 1751, was able to care for the poor, who made up more than a third of its patients, because the legislature voted it unclaimed dividends of bankrupts' estates and other favors. The American Philosophical Society petitioned the Pennsylvania legislature in 1768 for funds and equipment to assist David Rittenhouse to observe the passage to Venus across the sun the following year—observations on which, it was argued, "the Promotion of Astronomy and Navigation, and consequently of Trade and Commerce, so much depends." The legislature was persuaded and voted the money; at the same time it gave the Society an additional matching grant for encouraging the development of silk culture.[2]

But in no portion of the Third Sector was the fluid interrelation of all interests more clear than in higher education. Consider the New World's first institution of higher learning, Harvard College. It began as a collaboration of church and state; the College was founded when the General Court of Massachusetts Bay Colony— a homogenous, theocratic community of Calvinist Puritans— granted a charter and £400 for the purpose of providing the colony a learned ministry. Rents from the Charlestown ferry were designated part of the College's income. It was also supported by a tax, the "colledge corne": every family was obliged to contribute a peck of corn or a pine tree shilling (or the equivalent in wampum) annually for its maintenance.

The 1650 charter established a mixed form of governance: the internal governing body, the Corporation, was chosen by the college; the local Cambridge community of clergy and magistrates chose the Overseers. Two years later, the commonwealth allotted to the College 800 acres of public land as a source of income; the next year it granted an additional 2000 acres "for the incouragement of Harvard College and the society thereof, and for the more comfortable maintenance and provision for the president, Fellows, and students thereof in time to come." In 1654, the General Court added an annual levy of £100 to aid the College.[3]

Harvard was far from unique in its church-state character. The charter of William and Mary in Virginia in 1693 made the college the beneficiary of a tax on furs and skins; in 1759, it received the receipts of a tax on peddlers. Connecticut Colony in 1712 relieved Yale students of tax and military obligations and shortly after awarded the college an annual appropriation of £100, as well as assigning to it the "avails of a French prize [ship] brought into New London by an armed vessel of the state."[4]

By the time of the revolution these patterns were well established. The role of government, checked only by Englightenment concepts of personal freedom and individual rights, was a comprehensive one—whether in the development of hospitals and almshouses, the encouragement of scientific enterprises, assistance to higher education, or the stimulation and control of the economy. In 1776, the year Adam Smith published his doctrine against governmental intervention in the economy, General Washington complained bitterly that private enterprise could not meet his army's need for manufactured supplies. On January 16, 1777, he therefore ordered the erection of a public factory for casting cannon at Yorktown, Pennsylvania.

The Advent of the Republic

Though the Constitution, adopted in 1789, built high and strong barriers between church and state, mapped the division of executive, legislative, and judicial powers within the Federal government, and marked off the powers reserved to the states, it changed very little in the relationship between government and the private sector, profit and nonprofit. Indeed, in the early decades of the republic, the determination to advance economic development and settle communities across the continent was so strong that the areas of public-private collaboration were steadily extended.

Alexander Hamilton, the first Secretary of the Treasury, in his famous *Report on Manufactures* in 1791, advocated the use of tariffs, bounties, patents, and a great variety of other means of encouraging and protecting new industries. Commercial interests were active in urging commercial treaties, navigation laws, discriminatory tonnage duties, and inspection laws. Agrarian leaders pressed for, and obtained, government aid for their agricultural societies and they persuaded many state legislatures to supply them credit through public loan offices.

The national and state governments, as the westward expansion developed, became major entrepreneurial forces in active partnership with private interests to encourage settlers to migrate, to create new transportation networks, and to set up new industries. Homesteading inducements were offered. Turnpikes were built as collaborative private-public ventures. The grand trunk canal systems were given Federal and state aid. Later, the railroads were built with the help of important concessions by government and with direct state and local government grants of land and money.

To suggest the extent to which "state capitalism" was accepted practice, Pennsylvania after the Revolution embarked on a policy of chartering business corporations. "In some of the corporations which it chartered," as Louis Hartz explains, "it subscribed to and owned as much as half of the stock. A kind of mixed corporation developed: the Auditor General appointed State directors to participate in the board meetings of firms partially owned by the government." Further, to see that the public treasury received its full share of dividends, State legislative committees periodically authorized public audits. "When, in the field of transportation, the mixed corporation failed to satisfy the ambition of an expanding domestic commerce, the government itself embarked upon a vast system of public works. This program involved a total expenditure of more than one hundred million dollars, the construction of a large administrative machinery, and the expropriation of private property for public use. . . . It was accepted almost as a matter of course that the State had the power to license business enterprise, to inspect and impose standards on commodities, to regulate factories, to limit child labor, and to initiate many other controls."[5]

During these same years, the economic theories of men like Adam Smith in Britain and the French Physiocrats had crossed the ocean, and voices were beginning to be raised in behalf of the new idea of *laissez faire.* Benjamin Franklin himself was among these: "I find myself inclined to adopt that modern view which supposes it best for every country to leave its trade entirely free from all incumbrances." But as historian Frederick K. Heinrich has pointed out, these were minority and often contradictory voices: "Every single *laissez faire* theorist was also an advocate of some kind of intervention. . . . It is apparent that the overall picture of American policy was far more interventionist than *laissez faire*. . . . The simple fact is that when our republic was being established, Americans wanted both liberty and control. Each interest campaigned for the particular form of intervention that would help it most, and at the same time decried any interventions that would injure it, while helping someone else."[6]

In the nonprofit field there was even less inhibition to public-private collaboration than in business matters. New hospitals, for example, were built on the basis of a variety of ingenious combinations of philanthropic, religious, and official contribution. Massachusetts General Hospital, founded in 1821, was funded largely by the state government, and only in part by philanthropy. The construction funds for Louisville General Hospital (1823) came from private donations, but the maintenance was financed by a 2 percent auction sales tax and an annual grant from the Federal government; its management was entrusted first to the state of Kentucky, and then to the city. Maryland's government in 1823 took over control of the formerly private University Hospital in Baltimore, and in 1840 the Mississippi government took over the formerly private Natchez Charity Hospital. While the Catholic hospital and nursing movement gained momentum only after 1840, even before that year there were collaborative enterprises with government: Mobile, Alabama, in 1830 and Augusta, Georgia, in 1834 established city hospitals with the intent that Catholic sisterhoods should manage them.[7]

The same unconstrained relation with government also obtained in efforts made for the advancement of science—all of which served highly utilitarian purposes. George Washington's first annual address to Congress contained a plea for the public support of inventions and inventors: "The advancement of agriculture, commerce, and manufacturers by all proper means will not, I trust, need recommendation," he wrote in 1790, "but I cannot forbear intimating to you the expediency of giving effectual encouragement as well to the introduction of new and useful inventions from abroad as to the exertions of skill and genius in producing them at home." This in time was done.

John Quincy Adams's first annual message to Congress in 1825, under the rubric of promoting internal improvements, supported assistance for expeditions to the interior of the continent. Though these were meant primarily to serve military, commercial, industrial, agricultural, and mining interests, the explorers were also carefully briefed on the needs of botanists and zoologists, were urged to bring back appropriate specimens, and on occasion took professional naturalists and academic scientists along with them.

Through the first half of the nineteenth century, this kind of limited, episodic public funding continued. As George H. Daniels in his social history of science in the United States has observed, "Little thought was given to the idea of public support for science per se: it was only specific enterprises that could be viewed as necessary instruments for securing some public purpose which the democratic society could properly patronize."[8]

Even though the amount of public subvention at the time was extremely limited, there was already misgiving on the part of some scientists about the value of it, or at least about the means by which it was dispensed. Louis Agassiz told the new American Association for the Advancement of Science in 1849 that government patronage was "not worth the time consumed in imploring it." All the governments on earth, he said, would not develop as much scientific knowledge "as one humble individual, whose lot is cast in a garret."

In higher education, government funding of privately governed colleges continued—including grants of the Commonwealth of Massachusetts to Williams College, of New York State to Columbia, and of Pennsylvania to the private University of Pennsylvania. But the practice encountered two kinds of increasingly severe obstacles as mid-century approached. First, it was swamped by denominational splits among various religious groups which at the same time were fired with a college-founding fervor. Not less than 700 small sectarian colleges were created in the early decades of the century, all jealous of their individuality, all inadequately financed, and all endlessly petitioning state governments for relief. This the legislatures for political as well as budgetary reasons were less and less disposed to offer, with the result that a good proportion of the newborn institutions quickly expired.

But the more fundamental resistance to the habit of state subsidy derived from rising pressures for the establishment of outright public institutions. Allen Nevins summarizes these under the following headings: (1) Growing criticism of the inadequacy of the classical curriculum followed in the private colleges and growing demand for greater emphasis upon the teaching of science, political economy, history, and modern literature; (2) growing demand for the training of professionals who could contribute to the industrial transformation and expansion of the country, including land surveyors, road builders, and agricultural specialists; (3) the new spirit of regionalism, and the belief that educational institutions should have relevance to the needs of individual states and areas (e.g. Wisconsin and dairy farming); and (4) the spreading commitment to the idea of a universally educated citizenry: Men like Horace Mann and Ezra Cornell believed that "a people who mean to be their own governors must arm themselves with the power that knowledge gives" and they therefore argued that all citizens have the opportunity to acquire education, including higher education, without restrictions of wealth, social class, sex, or religious affiliation.

A state university had been established in Georgia by 1783, and in North Carolina by 1795. By 1801 there were six. Then in 1850, Jonathan Turner put forth a plan for the creation of public colleges throughout the West: "If the farmers and their friends will now but exert themselves, they can speedily secure . . . for each State in the Union, an appropriation of public land adequate to endow in the most liberal manner a general system of popular industrial education."[9] By 1862, this dream was realized in the Morrill Act, which allocated a total of 16,000 square miles of Federal land which the states could sell to create a network of "land grant colleges."

These same public pressures for democratic control over higher education also took the form of demands for greater "accountability" to the people by private colleges receiving public funds. The story of their rise is contained in cameo in the case of Harvard from 1780 to 1850.

In that earlier year, John Adams wrote some clauses in the Massachusetts constitution which continued both Harvard's aristocratic autonomy and its financial privileges, whereupon many Massachusettes towns balked. Middleboro, at its constitutional ratification meeting, demanded that a complete accounting of all funds of any kind "heretofore and now Belonging to Harvard College . . . be given annually to the Senate and House of Representatives in order that it may be fairly known what further privileges or grants are Really Necessary." In the town of Bellingham, the Harvard clauses were defeated, on the grounds that the "Inhabitants have a right to know the Annual Income to and for said University, and how the Same is annually expended, and the want of which has been Greatly Complained of."

While new issues had pointedly been raised, the Massachusetts General Court did not interrupt financial support, awarding the College $10,000 annually from 1814 to 1823. But because the legislature refused to make regular appropriations for the salaries of the president and faculty and confined its payments to an *ad hoc* basis, the College began to turn to men of property for its Corporation members, giving rise to a tradition of dependence on private fund-raising.

Just before the Civil War, a General Court committee—chaired by a Democrat soon to be elected Governor, George Boutwell— issued a report on Harvard which castigated the College for leaving unmet the educational needs of all but an already advantaged few. The College, charged the report, "fails to answer the just expectations of the people of the State"; it called for a more practical curriculum than Harvard's rigid adherence to the classics; it demanded that Harvard be opened to all those who "seek specific learning for a specific purpose"; and it proposed a bill requiring not only that the Harvard Overseers be directly elected by the State House and Senate, but that faculty be paid according to the size of their classes. The bill, sponsored by Boutwell and a coalition of Democrats and Free Soilers, failed to pass. But as one newspaper editorial of the period put it, "Harvard College belongs to the people of Massachusetts and by the grace of God, the people . . . will yet have it and hold it, if not in one way, then in another."

For 200 years the proposition that "Harvard College belongs to the people of Massachusetts" would have been relatively uncontroversial. But in 1850 the Harvard Corporation, in response to the growing challenge to its autonomy, rewrote two centuries of higher education history by declaring that the Massachusetts General Court had given away its controls on the College's governance in the 1650 Charter. In 1855, the Corporation similarly—and again unhistorically—suggested that the Overseers had no legitimate right to confirm faculty appointments or salaries, and it began electing its Overseers from among its wealthy alumni. On the one hand, as Samuel Eliot Morison writes, the state had retreated from the legislative control it might have exercised over Harvard by denying it further allocations; on the other, the College felt "that to protect academic freedom she must at the earliest opportunity free her government from political elements; and that, as a price for freedom, she must look to her own alumni . . . not to the Commonwealth, for support."[10]

Democratic Advance, Third Sector Withdrawal

In the genesis of Harvard as a "private university" is reflected both the enormous penetration of conceptions of popular democracy into every aspect of national life in the period leading up to the Civil War as well as the tactical and ideological responses of the private economic and nonprofit sectors to the spread of such ideas.

Participation of the "common man" in public affairs was rapidly on the rise after Independence. The country teemed with private societies and associations "to resist enemies which are exclusively of a moral nature" as a Frenchman, de Tocqueville, observed during his travels in the early ninetenth century, "In no country in the world has the principle of association been more successfully used, or more unsparingly applied to a multitude of different objects, than in America."[11] Innumerable private groups were organized to promote reforms in the care of the poor and the handicapped, the improvement of prisons, women's rights, the abolition of slavery, and dozens of other idealistic purposes; and they were of powerful influence.

The election of Andrew Jackson signalled the advent of mass politics and fueled the further advance of what began to be called by many of the displaced generation of Founding Fathers "radical democracy." Militant demands that government should offer "equal protection and equal benefits" to all the people became a dominant theme of public debate.

As the century advanced, and especially after the Civil War, the ideological crosscurrents became increasingly evident. Native egalitarianism was reinforced by socialist theories from Europe, brought in part by the successive waves of immigrants then streaming to American shores, and the sweep of what came to be known as populistic and progressive ideas became very strong. But they were not uncontested. At the time, the terms "democrat" and "liberal" denoted opposing political philosophies, and the liberal countercurrent was also becoming more vigorous. The liberals were more concerned with ensuring "freedom from" arbitrary rule and excessive government power than with ensuring popular "freedom to" shape public policy. Their position had its intellectual roots in the seventeenth and eighteenth-century writings of men like Locke and Montesquieu. After the mid-nineteenth century it was reinforced by those of John Stuart Mill in Britain and of Social Darwinists like Herbert Spencer, which evoked strong response among middle- and upper-class groups in the United States.

These intellectual influences provided the rationale, but another factor provided the wherewithal by which liberalism in its nineteenth-century definition put its own enduring stamp on the nation's subsequent development. That other factor was the rise of a new class of rich and influential industrial entrepreneurs. After mid century, the extraordinary development of the joint stock company and the revelation of its almost unlimited potentialities for the assemblage of private wealth and power caused many business leaders to conclude that they no longer needed the intervention of government to assist their undertakings and indeed now found it a hindrance. *Laissez faire*, which became their battle cry, thereupon leapt into American affairs not as the new slogan of a special interest group, which it was, but as a sacred American relic, something which had allegedly been a continuous presence in the American economy from the beginning, and which was now being sullied by an intrusive public sector. This misconception, as Oscar Handlin puts it, "will be found not only in the pretty publications of the National Association of Manufacturers where it might be expected, but also in the serious works of our most careful scholars into which it obtrudes almost automatically."

In plain historical fact, *laissez faire*—"the abstention by government from interference with or participation in economic processes and the restriction of its functions to certain narrow police powers, mainly the protection of life and property," as Handlin defines it—was largely an invention of the Civil War era. Speaking of Massachusetts, he writes that there was never a period in its history" when this conception was of the slightest consequence. From the very first organization of the Commonwealth in 1780, the state actively and vigorously engaged in all the economic affairs of the area, sometimes as participant, sometimes as regulator." [12]

In Pennsylvania, where the public-private partnership was also a tradition, there arose a movement in the 1840s and 1850s to sell the public works chartered by the state to private corporations. "The impetus behind this movement," writes Louis Hartz, "came less from the fact of government inefficiency than from the fact that private capital was now in a position to own and operate the improvements at a profit." Yet it was not the accumulation of capital which was invoked to explain the switch. Rather, a more elegant, revisionist approach was taken. The Pennsylvania house committee which reported on public-private collaboration in 1854, Hartz says, "looked back to a happy time in the past when government and business were confined to separate spheres." Committee language reflected the imaginative reinvention of separate sectors and the emergent ideological concepts of proper roles and improper "interventions." "The objects of government should be as few and simple as possible," it declared. "To mingle it with business, whether mercantile or mechanical, is inconsistent with its object, and . . . is alike destructive of sound morals and private enterprise. . . . The separation of politics and trade would do much to restore our government to its original purity, and would be heralded by every virtuous citizen as the dawn of a brighter day. . . . The union of trade and politics must ever be dangerous. . . . Governments should be restrained to purely political powers necessary to the existence of society."[13]

The myth of original purity would animate much subsequent discussion of government's relation with the economy. It would be invoked to explain why regulation was wrong, and why joint ownership was harmful. From it would develop the false presumption that the Founding Fathers had carefully delineated the rightful spheres of government and business, and the accusation that government was dangerously overstepping its bounds. The myth, however useful politically, was counterfeit, and no less so in the government–economic realm than in the government–Third Sector relation to which it was also appropriated. The American tradition of private initiative in the nonprofit as well as in the profit-making sphere was a fact, but it was never the fact that it operated in isolation from and abhorrence of government.

The Drive for Disengagement

After the Civil War, the private colleges found their petitions to state legislatures for support generally unavailing, as public funds increasingly were channeled to public institutions. At the same time they began to find new means of support among their alumni and among a body of millionaire benefactors. With their recognition that the day of public support had ended and that a new day of private support had possibly begun, a remarkable lapse of memory occurred. Their lips, it seemed, had never tasted the public drinking cup; and in the liberal and *laissez faire* spirit of the time, the myth of the pristinely private college was born.

Before long, college presidents like Eliot of Harvard would be talking, as Frederick Rudolph explains,

as spokesmen for rugged individualism, for the virtues of independence and freedom from state support. A partnership in public service, which had once been essential to the colleges and inherent in
the responsibilities of government, now became insidious, or it was
forgotten altogether. . . .

In time the friends of the American college would be asked to
increase their benefactions in order to avoid that awful day when
the privately endowed independent college would have to turn to
government for support. In time the myth of the private college
would bury its honest, respectable past as a creature sustained in its
most trying days by the responsible assistance of the state.

The new educational ideologues then became lobbyists for a
new interest group, the private colleges, against any government
aid to higher education. By 1872, when Congress was debating
whether to increase the Federal endowment of the land-grant
colleges, Presidents McCosh of Princeton and Eliot of Harvard
railed against such governmental assistance. Rudolph writes that

> In opposing supplemental federal aid for the land-grant institutions
> in 1872 and subsequent years men of the caliber of McCosh and
> Eliot indulged in one of the shabbiest episodes in American aca-
> demic history, not only because they were prepared to deny, on
> principle, to the new colleges the kind of support that so many of
> the older colleges had in the past found vital for survival, but also
> because they often combined their opposition to the new popular
> colleges with an unconcealed condescension. That "excellent col-
> lege at New Brunswick, managed by a few Dutchmen" was the
> President of Princeton's not altogether friendly way of referring to
> the land grant institution at Rutgers.

Speaking in 1873 against the creation of a tax-supported national university, Eliot advanced the argument that "our ancestors
well understood the principle that to make a people free and self-
reliant, it is necessary to let them take care of themselves, even if
they do not take quite as good care of themselves as some superior power might." Had this principle actually been well understood by Mr. Eliot's ancestors, as Rudolph points out, "there
would have been no Harvard and no presidential office there for
him to use against the principle of government-financed education. . . . Indeed, Harvard, Yale and Columbia could not have

survived the colonial period without the support of the state."[14]

By the 1880s, the sounds of a developing drive for disengagement from government could be heard coming from several additional segments of the Third Sector. In science, a doctrine was formulated asserting its right to be free of influence even as it demanded increased government funding.

Men like Alexander Winchell were alarmed, in 1886, at the consistent legislative prejudice for "science" that would produce fiscal returns and against public support of pure research. Scientists wanted government money for basic research and objected that it was going only into projects with demonstrable military or industrial benefits. This new push, which resembled the earlier demand of the educators for public money without "accountability," was a sharp break with past practice. Indeed, as Daniels writes, it sought to impose new requirements

> in utter conflict with the prevailing democratic assumptions about the political process. It was the pure-science ideal that now made the formerly satisfactory situation seem unsatisfactory, and it was the new demands upon government introduced by the ideal that led to frequent clashes with legislators, administrators, and the general public. . . . The pure-science ideal demands that science be as thoroughly separated from the political as it is from the religious and the utilitarian. Democratic politics demands that *no* expenditures of public funds be separated from political control . . . , that no power be granted without responsibility—which always includes public accountability.[15]

The result of such diametrically opposed assumptions was an impasse, followed by reversals of view and new rationalizations. In the last years of the century voices could be heard asserting that government should stay out of pure research altogether. Thus, the editor of the journal *Science* warned of the dangers of governmental support for nonpractical work, saying that such scientific activity would unfortunately be "far removed from that public criticism which is so conducive to efficiency in other branches of the service." During that same period the *New York Evening Post* editorially took the view that "the scientific establishment should be kept safe from the political spoilsmen."

Even in the cultural field, which had developed more slowly than education and science, demands for nonaccountability and the noises of another myth of privateness under construction became audible. It was the Civil War era that saw the first important American art institutions opened to the public. Their founding, in the characteristic American pattern, typically was based on a public-private partnership; often the financing involved profitable real-estate speculation and political wheeling and dealing; and the motives behind the creation of the institutions included both cultural evangelism and the desire to give a boost to the economy.

The Metropolitan Museum of Art in New York, for example, was the product of such a mixture of elements. At a Union Club meeting in 1869 attended by over three hundred people—bankers, businessmen, lawyers, municipal officers, educators, and most of the city's artists—William Cullen Bryant stressed that "New York was growing with unparalled and chaotic speed, and attracting not only those who were "eminent in talent" but also the more sinister elements—those "most dextrous in villainy" and "most foul in guilt." "My friends," Bryant said gravely, "it is important that we should counter the temptations to vice in this great and too rapidly growing capital by attractive entertainments of an innocent and improving character." Art, the great moral teacher, would redeem the wicked while refining the good.

Joseph Hodges Choate, one of the trustees, placed the accent on the economic virtues of art. Appealing to those whom Choate called "men of fortune and estate," he explained that "The wealth and prosperity of Dresden rest largely upon the throngs that report to its vast galleries; and whole cities in Italy live upon their inherited treasures in art." Calvin Tomkins in his history of the Museum summarizes Choate's cost/benefit case in these words:

> But even more important than the pilgrimages of art lovers were the benefits that *manufacturers* would reap from the development of museums. . . . In fact, according to Choate, "every nation that has tried it has found that every wise investment in the development of art pays more than compound interest. . . . Think of it, ye millionaires of many markets," he exhorted them, "What glory may yet be yours, if you only listen to our advice, to convert port into

porcelain, grain and produce into priceless pottery, the rude ores of commerce into sculptured marble, and railroad shares and mining stocks into the glorified canvas of the world's masters." [16]

The museum was duly established by an act of incorporation in the New York legislature in 1870. Its board was a public–private mix, including as ex officio members the mayor, the governor, and the head of the Department of Public Parks. But the new museum was unable to raise much money from the millionaires to whom Choate's fervent appeal had been addressed; most of them objected that without massive state aid their donations would be money down the drain.

Choate and the trustees thereupon devised a brilliant solution, trading on the power of their friends and the political realities of New York. They drew up a petition asking for $500,000 from New York City taxes and it was signed by most of New York's wealthy and prominent citizens. A delegation took the petition to Boss Tweed and his aide Peter Barr Sweeny, who approved the appropriation. "There was no mystery about Tweed's sudden espousal of high culture," Tomkins writes. "The names on the petition represented more than half of the real estate of New York City."

Yet, despite this essential public assistance, within fifteen years the trustees had invented a vision of the Museum's immaculate conception and a fiction of its purely private character. As one wrote to another in 1885, "Now they think the Museum is a public institution, in the management of which the public has a voice. They must be forced to think of it as a private institution. . . . They must stop thinking they support the Museum, and be compelled to see that we own and support the Museum and give it in pure charity for public education." [17]

The rationale by which the impulse for disengagement was expressed in education, science, culture, and other fields differed, but there was no mistaking the general direction of the drive. The spokesmen for higher education not only reinvented the past and insisted on the pure privateness of their institutions but they attempted aggressively to block the spread of publicly supported higher education. The spokesmen for science, on grounds of a newly discovered principle of freedom of inquiry, sought to achieve institutional privateness, or at least a diminution of direct government influence. The spokesmen for culture made full use of their political power to obtain public subsidy without strings.

What was common to all, however, was a determination somehow to carve out a distinctive sphere of absolute sovereignty for private nonprofit institutions on the basis of a still largely unarticulated conception that if society would grant them such a privileged place, it would reap precious benefits in the form of excellence, creativity, and diversity in national life. Such a proposition, if it had been so baldly stated, would in the context of the times have seemed absurd. Few of the claimants had ever known, or even previously wanted, such separation from government. The self-interest of many of them in putting forth the new doctrines was readily apparent and most of them were hardly models of the excellence and innovativeness they presumably espoused. In 1870 the Harvard Medical School, for example, which was one of the two or three best of a very bad lot at the time, refused to consider requiring written examinations as a condition for graduation on the interesting grounds, in the words of its dean, that "our students cannot read or write well enough."[18]

Most important, the demand they were putting forth—essentially for public rights and privileges without counterbalancing private responsibilities—ran directly counter to the Populist and Progressive political spirit of the times. So it should have quickly dissipated and disappeared. But contrary to all reasonable expectations it did not. Instead, over the closing decades of the nineteenth century and the opening decades of the twentieth, the mythological, idealized vision of a splendid and isolated Third Sector—thanks to the instrumentality of a great new social invention—acquired a substantial degree of reality. That instrumentality was the concept of the modern philanthropic foundation. Its inventors came from the ranks of the new industrial barons. The field of action in which the potentialities of private, independent institutions in serving the general welfare was most spectacularly demonstrated was that of health care and medicine—which at the beginning of the period was in a miserably low state.

Myth into Reality

The two towering creative figures who invented the modern foundation were the ebullient little Scottish steelmaker Andrew Carnegie and the steel-cold and even wealthier John D. Rockefeller. Both were men of strong religious belief who were able to combine an urge for "good works" with the kind of entrepreneurship and aggressiveness which characterized their business dealings. The result was to transform the venerable private foundation from a means of distributing simple ameliorative charity into a powerful engine of social innovation. The invention of these donors was to use planned and purposeful philanthropy to create new institutions, to trigger public outlays in new fields, and to support scientific research as a means of attacking the causes of social problems.

Carnegie, in an article for the *North American Review* in 1886, entitled "The Gospel of Wealth," stung the conscience and stirred the thinking of many of his fellow tycoons by arguing that "he who dies rich dies disgraced." Practicing what he had preached, he then proceeded to devote the last thirty years of his life to dispensing the fortune he had acquired in the first fifty. His example helped set a new trend among the super rich, and hospitals were among the first beneficiaries.

Hospital care until then was uneven at best, and at worst— especially in the great urban centers—close to barbaric. About the Bellevue of 1870, Mary Risley in *House of Healing* wrote that "New Yorkers fought like tigers, if they had the strength, to avoid being sent there when they were ill." [19] But by the later years of the century, improvements in nursing methods and the introduction of new scientific discoveries such as anesthesia and antisepsis made hospitals, which had been largely warehouses for the sick and poor, attractive to the upper classes. Hospital buildings suddenly became as fashionable for America's rich as constructing summer palaces at Newport or embarking on the Grand Tour of Europe. The Rockefellers, the Astors, the Vanderbilts, and the Morgans were persuaded by physicians like Dr. J. Marion Sims and Dr. Simon Flexner to donate huge sums. Edward Harkness alone gave more than $34 million to Columbia Presbyterian Hospital in New York. Actually, the motives of all were mixed. Some of the donors were inspired by personal tragedies; some by humane concerns. To become known as a hospital benefactor was also to silence criticism and to acquire social prestige. But whatever the motivation, the results were a boon to the entire community.

A second way by which private wealth transformed health care—and one more revealing of the potentialities of the modern foundation—was the revolution it accomplished in American medical education. Until then, the training of doctors had been done on a purely profit-making basis. As Dr. L. Connor told the American Academy of Medicine in 1898, the profession had in consequence come to consist of

> a vast number of incompetents, large numbers of moral degenerates; crowds of pure tradesmen, blatant demagogues; hospitals organized and conducted to the damage of the profession, patient, and people; . . . medical colleges organized for the advantage of the few at the expense of the many; . . . medical societies so conducted . . . as to advance the financial profit of their leaders; domination by common interests of drug manufacturers.

Shortly after the turn of the century, one of the Carnegie foundations commissioned Abraham Flexner to study the problem of improving the medical schools. His report, published in 1910, caused a sensation. He had visited each of the 155 medical colleges then in operation and concluded that all but 31 of them should be abolished. "Dirty and disorderly beyond description," he said of a typical college, "its outfit in anatomy consists of a small box of bones and the dried-up filthy fragments of a single cadaver." Summarizing the situation, he concluded that the schools were "essentially private ventures, money making in spirit and object."[20]

On the basis of his recommendations for drastic action, state licensing boards began to apply stricter standards—against the passionate protests of the medical profession and the faculties of the schools—and within a few years dozens of the worst institutions had been shut down. Even more significant in the long run, Flexner persuaded the Rockefeller philanthropies to make a series of substantial grants to strengthen the major university centers of training in scientific medicine. These benefactions went first to Johns Hopkins and Harvard, then to other private schools such as Vanderbilt, Chicago, and Rochester, and eventually to state universities in Iowa, Colorado, Oregon, Georgia, and elsewhere.* *In toto,* tens of millions of dollars were poured into the task of radically upgrading American medical education on a nationwide basis. And within the brief span of a couple of decades, the heroic undertaking had largely succeeded.

The third dramatic change in health care wrought by private philanthropy was its strengthening of the research and scientific base of modern medicine. Grants on a large scale were given both to medical schools in the universities and to newly founded research institutes. Of the latter, the earliest was the Rockefeller Institute for Medical Research established in 1901, which made a series of important contributions to the control of major diseases such as malaria and yellow fever. In 1909 a Rockefeller Sanitary Commission was established to check the incidence of hookworm in the southern states, and its striking effectiveness led to the creation of a private International Health Board in 1914, which then mounted a massive scientific attack on a variety of infectious diseases in 63 countries on six continents.†

The direct results of this period of stunning philanthropic achievement were important enough in themselves. American medical teaching and practice were lifted to a level equal to the best in the world at that time, and the medical profession, that collection of "degenerates, demagogues and profiteers" of the earlier period, was transformed into a respectable and relatively progressive body—at least temporarily. But the indirect effects in causing the whole Third Sector to be seen in a new and better

---

* The first time Flexner proposed the inclusion of a state university, Iowa, in the list of grantees, he encountered the strong opposition of Mr. Rockefeller's closest advisor, Frederick Gates, on grounds that the state universities were "creations of politics and subject to the whims of uneducated legislatures." Gates argued that "it would be against public policy for a cent of Mr. Rockefeller's money to be given to them" and that the best service would be "to protect them in freedom of teaching by throwing around them in every state a cordon of strong, free, privately endowed colleges and universities."[21]
† The Rockefeller philanthropies over half a century put more than $300 million into these programs. Following the Rockefeller lead, by 1930 about forty foundations were giving substantial sums to medical research and education.

light were at least equally important. Whereas private nonprofit institutions had traditionally been perceived as, and had often behaved as, agencies serving the special tastes and interests of the privileged classes, of industry, and of the various religious sects, they came to be accepted as genuinely *pro bono publico*. The private colleges, with the help of private benefactions, came to be seen as "peaks of excellence," and pure scientific research, privately financed and free of government constraints, was almost canonized as a vehicle of human progress. The philanthropic foundations which had not only brought about highly beneficial reforms in private institutions but also in government policies and programs, came to be regarded as a major source of the precious "venture capital of society."

Given its accomplishments, the wave of public approbation for the Third Sector was understandable. But that it occurred during the decades around the turn of the century was curious, for those were the years when Populism, Socialism, Progressivism, and Woodrow Wilson's "New Freedom" were moving government—with temporary interruptions during the presidencies of McKinley and Taft—toward imposing restraints upon the freedom and power of business corporations, extending governmental responsibilities for protecting the weak (including women and children), protecting industrial workers and consumers (against unsafe workplaces and impure food and drugs), and playing a more active role in behalf of greater social justice. Popular pressures were compelling government to extend its reach into areas of national life which had previously been the province of the private sector, while at the same time they paradoxically encouraged the strengthening of the independence and activism of private nonprofit agencies.

Despite the apparent contradiction of tendencies and confusion of concepts, those decades were a remarkably fruitful historical interval, a time of highly constructive tension between the relatively balanced forces of governmental and private initiative in many fields.

Within a few brief years after World War I, however, that bright interval was extinguished. Government fell under a blight of banality, corruption and orthodoxy during the presidencies of

Harding, Coolidge, and Hoover. Private philanthropy for some reason also largely lost its genius. And the capability of private organizations was overwhelmed by the advent first of the Great Depression and later by the demands of World War II. By the 1940s, whatever balance had been achieved in the earlier period was drowned in the massive extension of government activity in social, educational, and scientific fields. Since then government has grown rapidly while the private sector has fallen far behind in relative size and also in vigor.

This contradictory and somewhat circuitous evolution of relationships between government and the Third Sector is often ideologically interpreted. For those to whom the Third Sector's privateness and autonomy remains a motivating idea, the "impurity" of its relationships with government during the first two-thirds of American history tends to be overlooked or denied; the interval of dynamism and disengagement which spanned the decades at the turn of the century is seen as a Golden Age the memory of which still hangs nostalgically in the air, and the recent decades of re-engagement and coalescence are seen as a deplorable departure from sound principle. Many others, however, see that supposed Golden Age as a relatively inconsequential aberration. To them the main theme of the American story has been and remains the progressive achievement of social democracy through the instrumentality of government.

A more comprehensive and accurate reading of the twisting tale, however, would seem to be the following: Collaboration, not separation or antagonism, between government and the Third Sector (and the private economic sector as well) has been the predominant characteristic. Such intimate association has also, on the whole, proven to be highly productive—in settling the continent, in advancing its economic and social development, and in fighting its wars. But from the beginning, the Third Sector, though often its partner and beneficiary, performed an initiatory, stimulative, and critical function vis-à-vis government. Never a merely passive agent, it served both as collaborator and as countervailing force. Even during those decades at the close of the nineteenth century and the opening of the twentieth, when the pretensions of the Third Sector to independent and autonomous status were at their zenith, the interrelationships with the public sector remained important. As for the great achievements of private philanthropy, it was the effect of Carnegie grants for libraries in drawing public funds into the support of a public library system, and the grants of the Rockefeller General Education Board and the Rockefeller Foundation in drawing government into new programs of Negro education and public health, which greatly magnified their impact.

The increasingly troubled relationship now existing between government and the private nonprofit sector is not therefore the simple result of violations of fixed jurisdictions and of transgression of clear precepts. The underlying problems are rather those of balance and of degree within a context of collaboration; of redefining roles in response to changing values and public attitudes; of preserving essential elements of independence within interdependence and mutual dependence.

Solutions cannot be found by seeking separation of the sectors, or by attempting to reverse the tide of current history, which is steadily moving toward the enlargement of government and the broadening of its responsibilities. They can only be found in adjustments, accommodations, and conceptual calarifications—all for the purpose of preserving a mixed, pluralistic, interactive system, which is the true American tradition.

To cope with present-day problems, even to understand them, is especially difficult because of the whirlwind of change which has struck every aspect of American life since the 1930s and most especially since World War II. In order to grasp the nature and meaning of those developments, it is necessary to move from a review of overarching historical trends to an examination of key subsectors—private higher education, health services, basic scientific research, cultural institutions, and the social-action movements.

Each of these institutional categories has its own particular financial and operating problems, its own particular pattern of relationships and problems with government. And in recent decades each has felt the impact of social, political, and value changes in distinctive ways. In following chapters I shall attempt to draw their individual portraits and to lay the groundwork for some overall conclusions and public policy recommendations.

II

THE PREDICAMENT OF
KEY SUBSECTORS

3 ▶▶▶▶

Higher Education:
Duality, Dependency, and Decline

HIGHER EDUCATION provides the natural starting
point for a closer examination of the key portions of the Third
Sector, partly because of its scale and inherent importance, and
partly because it embraces in some degree all the others. In addition to providing instruction, the colleges and universities supply
the setting for most of the nation's basic scientific research, for
medical training and much medical research, for a very large
amount of cultural activity, and for a number of the major protest
and reform movements of recent decades. In addition, higher education has long served as the main bastion for the protection of
intellectual and scientific freedom generally. In a sense, therefore, higher education is the anchor of the integrity of the whole
nonprofit sector. Which is why its present distress and dislocation
is properly of such acute concern.

By the end of World War II, American higher education had
reached a state of high and balanced development. From the last
century's multitude of small private colleges and scattering of
state-supported institutions devoted to training in "the agricultural and mechanical arts" had emerged a large, richly diverse assemblage of institutions. About one out of three high school graduates in the country went on to higher education. Of these about
half were enrolled in private institutions and half in public ones.
And of the 1700 schools then in existence roughly half were pri-

vate in their governance and funding; the remainder were government supported. Moreover, with each sector substantial differences existed. Among the private schools there were several hundred small residential liberal arts colleges, including many which were church-related; dozens of urban institutions with large commuting populations; an array of special-purpose institutions for music, art, or science; and some 50 "research universities" of which about half were public and half were private. In addition to undergraduate and graduate teaching, these carried on significant programs of basic research.

In the public sector the land grant schools had developed into full-blown universities, leaving their "cow college" image far behind. In addition there were many additional universities and colleges supported by state funds and a growing number of community colleges, mostly of the two-year type, supported by their localities.

From 1945 to the early 1960s the private institutions received some Federal support for research and training projects related to defense and space technology, but otherwise they were essentially privately financed. The public institutions were supported principally by state funds. The role of the Federal government was relatively minor.

The diversity and the substantial freedom of each institution to determine its own mission and programs was protected by an ingenious pattern of buffering and governmental self-denial. Direct Federal regulation was minimal since the requirements of social legislation such as Social Security and Workmen's Compensation generally exempted educational institutions. And the diversity of public institutions was protected by the fact that the various states chose to regulate and support them in varying ways; boards of trustees had been strengthened to provide a significant degree of insulation from direct legislative or administrative control, and the chartering power which the states exercised over public and private institutions of higher education was generally exercised with restraint so as not to impose upon their educational autonomy.

The result was a complex, radically decentralized, intricately counterbalanced educational apparatus. It had many virtues but it was by no means flawless. In the 1950s it was still largely segregated racially; access to the best private institutions for all but the most extraordinarily talented of the children of low income families was difficult; and the total capacity of the system—certainly as compared to what came to exist only twenty years later—was still relatively restricted.

Still, the total structure offered an abundant choice of educational fare; a good many of its best institutions ranked with the finest universities in the world; and the individual institutions composing it enjoyed a degree of educational freedom rarely to be found.

In comparison to the university system of other advanced nations, perhaps its unique characteristic was its duality—the parallel operation of major public and private elements. Each of these subsectors has developed its separate (and sometimes self-glorifying) definition of itself. Their partisans claim that the major qualities of the private institutions are diversity, liberal learning, independence, excellence, and experimentation. On the other hand, relevance, responsiveness, and representativeness have always been, according to their advocates, the special attributes of public institutions. But such dispassionate words do not convey the depth of feeling which those who believe in the private schools share about the values they are felt to embody and the class affinities they represent. Conversely, state-supported colleges and universities for many ordinary people of the United States—from the early farmers, artisans, and frontiersmen to the later waves of immigrants and still later the urban poor and the racially disadvantaged—have long symbolized equality and opportunity and have represented their main thoroughfare to higher status and social integration.

As a result of these strong underlying feelings, arguments about the merits and deficiencies of the two sectors have often tended to exaggerate the differences between them. In reality, the existing distinctions in quality and academic emphasis are becoming increasingly blurred. There is great doubt, for example, based on available educational research, whether there are now significant differences between public and private institutions with regard to student achievement, especially undergraduate achievement. But despite the lack of hard evidence proving the unique benefits of private institutions, their advocates are firmly convinced they exist.

A good many faculty members, even at private institutions, also seem to share the view that "What goes in comes out: bright, bright; dim, dim. What is transmitted differentially at, say, Harvard, is not learning but status." A harsher, Marxist view is that of Samuel Bowles and Herbert Gintis in their recent book, *Schooling in Capitalist America*.[1] According to them, children of the property-owning class go to elite institutions which prepare them for future leadership positions; the others are sent to numbing public institutions, where their talents are blunted, their expectations are lowered, and they are prepared for life sentences to dull and subordinate positions in the factories and bureaucracies of large corporations.

Nevertheless, there are two demonstrably valuable contributions the private institutions make to the character of the total system. The first relates to diversity. The Carnegie Foundation for the Advancement of Teaching reported that as of 1975, 56 percent of the higher education institutions attended predominantly by black students were private. Of those institutions with small enrollments of less than 500, 94 percent were private, as were 93 percent of all men's colleges and 99 percent of all women's colleges. And of course 100 percent of those institutions with religious affiliations are private.[2] Public colleges and universities are by no means homogeneous, but the existence of a private sector unquestionably adds significantly to the actual diversity of American higher education as a whole.

Secondly, that the private institutions play a special role in maintaining standards of quality is more than a mere boast. The evidence is not one-sided, however, and must be interpreted with discrimination. Institutional excellence is clearly not confined to the private schools. There are public institutions which are equal in every respect to the best of the private ones, but it remains true that a disproportionate number of the private schools are of the highest quality. Although they enroll less than a fourth of the total number of students in higher education, they include more than half of all graduate departments with "distinguished" faculties.

In 1970, the American Council on Education found that 12 of the 22 top-rated universities and 26 of the top 49 were private. The real significance of such numbers, which goes beyond the merely statistical, is that they give proof that in the intellectual and scientific life of the United States a good many of the strongest and most creative centers of social and scientific thought are privately controlled and to a degree still independent of government. Which is an incentive and a protection for all elements of the system.

However great their various disagreements, the advocates of both the private and the public institutions almost unanimously agree—and this is probably the most important of all—that the duality of the American system is essential to maintain. The operative consensus was well summarized in the Newman report (1971), produced by a special task force to the Secretary of HEW: "The issue is not whether private education is more effective or more diverse than public. The combination of public and private *is* more effective and more diverse than public alone. More important than ever is the point that the relative independence of some institutions helps insure the vitality and freedom of all."[3]

This view has become part of the American credo; hardly a respected voice can be heard to challenge it. Odd, then, that the effect if not the intention of public policy in recent years has been, progressively and cumulatively, to undermine that duality. In the words of Stanford president Richard Lyman, the country may well be on the way to getting "a single tax supported system without ever having consciously willed that this should happen."[4]

The Postwar Transformation

The story of the deep alterations which have been made in the character of American higher education since the 1940s begins with money—its volume and its changing sources. Even though it may recently have begun to abate, the enthusiasm of the American taxpayer for education in recent decades has remained very strong. In GNP terms, for example, government in the early 1950s spent 3.8 percent on education at all levels; by 1963–64, this had risen to 6.1 percent, and by 1976–77 to 7.7 percent. Within these totals, expenditures for higher education have risen much faster than those for elementary and secondary education: the latter, during these 25 years, rose about 50 percent, the former more than 90 percent.

State and local appropriations have traditionally been the predominant source of government funding for higher education, but in recent years the Federal portion has become almost equal. From a level of less than $100 million in 1944 Federal outlays shot to $2.2 billion by 1963 and to some $10 billion in 1979. By the late 1970s the Federal government was providing about 30 percent of the total expenditures of public and private higher education, virtually the same as the state and local share.

This Federal money has flowed into higher education in three broad streams—to support research and development in certain fields, to construct new facilities, and to provide aid to various categories of students.

Based on wartime precedents, the Federal government after 1945 increasingly employed the universities as its research arm. They were counted upon by the government to develop technological innovations for space exploration, war making, and heavy industry; for strengthening the scientific basis of the burgeoning electronic, computer, and pharmaceutical industries; and for providing expertise in fields ranging from economics and foreign policy to child development and cancer research. At present the nation's major universities, both public and private, with Federal assistance, train the upcoming generation of scientists and perform two-thirds of the basic scientific research done in the United States.

The Housing Act of 1950 authorized Federal loans for the construction of dormitories and other campus facilities. The same act as amended in 1959 permitted educational institutions to undertake large-scale urban renewal projects in cooperation with city governments. In 1963 the Higher Education Facilities Act put the government permanently into the business of providing regular support for campus construction. Thereafter funds in increasing amounts were provided for laboratories and undergraduate and graduate facilities. By the late 1960s Federal construction expenditures had reached a level of more than $700 million per annum. Since then, because of initial overconstruction followed by declining student enrollment, such loans and grants have declined sharply.

Student aid on the other hand has become the centerpiece of Federal policy toward higher education—given in steadily mounting volume and, since the mid 1960s, mainly in pursuit of egalitarian objectives. The several programs in parallel operation at present provide aid to nearly half of the 11.5 million students in colleges and universities, at an annual cost to the Federal government of more than $9 billion. It is this great flow of targeted funds which has now made Federal influence upon the shape and direction of American higher education decisively important.

Since the end of World War II, Federal funding for student aid has come in several surges. The first began with passage of the GI bill in June 1944, as part of the demobilization program for war veterans. More than 15 million persons were eligible for assistance under the Act; nearly 8 million of them availed themselves of its provisions at a total cost to the Federal government of $14.5 billion. Of these about 30 percent attended college, and the program thus had great financial impact on institutions of higher education. In addition the mature, highly motivated former servicemen and women who attended under the program proved to be able students, and, at the same time, brought the colleges and universities a new diversity of skills and backgrounds. In the words of Donald M. Stewart, President of Spelman College, "they helped democratize higher education and move it from its elitist moorings."[5] Clearly higher education had become a significant instrument of national policy, including noneducational policy. The GI Bill, using the schools and colleges as its vehicle, had created a veterans' readjustment facility as well as a hedge against massive unemployment. At the same time a precedent had been set for Federally planned extension of economic opportunity through education for whole groups of the population selected on a basis other than individual academic aptitude or achievement.

The National Defense Education Act of 1958 marked the second surge of Federal student assistance. Stimulated by Soviet success in launching the first Sputnik, the program sought to assist students of exceptional ability, especially in science and engineering. Both graduate fellowships and subsidized student loans were provided at a cost totalling some $5 billion over the following 20-year period.

The Higher Education Act of 1965 began the third surge. It was enacted in an atmosphere of political concern for the poor and accordingly offered a variety of kinds of student assistance, especially for those from low-income families.

A series of amendments in subsequent years modified it to the point where it now consists of six major financial aid programs. The biggest is the Basic Educational Opportunity Grants (BEOG) program, organized in 1972 and still growing rapidly. In its first year of operation it provided needy students with $50 million; in 1978 it distributed more than $2 billion to them, and in 1979, to accommodate the demand of middle income families for student aid, this total could exceed $2.5 billion. The Supplemental Educational Opportunity Grant (SEOG) program for "exceptionally needy students" will expend some $340 million in 1979–80; the National Direct Student Loan (NDSL) program will make new loans of $330 million; the College Work-Study program, primarily for students from low income families, will spend about $600 million; the Guaranteed Student Loan (GSL) program will insure student loans by banks and other agencies at an annual cost to the government of $800 million; and the State Student Incentive Grant (SSIG) program will spend $77 million in the form of matching grants to encourage state governments to increase their scholarship programs.

In addition to these activities administered by the Office of Education in HEW, the Veterans Administration provides large-scale assistance to war veterans enrolled in institutions of higher education. The annual cost of these programs, because of the Korean and Vietnam conflicts, rose spectacularly from $340 million to $1.9 billion between 1967 and 1976. By 1979, as these veterans finish their studies, the total will have dropped back rather abruptly to $780 million.[6]

The other major program operating outside the Office of Education—and one that is little known although very large—is the student benefit program of the Social Security Administration. It provides assistance to "18–21 year-old unmarried full-time student dependents of dead, disabled and retired workers." In 1979, this program will distribute more than $2 billion to 900,000 beneficiaries. Unlike the GI program, which is declining in scale, Social Security Administration benefits have risen steadily, increasing fivefold between 1966 and 1978. In early 1979, however, the Carter Administration in a reversal of policy proposed the elimination of the entire program over a four-year phase-out period.

In most of these Federal programs, the criterion for assistance has shifted from academic achievement to need. The widening of access to higher education for the disadvantaged has now overwhelmingly become the dominant objective of higher education policy, and higher education is being utilized on a major scale as a vehicle for social change and equalization of opportunity.

By comparison, state student assistance is relatively small, totaling $746 million in 1978. But it is growing rapidly under the stimulus of the Federal SSIG program.

The immense volume of Federal, state, and local government expenditure on American higher education in the postwar period has had several major impacts. These are most clearly seen in the improvement of the physical plant and in the changed size and composition of the student population. Public institutions in particular have flourished. Gleaming new campuses have been created all over the country. Kent State in Ohio, Stony Brook in New York, and California State University at Long Beach were little-known institutions only a few years ago, but today Stony Brook has a student body of more than 15,000 and Long Beach and Kent State each enroll 25,000 students or more. In 30 years the total number of colleges and universities has grown from 1700 to 3000; over the same period, the number of community colleges has leapt from some 500 to more than 1100.

Equally dramatic has been the increase in total student population: in 1950, one of three American high school graduates went on to college. In that year, of a national population of 150 million,

2.3 million students were enrolled in institutions of higher education. By 1977, more than one of two high school graduates went
on to college. The student population had more than quadrupled
and out of a national population of 217 million, 11.4 million (or
more than 5 percent) were enrolled in higher education, 4 million
of them in the mushrooming community colleges.

The composition of the student body in higher education had
also changed markedly in the intervening years, the proportion of
women, blacks and students from lower income families having
greatly increased. Of a total enrollment of 2.1 million in 1946,
there were 1.4 million men and 660,000 women; thirty years
later, of a total enrollment of more than 10 million, there were
5.5 million men and 4.6 million women. The overall student population had increased fivefold, and the number of women seven-
fold.

The more recent growth in the number of black students, following passage of civil rights and equal opportunity legislation,
has been equally rapidly. Of a total student body of 4.6 million in
1964, 4.3 million were white, less than 250,000 were black. Ten
years later, the total population was about 9.5 million, with
8,516,000 whites and 940,000 blacks. The total college population
had more than doubled while the number of blacks in higher education had quadrupled.

Historically, the children of poor families have gone on to
higher education far less often than those of middle and upper income families, but this is significantly less true today. In 1967, for
example, 40 percent of college freshmen came from families in
the top quartile of income; but by 1975, only 32 percent did.
By contrast, whereas only 11 percent of the freshmen in 1967
came from families in the bottom income quartile, in 1975 16
percent did.[7]

Postwar educational policies have thus had two triumphant results. They have sustained and broadened the nation's world leadership in scientific research and they have gone a long way toward
making higher education a possibility for nearly every young
American, black or white, male or female, and to some degree,
rich or poor.

At the same time a train of other consequences, not insignificant and not generally beneficial, have accompanied these successes. One set has to do with the internal affairs of individual institutions, both public and private. The growth of government research grants has changed teaching practices, patterns of research, and faculty relationships in many schools. Because such grants have supported primarily the "hard" physical and natural sciences and the quantifiable aspects of social science and even the humanities, they have distorted research priorities and methodologies accordingly. They have deflected thousands of academic careers toward fields of interest to government and have made research, consulting, and graduate instruction so absorbing and prestigious that undergraduate teaching has been seriously downgraded. By pouring money into projects, studies, and institutes—all new and superimposed on existing academic activities—government has added to the administrative burdens of universities, while "creating on the rim of the central structure vested interests whose allegiance is to the outside source of funds, not the institution they happen to belong to. The unity and sense of loyalty of large companies of scholars have thus been undermined."[8]

The words are those of Jacques Barzun in his *House of Intellect*. Speaking of the effect of both government and foundation grants, he goes on to say bitterly that the judgment that teaching is inferior to research

> is expressed in the coveted research professorships, and even more vividly in the inducements recently held out by the wealthier state universities to the members of poor ancient ones; the distinguished man is offered a high salary, frequent leaves of absence, funds for research, and no duties. The highest prize of the teaching profession is: no teaching. For the first time in history, apparently, scholars want no disciples. And perhaps seeing those that come forward, they are right. In any case, they accept sterilization at a high fee, while the funds voted by legislatures and foundations to increase facilities serve in fact to remove the best minds from the classroom.[9]

Government, especially the Federal government, has also on occasion, as a condition of its funding, transgressed upon traditional rights and operating principles of higher education. The

National Defense Education Act in 1958 required that students sign a loyalty oath in order to benefit from its assistance. In letting research contracts, government has in some cases required security clearance of personnel, the classification of data, and conformity to other official demands which have strained the elasticity of the concept of academic freedom to its limits and sometimes even beyond.

Still more serious abuses of the relationship have recently come to light. For example, it now appears that the CIA in the 1950s and 1960s was able to persuade—or mislead—dozens of schools to collaborate in research programs which not only imposed obligations of secrecy but also involved unethical activities.

Admiral Stansfield Turner, the Director of Central Intelligence, said in Congressional testimony in August of 1977, that the CIA covertly sponsored research at 80 institutions, including 44 colleges and universities, from 1953 to 1963. One part of this research was the project codenamed MK-ULTRA, which sought to modify the behavior of unwitting subjects through such means as hypnosis and drugs. When the Senate Health Subcommittee invited the heads of 20 of the institutions involved to testify on the program, all but one declined on grounds of previous engagements.[10]

The most sweeping effects of increased government funding and of new policies, however, have been on the general equilibrium and decentralization of the entire structure of American higher education. First among these has been a drastic dislocation in the preexisting balance between public and private institutions. With governmental encouragement and financing, the publics have now become the dominant factor; the private schools, which less than 30 years ago were the equal of the publics in terms of enrollment, have been reduced to a quantitatively minor position. As late as 1950, private institutions accounted for 50 percent of total enrollment in all institutions of higher education. Since then, the proportion of students in private schools has dropped steadily: 44 percent in 1955, 41 percent in 1960, 34 percent in 1965, 27 percent in 1970, and 22 percent in 1977.* To

---

* It must be emphasized that this has been a *relative* decline. The actual number of students during the period in private institutions doubled—but the total student population over the same years more than quadrupled.

some degree these figures are the result of decisions by a number of private schools not to increase their enrollments, or to increase them only moderately, in a time of rapid expansion; but basically they are the result of governmental policies to enlarge the system of higher education and widen educational opportunity, which in the event was accomplished principally by expansion of the public sector.

In addition to a general reduction of the relative position of the private sector, government policy has equally diminished the special position formerly enjoyed by private institutions in certain fields. Title IV of the National Defense Education Act in 1958, for example, was specifically designed to establish an entirely new system of graduate education by breaking up the traditional hegemony of the Eastern, mainly private, schools and creating a string of new graduate centers, primarily in public institutions, throughout the South and West.

In parallel with this shift toward public predominance, the pluralism of the system of American higher education has also been curtailed by government action over the past 40 years. It has, for example, contributed greatly to centralization at the state level in certain areas of decision-making. Thus with passage of the Higher Education Facilities Act by Congress in 1963, a network of state coordinating boards came into existence to oversee the location and expansion of new buildings. Their role varies greatly, but in terms of authority exercised, four-fifths of them now have jurisdiction over both private and public institutions, and more are attempting to incorporate the private sector in their planning efforts.

Their power over individual institutions derives in large part from their authority to require compliance as a condition of receiving funds. The boards were originally put in place during a period of expansion to guide institutional growth; but now that the time of affluence has ended, they are tending to become the means by which governmental control is exercised over the statewide balance between private and public higher education, and over individual institutional priorities, both financial and academic. The growth of their centralized authority has been directly at the expense of that of the governing boards of individual institutions.

The Educators' Nonresponse

Perhaps because these enormous shifts occurred slowly and piecemeal, or perhaps because of the anesthetizing power of money, they left educators largely undisturbed through the 1960s and even into the early 1970s. To the extent there was protest, it focussed principally on the growth of state rather than Federal authority. Thus in 1957, a Committee on Government and Higher Education was created by the Carnegie Corporation out of a concern that "the legal autonomy of governing boards of public colleges and universities is being eroded by an expansion of administrative supervision from the offices and agencies of state government."

But the possibility of Federal encroachment was not taken seriously. In 1962, for example, presidential advisor McGeorge Bundy, who had been Dean of Arts and Sciences at Harvard until the year before, called the Federal dollar on the whole "as good as any other" and said that it had done much "to enhance the freedom and independent strength of American colleges and universities."[11] A 1968 study of the views of 1200 college and university presidents showed that virtually none of them were worried about intrusion of the Federal government.[12] An ACE study in 1969 reported similar results: In a poll of student leaders, faculty members, administrators, and trustees, the statement, "As a corollary of tax-dollar support, government agencies will have increasing influence over private colleges and universities" was ranked very low in probability of occurrence by most respondents. As late as 1973, Professor Dael Wolfle, long-time Executive Officer of the American Association for the Advancement of Science, wrote that the administrators of Federal higher education policies "have accepted and honored the proposition that education decisions should be made by educators and scholars and not by the Federal government. Deliberate infringement as a matter of Federal policy can be dismissed; it is not a major threat. Leaders of the Federal government join with professors in repeating the hallowed principle that universities should be free from government influence."[13]

Curiously, it was from persons outside the educational establishment—and even from government itself—that some of the sharpest warnings came. President Eisenhower in 1961, in his farewell address to the nation, after delivering his famous caution about the "military-industrial complex," went on to say in a less remembered passage that "The prospect of domination of the nation's scholars by the Federal government, project allocation, and the power of money, is ever present, and is gravely to be regarded." Gerard Piel, publisher of the *Scientific American,* told a Congressional committee in 1965 that the colleges and universities, "in their avidity for government funding, were becoming mercenaries of science and scholarship," and that their integrity was being steadily undermined. The report of those hearings, published in the midst of the boom years for higher education by the House Committee on Government Operations, concluded that Federal funding was not only reshaping academic research priorities but was also having an unplanned and unacknowledged impact on educational policies and practices in general. And yet, although the concern of others was obviously growing, the educators themselves were mostly still drugged by dollars.

Willing Mercenaries, Unwilling Draftees

However, disenthrallment has finally come and the air is now increasingly filled with cries of alarm. In harnessing the nation's system of higher education to its various purposes—military, economic, and social in the 1940s and 1950s—government in effect hired the institutions for their services. The demands placed upon them were accompanied by full—even lavish—funding. But beginning in the 1960s, the Federal government established an additional series of national goals which all institutions, including colleges and universities, are now obliged to pursue, such as equal employment opportunity, environmental protection, and job safety. These new programs seek to accomplish their objectives by regulation, not contracting or subvention, and they do not on the whole provide financial inducements and benefits for the affected institutions. It is this new development, combined

with generally adverse economic trends, which has mainly roused
the educators to protest.

From the viewpoint of higher education, the major milestones
on the road to this new phase of Federal intervention have included the following:

Equal Pay Act of 1963
Equal Employment Opportunity (Title VII of the Civil Rights
    Act of 1964, as amended)
Affirmative Action (Executive Order 11246 issued in 1965 and
    amended to include discrimination on basis of sex, 1967)
Age Discrimination in Employment Act of 1967, as amended
Unemployment Insurance (Social Security Act—Employment
    Security Amendments—1970)
Social Security tax increases (Employment Security Amend-
    ments, 1970)
Wage and Salary Controls (Economic Stabilization Act, 1970)
The Occupational Safety and Health Act of 1970
Environmental Protection Act of 1970
Health Maintenance Organizations, 1974
Pensions—ERISA, 1974 (note: Public institutions excluded)

The Multiple Consequences

Increasing regulation in combination with heavy dependence
on Federal funding now subjects college and university administrations to the most minute and detailed scrutiny in the name of
accountability, to laborious and frequently duplicative reporting
requirements, and to aggravating and costly bureaucratic procedures. From 1964 to 1976 there has been a 1000 percent increase—from 92 pages to nearly 1000 pages—in the quantity of
Federal regulations with which educators must comply.

In the words of Earl F. Cheit, of the University of California at
Berkeley and an advisor to the Ford Foundation, these administrative burdens have produced "a new purgatory right here on
earth. . . . The new regime in higher education is one of review
procedures, regulation, litigation, and demands for information.
Together these now account for so much of the energies and at-

tention of college and university officials that the whole House of Intellect could soon be buried in an avalanche of paper. . . . Higher education may be a faded passion of the 1960s, but it is a fully established bureaucratic enterprise of the 1970s."[14]

It is of course a commonplace of the American political tradition for interest groups of various kinds to demand government benefits and protection while at the same time to denounce the administrative restrictions which accompany them. Indeed, many of the recent statements of university leaders, such as the Report of the President of Harvard in 1976, resemble in tone and content the old diatribes of the National Association of Manufacturers about "creeping Socialism." To a degree, therefore, they can be discounted as outcries of an offended vested interest. But it is also the fact that the Federal government has now generally fallen into regulatory habits which are at the same time extraordinarily burdensome and notably ineffective. In no field is this more apparent than in higher education.

Change magazine has estimated, for instance, on the basis of figures compiled by the American Council on Education, that the additional costs imposed on colleges and universities to comply with new social regulation amounted in 1975 to $2 billion, *or the total of all voluntary giving they received that year*. Among examples of bureaucratic exaggeration and mindlessness it cited were: requirements by Federal agencies of lists of names and addresses of all incoming students, detailed analyses of how faculty spend their time, and the compilation of follow-up data on all recent alumni; requirements by state agencies for complete accounting of every professional membership fee paid, every journal subscription, and every gross of paperclips purchased.[15]

At the state level too, a mounting interest in controlling even the most detailed aspects of higher education is evident. At the 1975 session of the California State Legislature, for example, nearly 600 bills were introduced to regulate the affairs of educational institutions—designating, for example, smoking and nonsmoking areas on campus; levying fees for employee parking; and establishing whether librarians are to work 10 or 12 months of each year, and whether a staff vacancy can be filled with a nonemployee before the position is posted for at least 10 days.

Division and Disarray

The perceived threat to their position has now stirred both public and private institutions to action, or at least to some action, and they have, at least on some issues, joined forces. Thus, with a unified voice they have decried bureaucratization and growing regulatory costs, demanded a greater voice in the shaping of Federal education policy, and appealed for more money. In one of a number of similar *démarches* organized in recent years, a coalition of groups and associations in early 1977 joined to ask the Congress to appropriate some $2 billion more to higher education than President Carter had proposed—including increased student aid funds to check the decline in enrollments, institutional allowances to cover costs of administering Federally mandated programs, and special grants to enable schools to comply with new occupational health and safety requirements and to make their facilities more energy efficient.*

The need for mobilization is now widely accepted, but whether it can be achieved even under present circumstances remains unclear, for higher education has never been very effective in assembling its forces to importune or influence government, especially at the national level. The Federal government has been munificent in responding to the needs of colleges and universities in the years past—but higher education did little to assert those needs. It was largely acted upon rather than acting, and the pressures which impelled government to raise the priority of higher education in national policy arose largely from other elements of the political system.

In the executive branch, responsibility for higher education is highly diffused and heavily layered over in the hierarchy. Perhaps for that reason, university and college spokesmen in recent decades have hardly been able to get into the antechambers of power while those of science, for example, have had direct access

---

* To suggest its scope, the coalition included the American Association of Community and Junior Colleges, the American Association of State Colleges and Universities, the Association of American Universities, the Association of Jesuit Colleges and Universities, the American Council on Education, the National Association of State Universities and Land-Grant Colleges, and the College and University Department of the National Catholic Educational Association.

to the inner sanctum itself, namely the White House. Indeed, during the Nixon years an atmosphere of hostility, and at times almost total noncommunication, prevailed between government and the educators. The Carter Administration has now proposed raising education to cabinet rank for the first time. The new department, if and when it is created by Congress, would give education greater visibility than ever before—but whether its establishment would have the effect of increasing the influence of educators upon the Federal government, or of the Federal government upon the educators, remains a moot question.

Vis-à-vis the Congress, the lobbying efforts of higher education have likewise been indifferent compared to those of the forces of elementary and secondary education, for example. Because of historical, ideological, religious and other differences, colleges and universities have always had great difficulty in coalescing around an issue. They have also characteristically displayed an uneasiness about the work of influencing legislation. In the words of Derek Bok, president of Harvard, entering the dust and heat of the political arena "is not a congenial task for educators, who dislike the thought of seeming to play the part of lobbyists." According to Stephen Bailey of the American Council on Education in Washington, "we have a reputation—at least in this town—for being exclusive, self-indulgent, patronizing and sloppy. . . . The simple fact is that educators have not been adequately helpful to those who are trying to be helpful to them." Representative John Brademas, Democrat of Indiana, one of the stalwart Congressional supporters of aid to education, referring to the often condescending attitude of the witnesses who came before legislative committees, has called for "a little more information and a little less admonition from the higher education community."

The political coalitions of higher education are thus inherently fragile and frequently inept. They tend also to be inert since many individual institutions are riven with internal conflict. Time was when collegiality and consensus regulated their affairs. But beginning with the student unrest of the 1960s, competing interests and groups within the institutions have increasingly vied for power. The campuses have become deeply divided as to the nature of their academic mission and increasingly politicized. "Student power" has been followed by "black power," "junior faculty power," "senior faculty power," "women power," and "union power"—now the most rapidly growing of all.

It is estimated that more than 100,000 of the country's 600,000 faculty members are already members of one of the three principal bargaining agents—the National Education Association, the American Association of University Professors, and the American Federation of Teachers—and the number is increasing rapidly. Many observers believe that in the not too distant future faculty unionization and collective bargaining will become the national norm.

Confrontation has become the rule, and policy issues tend to end in stalemate or in a decision reflecting the lowest common denominator among all interests involved. The old consensual processes were never very efficient or expeditious, but for purposes of participating in political action with other institutions, the effect of the new situation is paralyzing.

The organizational and tactical problems higher education faces in mounting an effective defense of its interests are therefore considerable. A number of leading educators and organizations are hard at work to build a new solidarity, but already a deep historical split has reappeared—that between the private and the public institutions. And it is widening steadily. Higher education is therefore entering a difficult and dangerous period with its forces in disarray.

The Plight of the Privates

That disarray and division will very probably become worse. A time of stringency and shrinkage is at hand, and the consequences will not fall equally upon the strong and the weak, nor equally upon the publics and the privates. For the former, the problem is one of moderating and managing a prospective decline. For the latter, at least in their own view, the problem is quite simply survival.

Without much question the private institutions are in special difficulty. But just how grave their situation is is a matter of considerable dispute. The facts as the private institutions see them are ominous. A few institutions are strong because of their endowments and the wealth of their alumni. They tend also to be prestigious, which enables them to attract large numbers of well-qualified applicants for admission. But the great majority lack all these strengths. They are small, poorly endowed, and obliged to compete actively for their students not only with state-supported schools but also with their private rivals. Their traditional sources of sustenance (often religious) have been drying up and they do not have rich new sources of private support to which they can turn.

It is true, spokesmen for the private institutions will admit, that over the past decade the number of outright bankruptcies has been small. But they emphasize that this is because nonprofit institutions of all kinds, and particularly small colleges, have a strong instinct for survival and the capability to mask their budgetary difficulties for long periods by all manner of sacrifices and expedient measures. Among these are deferring plant maintenance, delaying the payment of bills, reducing services, and holding off salary adjustments. It is only by such painful efforts, they point out, that they have been able to cope.

But now, even demography has turned against them. Because the "baby boom" of the early postwar years ended in the 1960s, the growth of the 18- to 24-year-old segment of the population has been slowing sharply; it will soon begin a steady decline that will continue for another 15 years. At the same time, college enrollment rates, especially for males, have begun to drop. It is therefore to be expected that the enrollment of colleges and universities will not only decline but will decline at an even steeper rate than the size of the 18- to 24-year age group for at least another decade.

The situation would be aggravating enough if it were the result of inexorable demographic or economic forces. But many leaders of the private sector believe that their institutions have been victimized by a pattern of prejudicial Federal educational policy. In their judgment, the public institutions were vastly overbuilt during the 1950s and 1960s; now that student enrollment has begun to taper off, the private schools have been placed in fearful jeopardy. Public universities have become much more aggressive in their efforts to attract students, since their state appropriations are linked directly to their enrollments. Moreover their deficits are simply passed on to the taxpayers via legislative appropriations and are not necessarily reflected in their fees.

On the other hand, the private institutions, faced with a growing gap between income and expenses, say they have no alternative but to raise tuition charges. (Between 1965 and 1975 the gap in student fees between the privates and publics doubled from about $1000 to more than $2000.) But they thereby run the risk of pricing themselves out of the market. "In the absence of large public subsidies," a task force of the National Council on Independent Colleges and Universities has said,

> the private institutions have been thrown back on their only available source of substantially increased income—student charges. Tuition and fees charged by private institutions, starting from a higher base at the onset, have risen much more sharply than the corresponding charges of public institutions. Needless to say, this has gravely weakened the competitive position of the private sector. It is in the position of a thriving business that finds itself confronted with an inherently strong and heavily subsidized competitor which can sell its product at one-fifth the price.[16]

Moreover the procedures and conditions of Basic Educational Opportunity Grants, the principal form of Federal student aid, intensify the competition to the disadvantage of the private schools. The funds are put directly into the hands of students to use at schools of their choice, and grants can cover a maximum of one-half the total fees. Such policies in combination invite students to shop around, the private colleges claim, and predispose them to choose the cheaper institution.

The effects of government policy are not, however, all one-sided. The private schools, even from the BEOG program, derive some students and financial benefits. And some 40 state programs of assistance now distribute most of their funds to those who attend private institutions. These programs are particularly important in a few states—New York, California, Illinois, Pennsylvania, and Ohio—which also happen to have many private schools.

Overall, based on the results of several recent research studies, it appears that the "plight of the privates" is difficult but not quite desperate. One of the most reputable and balanced of these was issued in December 1977 by the Carnegie Council on Policy Studies in Higher Education. It concluded that the financial situation for private institutions had substantially stabilized after the difficult period of the late 1960s and early 1970s when depression, inflation, and the expansion of low-cost public institutions dealt a serious blow to many of them. "Although some institutions have closed and a significant number of others are noticeably hard-pressed, there is no acute general crisis calling for drastic immediate increases in public support," the Council concluded.

Nevertheless, it estimated that about one-fourth of the private colleges are in distress and many others face an insecure and uncertain future, a condition that will persist through the 1980s.

Fighting Back—and In-Fighting

To defend their interests the private colleges have now moved to set up their own lobbies in Washington and at various state capitals. They are also in the process of assembling the argumentation and data to demonstrate that on a sheer dollars and cents basis it is more economical and effective for government to keep the private sector alive as a going concern than to allow it to expire and then to replace it with public facilities. They are therefore now demanding much more massive assistance, including tuition offset programs which might run into hundreds of millions or billions of dollars a year, for the private sector only.

As the militancy of the private sector mounts, however, the public sector has been spurred to assemble its considerable forces and its counter arguments. It contends that both it and the private sector are in difficulty; that public policy has already taken special measures to ease the financial problems of the privates; and that in principle no aid should be given to the private institutions at the expense of the publics.

In the rapidly approaching showdown, it is difficult to see how the privates can prevail. They have their supporters, but the public institutions command the big political battalions. The private institutions have a strong case to make, but the basically non-egalitarian position they are trying to defend is out of political fashion. Moreover, the natural leaders to whom they might turn, the Harvards and the Yales, feel they have little in common as a group with the small, lesser known schools and remain largely indifferent to their rising desperation. Even more crippling, these great schools seem to have lost confidence in themselves and their faith in what has historically been regarded as their unique role—setting and maintaining standards of academic excellence. Daniel Patrick Moynihan, a former member of the Harvard faculty and advisor on educational and social policy to several presidents before his election in 1976 as U. S. Senator from New York, is one of the sharpest critics of the private universities for having succumbed to the mounting pressures for unselectivity in all educational matters. These pressures come from government, which in his view constitutes not only a problem for the private institutions but a menace. "In the contest between public and private education, the national government feigns neutrality, but is in fact anything but neutral. As program has been piled atop program, and regulation on regulation, the Federal government has systematically organized its activities in ways that contribute to the decay of nonpublic education. Most likely, those responsible have not recognized this; they think themselves blind to the distinction between public and private. But of course they are not. They could not be. For governments inherently, routinely, automatically favor creatures of government. They know no other way. They recognize the legitimacy of no other institution." [17]

But even in the rare instances where government has shown an interest in aiding private institutions, Moynihan alleges that they have not responded as they should have in their own interest. As a case in point he cites the defeat of a proposal of President Nixon in 1970 (which he helped draft) to create a National Foundation for Higher Education whose object was to have been to channel unfettered money to institutions of special merit, essentially the older, prestigious private universities. This initiative, according to Moynihan, was a dramatic and unexpected recognition by government of the need to support quality as well as quantity in higher education. But the private institutions failed to give it their active backing. Instead, they submerged their interests into the preference of the public institutions for indiscriminate across-the-board aid and joined in denouncing the proposed Foundation as elitist and objectionable. These precious institutions, the creations and beneficiaries of privilege, thereby demonstrated, in the Senator's opinion, that they have in fact "become opposed in principle to the social arrangements which make their existence possible."[18]

The Prospect

Even without the handicap of the secret death wish the Senator perceives, private higher education is probably in for a difficult time, in part because higher education in general is in for a difficult time. It has just been through 30 years of growth and transformation at forced pace. Through that period, it has enjoyed broad public support, including a willingness to bear greatly increased costs.

But more recently there have been indications of growing taxpayer resistance to further increases in government budgets and a growing division of public opinion on major policy issues in education. Passage of Proposition 13 in California in 1978 has been followed by similar actions in other states and some observers see a true "taxpayers' revolt" in the making. Likewise, the strong egalitarian thrust of Federal educational policy of recent years has begun to encounter growing resistance, especially from middle-class groups who feel they are now being discriminated against. The decision of the U.S. Supreme Court in the controversial Bakke case has as one of its side-effects given encouragement to this view.

The heyday for higher education would therefore seem definitely to be past. From now on it will have to win its funding in a much more contentious political setting and in the context of an economy beset with sluggish growth and continuing inflation. Under these conditions, the conflicts within education will intensify and the financial noose around the necks of all colleges and universities will slowly but surely tighten. The public institutions will suffer severe strain but they will survive. Nor will the stronger private ones go under. But after the mid 1980s, with the prolongation of their financial difficulties and the gradual intensification of the battle for students, a growing number of the marginal private institutions in all likelihood may begin to fall by the wayside.

Such an erosion in the number of private institutions is not, in and of itself, significant. For American higher education to continue to maintain its effective duality, it is not necessary that there be an arithmetical balance between the public and private elements. But at the same time, imbalance cannot be allowed to go too far. Moreover, if the actual demise of some institutions should be symptomatic of a deterioration in the general health of the private sector of higher education, then there would be cause for serious concern. For if the interplay between public and private elements is to be corrective and stimulating the private element must be both sizable and vigorous. It is that degree of balance which is now in question.

If the private element withers, a degree of diversity and quality will be lost, and with the deterioration will come a gradual reduction of the creative, critical, and countervailing role of private institutions upon the entire system. This in turn would quietly but significantly alter the configuration of intellectual and political forces that will determine the outcome of many fundamental issues which American higher education confronts today: To what extent will it be a system devoted to traditional educational objectives and to what extent will it be employed as an agency for the achievement of social or political objectives? To what extent will it remain committed to truth and learning, and to what extent to public service? To what extent will the operative criteria for student admission be academic aptitude and achievement and to what extent financial need and ethnic or racial origin? To what extent will it be a decentralized, relatively autonomous collection of institutions pursuing their own definitions of role and to what extent will it be centralized around Federally defined priorities?

All of these issues arise today in particularly acute form because of the great period of growth and change from which American higher education has recently emerged. On the whole that period has left it bigger and fairer than ever before; but it has also left it far more dependent on Washington than ever before, more subject to its direction, more entangled in its procedures. The system has become more exploited in the sense that it is now increasingly employed as an instrumentality for the achievement of various noneducational purposes—economic, environmental, military, and social; more centralized in its decision-making, particularly at the state level; and more governmentalized in the sense that the public sector has become preponderant.

Such accompaniments to the progress that has been made in increasing and equalizing access to higher education for all groups now call for a period of reflection, evaluation, and further adjustments. These would be difficult enough to achieve even in a period of ease and stability. But it is the cruel prospect that they are going to have to take place during a period of great stress and friction caused by sustained demographic drop.

Historically the United States has been accustomed to dealing with problems of growth; it has been less familiar with and less apt in dealing with decline. In the 1950s and 1960s government—and educators as well—managed to cope with the expansion of higher education, but with something less than superb sensitivity and foresight. If the country is not able to deal with the task of managing the decline coming in the 1980s and 1990s with greater skill and forehandedness, one of the momentous consequences may well be the devitalization and possibly the liquidation of a good part of private higher education and thereby the duality of the American system.

4 ▶▶▶▶

Pure Science and the Public

THE RELATIONSHIP between scientific inquiry and government has been an intricate and troubled one for a very long time—from Galileo to Lysenko to yesterday's dispute about nuclear fall-out. And it has now, in the era of expensive instrumentation, become still more complicated by the necessity for science to depend heavily on government funding. At the same time, government is also heavily dependent on science, and a fine fluctuating tension exists between them, controlled by the power which each can exert upon the other.

From the scientists' perspective, the ideal would be subvention without obligation. In the words of Michael Polanyi in 1951: "The pursuit of science can be organized . . . in no other manner than by granting complete independence to all mature scientists. . . . The function of public authorities is not to plan research, but only to provide opportunities for its pursuit. All they have to do is provide facilities for every good scientist to follow his own interest in science."[1]

From the perspective of government, the ideal would be something quite different. Elmer B. Staats, U.S. Comptroller General, in a 1975 speech to the National Conference on the Advancement of Research, used football terms to define what he regarded as the proper balance between scientific autonomy and official responsibility. The metaphor may not have been elegant, but the message came through clearly. The modern R&D (research and development) game, in his words, "has become extremely sophisticated in its requirements for team unity and strategy, with every individual role adapted and committed to team effort for one objective, namely, to get the ball and move it forward until the goal is reached. Not only individual skills, but attitudes and team spirit are vital to success." Diversity may be a fine thing, he explained, but not when it leads to poor allocation procedures, duplication of effort, and a team running off in every direction. The need therefore is for "a coherent national strategy and a unity of purpose, spirit, and commitment that transcends the parochial preferences of each player. As in football, every individual player and specialty unit must function effectively with discipline, coordination and timing in accordance with the total team strategy." Therefore, he concluded, "to supplement the present pluralistic approach, some form of central focus and oversight is needed for evaluation, coordination, budgetary priority determination, and overall national policy."

These two statements made a quarter century apart summarize the evolution of government-science relationships which has now occurred in the United States, an evolution which Daniel Greenberg has called the change from the "old politics," when government money was given lavishly and without strings, to the "new politics," when it is given somewhat less lavishly and with a good many more strings.[2]

Polanyi's romantic vision of subvention without accountability has not been realized, but neither has Staats's managerial vision. This is the more remarkable because the institutions conducting basic research—principally university-managed laboratories—are probably more dependent on government funding than any other part of the Third Sector.

The Monopoly of Money

In 40 years, the scale of Federal support for science has leapt from the minuscule to the monumental. In 1979, Federal agencies provided some $28 billion for research and development. Some two-thirds of this figure was targeted for "development" (the translation of existing knowledge into hardware and gadgets), and one-fifth was for "applied research" (research directed specifically to the solution of some immediate, practical problem).[3] Most of this developmental and applied work is carried out by private industry under government contract.

The remaining one-eighth of the Federal R&D budget is spent for basic research, the search for new knowledge. This portion is crucial in the government-science relationship and it gives rise to the fundamental issues in their most acute form.

The Federal government currently provides some $3.6 billion annually for such research, 70 percent of the total national resources available for the purpose. Currently the areas of major concentration are defense, health, space, energy, and agriculture.[4] Two-thirds of the money goes to university-based laboratories. In its distribution a pattern of high concentration is evident; some 20 major research universities—such as MIT, Columbia, Stanford, and Harvard—receive the bulk of it. The remainder goes to government laboratories such as Oak Ridge and to some 35 federally funded research development centers, such as the Brookhaven Laboratory, which is operated by a consortium of universities on contract with the government.

Although the Federal government is now overwhelmingly the major source of funding of basic scientific research in this country, its authority over the scientific community is less than the arithmetic might suggest; its support is essential to the scientists, but their willing collaboration is indispensable to the government. The relationship, depending on one's preference in simile, is like two lovers in a hammock . . . or two scorpions in a bottle.

Rags to Riches—The Orphan's Enthronement

The intimate and fateful relationship which now exists between government and science began on August 2, 1939, the eve of World War II. On that day, a number of prominent physicists led by Albert Einstein sent a letter to President Franklin Roosevelt alerting him to the military potential of the atom. That letter was the first step in a train of events which led to the funding that year of a $2 billion atom bomb project called the Manhattan Proj-

ect, the creation of a wartime Office of Scientific Research and
Development (OSRD) which organized a still more vast program
of government-science collaboration in many fields, and eventually, in the postwar period, to acceptance by government of a continuing obligation to support basic science as a means to achieve
economic progress and national security.

Until the outbreak of that war, the American tradition had been
one of mutual aloofness between government and basic science.
Through the nineteenth century the United States was a net consumer, not a producer, of basic scientific discoveries. In Europe,
princely and commercial subsidy of fundamental research had
long been accepted, and the laboratories of Dalton, Faraday,
Gauss, and Helmholz were aglow with a scientific creativity
fueled by governmental funds. But in the United States, the official view, as reaffirmed by the U.S. Committee on the Organization of Government Scientific Work in 1903, was that science "on
the part of the government should be limited to utilitarian purposes." And leading scientific spokesmen on the whole agreed.

World War I brought the spheres of science and government
into somewhat greater contact but only a very limited collaboration. When the American Chemical Society, for example, offered its services to the Secretary of War at the outbreak of fighting, he replied that such help would be unnecessary. "He had
looked into the matter and found the War Department already
had a chemist."[5]

By the 1920s scientific progress was increasingly dependent on
costly equipment and full-time professional research workers. The
brute economics of these requirements began visibly to erode the
disdain of the scientists for potentially compromising funding. But
little of any kind was being offered. In 1925, then Secretary of
Commerce Herbert Hoover—with the encouragement of a
number of leading scientists—urged American industry to create
a fund to support basic research in the universities to help overcome the nation's lagging scientific development. Industry however did not respond. The scientists, with some misgivings, then
turned to the Federal government, but those initiatives, too,
were rebuffed.

Their continuing ambivalence about the risks of government

funding was reflected as late as 1934 in a letter from Karl T. Compton, then president of the MIT, who tempered an appeal for Federal research grants with the following words:

> I confess to considerable doubt as to the wisdom of advocating federal support of scientific research. . . . If government financial support should carry with it government control of research programs or research workers, or if it should lead to political influence or lobbying for the distribution of funds, or if any consideration should dictate the administration of funds other than the inherent worth of a project or the capabilities of a scientist, or if the funds should fluctuate considerably in amount with the political fortunes of an administration or the varying ideas of Congress, then government support would probably do more harm than good.[6]

Until the advent of World War II basic science remained an orphan—an impoverished but still prickly and sensitive orphan—caught between a desperate need for funding and a continuing fear of dangers of intrusions upon its autonomy by potential patrons. But after the Einstein letter, the orphan suddenly achieved not only affluence but also influence as a result of the enduring partnership which was forged. It is essential that the story of that achievement, and the political skills and scientific performance by which it was accomplished, be understood if the significance of what has occurred in the period since World War II is to be grasped.

Once President Roosevelt had given them the signal, the scientists who had approached him proceeded in a highly effective way to get a huge research effort underway in the shortest possible time—namely by enlisting institutions through the grant of funds rather than individuals through employment in government laboratories. As a result, university, industrial, and other facilities were rather quickly brought into a vast interconnected network of activity under broad governmental direction.

By executive order dated June 27, 1940, the President created a National Defense Research Committee (NDRC), which a year later was merged into a larger and more comprehensive Office of Scientific Research and Development (OSRD). Although created under the extraordinary pressures of war, these mechanisms were built on the basis of cooperation, not command, with special regard for scientists' sensibilities. The OSRD was a civilian scientist-controlled preserve reporting directly to the President. It worked for military objectives and in close liaison with the military, but it was independent of military control. In carrying out its broad assignment the OSRD was empowered to contract with university laboratories on a flexible basis which assured respect for their scientific independence. While obeisance was made to the idea of accountability, a degree of freedom was permitted the scientists which almost represented abandonment by government of its oversight responsibilities.

Dr. Vannevar Bush was the principal architect of both the NDRC and the OSRD. In his autobiography, *Pieces of the Action,* written years later (1972), he provided this revealing insight of the mood in which the new agencies were designed:

> There were those who protested that the action of setting up NDRC was an end run, a grab by which a small company of scientists and engineers, acting outside established channels, got hold of the authority and money for the program of developing new weapons. That, in fact, is exactly what it was. Moreover, it was the only way in which a broad program could be launched rapidly and on an adequate scale. To operate through established channels would have involved delays—and the hazard that independence might have been lost, that independence which was the central feature of the organization's success. The one thing that made launching it at all possible was the realization by the President that it was needed.[7]

Whatever violence the arrangements may have done to traditional concepts of proper public administration, they proved spectacularly successful. From the new war-born collaboration there quickly began to flow a stream of innovations of immense military importance—more sophisticated radar equipment, the proximity fuse, new kinds of underwater detection devices, and of course the atomic bomb itself.

Through their discoveries the scientists made a decisive contribution to the outcome of the war and by its end they had been exalted as public heroes by a grateful and somewhat awed nation. To the scientists themselves, what had been accomplished was taken as proof of the correctness of their conviction that science is best managed exclusively by scientists. The atomic blasts at Hiroshima and Nagasaki in the moment of final victory only intensified the public's admiration and solidified the scientists' determination that unfettered freedom had to be the basis of their future collaboration with government.

Even as the war began to draw to a close Vannevar Bush began to lay plans for ensuring that scientific research would be adequately nourished thereafter. The memory of the impoverishment of science up until the time of Pearl Harbor had not been erased by the luxurious and exhilarating wartime experience. In November 1944, President Roosevelt, at Bush's prompting, asked him to prepare a blueprint for the postwar relationship between science and government.

His report was delivered on July 5, 1945, to President Truman, three months after Roosevelt's death. Entitled "Science, the Endless Frontier," it proceeded from a central concern with basic research and from a realistic recognition that government funding was essential if national scientific achievement was not once again to be crippled by lack of resources. Its principal recommendation was that a National Science Foundation be created which would provide a channel for the flow of government money to the practitioners of science but which would screen out the possibility of political intrusion. The head of the Foundation would be chosen by a board composed only of civilian scientists. In effect the plan constituted a design for bestowing upon science a unique and privileged place in the public process—an enclave governed by scientists and paid for by public funds.

Dethronement and the Return to Administrative Normality

Bush's approach, formulated in the headiness of impending military victory and of public and political adulation of science, was by all conventional governmental concepts presumptuous in the extreme. The reaction it provoked from the politicians was predictably strong. There was virtually no disagreement about the necessity of large-scale and continuing government support of science. But there was much gagging at the demand that science should be exempted from the requirements of accountability and direction imposed on all other beneficiaries of the public treasury. Harold Ickes, Secretary of the Interior, spoke for many experienced public figures in flatly dismissing as plain "bunk" the whole idea that scientists represented a special caste, somehow superior to bureaucrats and politicians, that could be relied upon to spend public funds wisely and responsibly without oversight.

Convictions on both sides, however, were strong. Neither was disposed to give ground, and an intense five-year battle ensued. Senator Harley Kilgore, a leading Democrat, presented a bill which would have created a National Science Foundation (NSF) headed by a Presidential appointee, advised by a mixed board of civilians and officials. This the scientists vehemently opposed. Compromise bills by Senator Warren Magnuson and later by Senator Alexander Smith reflecting the Bush position were submitted, but when the Smith bill was finally passed in 1947, President Truman vetoed it on grounds that it represented "a marked departure from sound principles for the administration of public affairs" and that it would, in effect, "vest the determination of vital national policies, the expenditure of large public funds, and the administration of important governmental functions in a group of individuals who would be essentially private citizens. The proposed National Science Foundation would be divorced from control by the people to an extent that implies a distinct lack of faith in the democratic process."[8]

The proposed science legislation had come to an impasse. Meanwhile a parallel issue engaged the energies of scientists. It was at the same time a digression and a highly pertinent demonstration of the developing fragmentation of the scientific community and of its increasingly sensitive relationships with government. That issue related to postwar control of atomic energy. The bombings of Hiroshima and Nagaski had produced great concern among many of the thousands of scientists who had worked on the Manhattan Project about the military, economic, political, and ethical implications of nuclear research. Consequently, immediately after Japan surrendered, they formed themselves into a militant lobbying and advocacy organization to do battle on such questions as civilian versus military control and internationalism versus national monopoly. As splits among scientists developed, the outlines could be perceived of an "inner group" of many of the wartime eminences who were closely related to prestigious academic institutions, large corporations, and the military; and an "outer group" of generally lesser rank opposed to concentration of research under military influence and conducted in conditions of secrecy. The major effect of the struggle over control of atomic policy upon the prospects for science legislation was that it hardened opinions on both sides: to many scientists, it intensified their fear of governmental domination; and to many politicians, it intensified the feeling that the scientists tended to extremism in their policy positions.

Following many more months of wrangling, the National Science Foundation was finally established in 1950, on the basis of a tacit compromise. The Bush report had envisaged a highly centralized agency, with divisions of medical and military research, and with a director appointed by a private board. Instead a more decentralized system was established, including the newly created National Institutes of Health, separate research entities within the several branches of the military, and the new NSF—which would be headed by a Presidential appointee. By diversifying the sources of money for science among many agencies and military branches and by counterbalancing those agencies' natural preference for applied research with an emphasis on basic research in the NSF, a pluralistic structure of funding and administration was created which, in the judgment of the Congress and of the Truman Administration, would maximize both the autonomy and the accountability of the scientist and of scientific research institutions.

On the issue of control of the NSF, the scientists had suffered a signal defeat. But in a paradoxical way, they had also triumphed—at least for another decade—in their dual quest for ample funding and freedom of action. The reasons were three.

First, there was a seller's market for their wares. The year the NSF was created was also the year of the outbreak of the Korean War and the beginning of a period of greater chill in the Cold

War. Immediately after the Japanese surrender, when the money of the OSRD had begun to disappear, it had been the military services—especially the Office of Naval Research—which had come forward with more than adequate substitute funding, and this had not been interrupted during the years of debate over the establishment of the NSF and military versus civilian control of the atom. The services, recalling their prewar neglect of science and the great contribution of scientific discoveries to victory over the Germans and Japanese, were eager to embrace the scientists. After 1950, their "almost fanatic enthusiasm," as Harvard President James Conant called it, for research and development, combined with a certain amount of interservice rivalry, meant that they were prepared to enlist the cooperation of scientists on the latter's terms.

Second, the sheer scale and complexity of the collaboration made it impossible for subordination of science to governmental control to be established. If one agency tried to impose unacceptable loyalty requirements, another was able, and often eager, to offer the funds without such restrictions. If a bureau was blocked from funding basic research under one budgetary heading, it simply concealed it under another. There was the will, and in all the confusion it was always possible to find the way, to escape constraints.

Third, the scientists were able to live with the rules imposed upon them because they had largely written those rules themselves. During World War II and continuing into the postwar period, there had developed an indescribably intricate and extensive maze of governmental boards, advisory committees, and task forces on scientific matters in which civilian scientists played a highly influential role because of their expertise and because they took their advisory responsibilities seriously. In so doing, they served the government's needs, and at the same time they saw to it that the government did not neglect the needs of their institutions and the requirements of their profession.

By the end of the first postwar decade it could be said that although the scientists had lost an ideological battle over the NSF, they had won their war for sustenance and power. Living together with government under the resulting peace treaty was, however, less than perfect bliss, and by the late 1950s increasing strain and friction between the partners had become evident. While some agencies, such as the Office of Naval Research, had developed easy and excellent relations with scientists, others— most notably the Atomic Energy Commission (AEC)—had been convulsed with quarrels over questions of loyalty and secrecy, the Oppenheimer case being the most notorious example. In both Congress and the Executive Branch there was a growing feeling that the rapid increase of research expenditures, including those in the medical field, had led to wastefulness and even to the milking of the public treasury by a number of prestigious private centers of research. The situation was becoming ripe for reaction against the swollen affluence of pure science and against its position of de facto sovereignty over its own vital affairs despite its dependency upon public funds.

The discharge of that gathering sentiment was temporarily delayed by another accident of history—the launching of Sputnik I by the Soviet Union in October 1957. Instantly, if only briefly, the scientists were resanctified and Federal funding for research and scientific training increased vastly. In addition, the potentates of science were given direct access to the very center of political power. The Science Advisory Committee, previously buried in the Office of Defense Mobilization, was raised to the status of the President's Science Advisory Committee (PSAC).

The post-Sputnik honeymoon was ardent but short-lived, and by the early 1960s science was under growing political attack. An ill-starred project of the National Science Foundation called Mohole was one of the events which unleashed it. Initiated in March 1957, the project originally envisaged the drilling of an unprecedentedly deep hole into the ocean floor to study the earth's interior. The cost was initially estimated at $5 million. By August 1966, nine years later, the hole had still not been drilled and the project had become a public fiasco. Indeed it had achieved the unique distinction of being the only basic research project ever terminated by act of Congress.

The NSF's bungling began with a confused and inconsistent statement of the project's objectives and with a selection of the principal contractor which strongly smelled of politics. Frequent

changes in directing staff resulted in loss of all control over costs
and priorities, and then, as public criticism began to mount, the
NSF found itself embroiled in an increasingly nasty series of internal quarrels. When the Congress finally put the matter to rest,
the estimated costs had soared to $125 million and the per-
suasiveness of the traditional demand of the scientists to be free of
the usual forms of administrative oversight had been rather badly
undercut.*

Dr. Ivan Bennett of the White House science office summarized the state of affairs as of 1966 in blunt and chilling words:
"Science . . . can no longer hope to exist," he said, "among all
human enterprises, through some mystique, without constraints
or scrutiny in terms of national goals, and isolated from the competition for allocation of resources which are finite. . . . Unless
we . . . are prepared to examine our endeavors, our objectives,
and our priorities, and to state our case, openly and clearly, the
future will be difficult indeed." [9]

To many scientists these words sounded like the epitaph for the
"old politics" of pure science—namely its ample funding and unfettered freedom—and a sure sign of the advent of the "new politics" of tightening belts and tightening restrictions. This, however, proved to be an excessively melancholy interpretation. The
dramatic increase in funding which had prevailed from the early
1950s through 1968 leveled off, but during the following decade
support for basic science remained steady at about $2.5 billion an-
nually, which if discounted for inflation amounted to a 20 percent
decline in support in real terms, significant but not catastrophic.
This coincided with some increase in legal and administrative
constraints by government. In the words of Don K. Price, the nation's most distinguished observer of these matters, these constraints were also intrusions, imposed "not in the interest of the
quality of research but of short term practical results, regional distribution of funds, or other criteria more or less irrelevant to scientific excellence." [10]

* Concern about mismanagement and irregularities in the handling of government research
continues. In 1978, for example, the National Cancer Institute was accused of slovenliness
in overseeing its support of the Eppley Institute in Omaha; and the Harvard School of
Public Health was accused of misapplying some of its contract research funds. Neither of
these instances has ripened to the point of criminal proceedings, however.

Indubitably, some diminution in the status of science *vis à vis*
government has now occurred. At the height of postwar scientific
ascendancy in the 1960s, Price saw the preponderance of influence with the scientists, and in his view "the scientific estate" was
on the whole the invader of governmental sovereignty, not the reverse. He saw the "new scientific revolution" moving the public
and private sectors closer together, upsetting the traditional system of checks and balances established under the Constitution,
redefining the meaning of both economic and political power, and
reallocating such power, on balance, toward the scientists.[11]

But by 1976, William D. Carey, Executive Officer of the American Association for the Advancement of Science, felt the preponderance had shifted to the official side. In his view, the Federal
government now "holds most of the high cards which determine
the thrust and priorities of scientific research and development effort in the United States. Its policy goals and its budget preferences to a very great extent have shaped the environment in
which science and technology have been carried on since the
1940s. There is no reason to suppose that these arrangements will
change much, if at all, in the years to come."

These shifts are not inconsequential, but neither should they
be exaggerated. The extent of shrinkage in funding of basic
science, given the continuing fiscal crisis of government over
these years, has been relatively modest, and the prospects are
that the decline is about to be reversed. The Carter Administration, in contrast to the Johnson and Nixon Administration, has
shown a determination to develop good relations with the scientists and it has placed a high priority on support for basic science
in its budget proposals. Bureaucratic requirements and Congressional pressures on science have increased, but partisan politics
and political ideology have been kept out of the laboratory. To
judge by its continuing creativity and productivity, American
science remains healthy and strong.

Putting the fluctuations in its resources and restrictions in
broader historical perspective, one could reasonably conclude
that although the ability of science to wring appropriations from
and resist the importuning of its governmental patron has periodically weakened in the post-World War II era, it has just as regu-

larly been reinforced by the advent of some urgent new problem, national or international—the Cold War, Sputnik, or the energy shortage. This capacity of science to benefit from each recurrence of crisis is evidence that science is now so essential to the accomplishment of priority governmental objectives that it has achieved, as Don Price discerned years ago, a special and important kind of political power, which is its ultimate protection. The result is a relatively stabilized, even institutionalized, equilibrium leaving science in the United States not as sovereign as it once was but still enjoying a combination of ample resources and freedom unmatched in any other nation.

Science and Society—The Coming Confrontation

The balance which has been struck between science and government, however improbable, rests upon a combination of safeguarding elements: government funding is provided through the budgets of a number of separate departments and agencies; Congress is beginning to develop greater competence and independence in dealing with science policy; various public interest groups are now monitoring such policy; the major universities through which most of the funds are used have a degree of strength in resisting excessive government demands; and above all, the countervailing power of the scientists because of their essentiality to national purposes. Though not without its difficulties and even dangers, the totality represents a tolerable combination of tradeoffs: basic science, though dependent on government for its sustenance, is substantially protected against the direct exploitation of that dependency by government, which could otherwise destroy its integrity or stifle its quality.

The relationship of major elements of the Third Sector with the citizenry at large is on the whole increasingly troubled. Science (as is also the case with higher education, health services, and cultural institutions) is increasingly affected by changes in public attitudes, as its dependence on governmental appropriations, and therefore on the political process, increases. Moreover, the contemporary mood is to demand more social responsibility, responsiveness, openness, and public participation in the decision-making of all institutions.

Among the different subcategories of the Third Sector, the impact of these tendencies varies greatly. In higher education, student demands for participation in university governance, so noisy and disturbing in the 1960s, seem now to have subsided; on the other hand, the demands of faculty, especially junior faculty, for a greater role are rising; and the general public, in the face of rising costs and falling achievement scores, is increasingly disenchanted with the educators. In health, public pressures have resulted in great changes in public policy, but the role of the general public in shaping specific health policies remains secondary, and the ordinary citizen remains largely passive in the presence of his physician—incapacitated by ignorance and anxiety. In the cultural field, supporters of opera, chamber music and other traditional forms of "high culture" feel increasingly threatened by the power of the more numerous partisans of "popular culture" over the allocation of government subsidies.*

It is in the area of science, however, where the clash of, or the gulf between, the public and the professionals is the most profound and potentially the most destructive. The reasons are mostly self-evident. A great many people, now aware of the menace of atomic weapons, carcinogens, and other manifestations of what once was called Progress have simply stopped believing that science is necessarily as beneficial or benign as they once did. They have also stopped believing that scientists are as capable, disinterested, and trustworthy as they once did. The late Robert M. Hutchins once formulated this sentiment in characteristically irreverent terms: "My view, based on long and painful observation, is that professors are somewhat worse than other people, and that scientists are somewhat worse than other professors. . . . A scientist has a limited education. He labors on the topic of his dissertation, wins the Nobel Prize by the time he is 35, and suddenly has nothing to do. . . . He has no alternative but to spend the rest of his life making a nuisance of himself." [12]

* The social action movements are essentially expressions of public concerns rather than institutions confronting them, so in their case the problem of public disapproval, to the extent it arises, does so essentially in the form of a diminution of their constituency.

The intimate involvement of science with the military, which originally put the scientists on a pedestal, has more recently been a factor in knocking them off it. As a result of their long immersion in matters of weaponry and geopolitics, scientists are suspected of having developed a militarized mentality, a fascination with power and the instruments of death. The evil image of Dr. Strangelove has now been as indelibly etched on the public consciousness as the saintly visages of Pasteur and Banting were in former times.

Among those citizens somewhat more knowledgeable about scientific affairs, the naïveté, incompetence, and collusiveness of the National Academy of Sciences—the nation's most prestigious scientific body—have also been damaging. In addition to its honorific functions, the Academy is chartered to serve as advisor to government on scientific questions. Through a vast array of committees, it attempts to evaluate hundreds of questions put to it, trivial and important, by almost every official agency and department. To do so, however, it has not been given budget or adequate staff of its own and has to depend on funding by its clients and on the services of part-time volunteers. Perhaps as a consequence, it has often failed to meet even the most elementary standards of objectivity and independence. For example, it chose a retired associate director of the National Bureau of Standards to direct an evaluation of that bureau's research programs. Its Aeronautics and Space Engineering Board, which advises the government on matters ranging from the space shuttle to civil aviation, has been headed by a vice-president of Lockheed. Its assessment of the effects of the defoliation programs carried out by U.S. military forces in Vietnam was put in the hands of a scientist who had formerly served as a leading figure in the Army's herbicide research program.

In addition it has willingly operated under rules set by its clients, which has further compromised its position. Reports have frequently been submitted to them for "comment" before release; clients have been permitted a strong hand in, even a veto over, the composition of study panels; and if studies have sometimes turned out to be objectionable to the clients, the Academy has allowed them to be suppressed.

A catalog of such instances of apparent impropriety and complaisance was documented by Philip Boffey in his devastating book on the Academy, *The Brain Bank of America,* published in 1975. His general conclusion was that the body, for all its prestige, had not distinguished itself as a protector of the public welfare. In support of that judgment, Boffey cited the following episodes:

> In our examination of pesticides, for example, it was Rachel Carson who first sounded the alarm about deleterious side effects, whereas the Academy pooh-poohed the alleged danger. In the area of defoliation, it was the American Association for the Advancement of Science which led the investigation of harmful effects, while the Academy allowed itself to be used by the military and its supporters in an effort to head off the AAAS thrust. In the case of the supersonic transport, it was citizens' groups in Oklahoma and elsewhere that expressed resistance to the sonic boom, and the Academy was rushed in by the government to quiet the opposition. Then, when a scientist working on an Academy committee did raise disturbing questions about the SST's possible impact on the incidence of skin cancer, the Academy practically disowned him. And in the case of the Atomic Energy Commission's plan to bury radioactive wastes at Lyons, Kansas, it was local geologists who raised questions about the safety of the scheme, while it was an Academy committee, operating with incomplete information, that generally endorsed the AEC's plans.[13]

A gentle but telling summary of the meaning of Boffey's book was contained in the review of it in the *New York Times* by Stephen Jay Gould, a Harvard scientist:

> The members of the Academy are not evil schemers or conscious conspirators; they are, in general, good and fair men. But conformity and compromise too often characterize the illusory pursuit of influence—better to mute one's voice and retain a tiny office in the corridors of power. . . . A system lies most nakedly exposed because the best and the brightest are willing to operate so uncritically within its constraints.[14]

Serious as the new concerns of the public about the disinterestedness and wisdom of the scientific community may be, they are secondary to those which have developed about the dangers to public safety of scientific progress itself. These relate to such problems as carcinogens and environmental degradation; to gene-splicing and genetic manipulation; to nuclear reactor safety, plutonium reprocessing, and the storage of radioactive wastes; and to the rapidly advancing technology of modern weaponry, including biological and chemical weapons as well as nuclear ones. Indeed, millions of citizens are now aware that the future of American society itself—indeed of the planet—can be jeopardized by the consequences of scientific advance and that many of the cardinal choices of public policy which the nation will face in the future— that is, those which in the crudest sense will determine whether they live or die—turn increasingly on highly technical and arcane scientific considerations. Yet such matters are totally beyond the direct experience of most politicians and of the general citizenry. What can a democracy do, they ask, when many of its crucial decisions cannot be reached through democratic processes? The realization of the dangers and of their own incompetence to deal with them is immensely fear-producing.

The response to such intolerable anxiety has taken two general forms. First a demand is growing for greater social control over the directions and substance of certain scientific research. The most pertinent case to date concerns recombinant DNA research, popularly known as gene-splicing. Among scientists themselves, a hot debate over the propriety of such research has been underway for several years. When gene-splicing was first found to be possible, some foresaw great potential benefits, including important new food crops, new medicines, and cures for presently incurable diseases. But others saw great risks, including plagues of altered viruses or germs attacking humans, animals, and plants, as well as human genetic engineering for malevolent purposes. They therefore called for a world moratorium on certain types of experiments because of the dangers.

The debate was subsequently joined by philosophers, theologians, industrialists, labor spokesmen, and activists of many kinds. As a result, legislation has now been proposed which for the first time would impose government regulation over an important field of basic biological research. The various bills under consideration would create a permanent official commission to monitor and regulate all recombinant DNA research, license facilities housing such research, and impose heavy fines on scientists violating the governmental regulations. In addition to possible Federal action, various localities are moving to establish their own restrictions on the "biohazards" which might result from such research.

Proponents see such legislation, though it directly invades the laboratory, as essential to public protection. Opponents see in the measures governmental attempts to control the freedom of scientific inquiry, attempts which immediately evoke images of totalitarian oppression. Whether or not this particular issue will be resolved by some form of compromise which would make scientists themselves primarily responsible for regulating the research rather than a governmental mechanism, it is predictable that public demand for the direct regulation of certain kinds of scientific experimentation considered dangerous to safety, health, or morals will arise repeatedly in the future.

A second form of public response to the perceived dangers of scientific developments has been demands for greater "accountability" on the part of scientists, not in conventional financial or administrative terms but in sweeping and undefined social, ethical, and political terms. In part they are aimed at breaking down self-segregation and excessive secrecy on the part of science, and to this degree they are reasonable and can be satisfied.

Scientists have in fact shown a tendency to become first a fraternity and then an establishment, which resists the intrusions of unorthodox individuals and ideas, and also resists divulging full information about its activities to the citizenry—or at least does not devote itself energetically to that task.

From the public's perspective, such habits on the part of governing elites have in the past led to appalling mistakes of public policy and then to efforts to cover up those mistakes. Greater openness is therefore regarded as a minimal and essential safety measure. And in the field of science it is gradually being achieved—as the World War II generation of leadership is succeeded by a younger one less steeped in the military atmosphere and as the Freedom of Information Act produces greater and greater declassification of documents.

But the new demands upon science go far beyond openness. There is also the strong but undifferentiated demand for participation without specificity as to in what, by whom, or according to what procedures. Scientists are at least as skeptical about the utility and appropriateness of this impulse as is the public toward institutionalized secrecy. Scientists believe that by and large, on highly technical matters, the only relevant and useful contributions are those of persons with knowledge and understanding of them. This opinion has been confirmed to the scientists' satisfaction by many experiences before Congressional committees, for example, in which such topics as high-intensity proton beams have been raised in an atmosphere of such utter incomprehension that the discussion approaches comic opera. Nor has their sympathy for openness and wider participation been encouraged by the tactics of some activists in the past, such as fisticuffs and tomato throwing at meetings of the American Association for the Advancement of Science. They remain committed to excellence, not egalitarianism, in their professional domain and in this sense they are unrepentant elitists.

One of the most significant manifestations of what can be called a developing "anti-science movement" are the controversies involving the content of science textbooks which have now erupted in many parts of the United States. The Scopes trial of 1925 over the teaching of the theory of evolution in the schools issued from a deprived rural area of Appalachia. But current textbook disputes arise mainly from middle-class citizens, many of whom are technically trained, living in such areas as urban Texas and Southern California, the very centers of industry based on high technology.

According to Dorothy Nelkin of Cornell University, a leading student of the problem, three themes pervade these controversies: A disillusionment with science on grounds that it is threatening traditional religious and moral values; resentment against the domination of the science curriculum in the schools by professional scientists; and fear that the meritocratic process operating within science threatens more egalitarian, pluralistic values.

The very idea that questions of scientific fact and scientific education should be settled by public debate and that the teaching of science should "reflect community values and norms" leaves scientists amazed if not outraged. In Nelkin's words, "Concepts of pluralism, of equity and of participatory democracy, as they are defined in the political context, are incongruous in science. Scientific concepts are taught when they are generally accepted by the scientific community. In fact, it is precisely that acceptance by the scientific community that acts to validate one concept and reject another; acceptance by those outside the scientific community is irrelevant."[15]

Bridging the gulf between science and the rest of society on such fundamental problems as openness and public participation will be extremely difficult. But an even further range of demands is now being placed on scientists which is the most unrealizable of all because it almost constitutes a pathology of escapism by American society.

On such disturbing problems as carcinogens, environmental degradation, and nuclear reactor safety, the public apparently wants from the scientist not tentative opinion and equivocation but clear and final answers. Regrettably, these cannot be given. Scientists can only make conjectures about the way the world works, and then collect data in rigorous fashion to see whether those conjectures can be disconfirmed, thereby to improve them. Everything the scientist thinks he knows today can give way to some new notion, some new evidence, tomorrow. This does not mean that science does not work; this is precisely how it does work. But to a bewildered and fear-ridden public, there is no comfort in the cold and permanent fact that in science no one knows, or will ever know, The Truth.

The public seems also to want Prophecy from science— knowledge in advance about whether new discoveries will be harmful or dangerous. But scientists are engaged in the enterprise of understanding nature. The discoveries they make lead to applications which are determined by a complex interplay of politics and economic and social forces. Whether those applications are used for human betterment or destruction, and what the ultimate implications of their discoveries may be, are neither controllable or even knowable by the few scientists originally responsible. As Bernard T. Feld and Victor F. Weisskopf, physicists at MIT, have written:

Intercontinental ballistic missiles involve the same technology as rockets used to study the upper atmosphere. The technology of multiple warheads and of maneuverable re-entry vehicles is the same as that which permits landing and takeoff of aircraft in bad weather, manned landings on the moon and the exploration of the planets. The same lasers that make possible "smart bombs" are being used to perform delicate eye surgery; they may eventually result in cheap fusion power.[16]

Ultimately the public seems to ask from the scientist not only Truth and Prophecy but also Wisdom; it is not enough that he be authoritative in judging matters in his special field of knowledge; he must also be sensitive, ethical, and responsible in advising on the great public issues of science policy.

In fairness it must be said that the scientists, for all their establishmentarianism, have been at least as aware of and concerned about their broader social and ethical responsibilities as members of any other profession. Compared to the social performance of lawyers, accountants, and medical doctors, for example, their record is a proud one. Some of them tried in vain to alter the decision to drop the atomic bombs on Japan. Immediately after the war they helped devise a generous and farsighted plan for placing the peaceful development of nuclear energy under international control. They called attention to the dangers of atmospheric testing of nuclear weapons and were influential in achieving the nuclear test ban treaty of 1963. They deserve credit for goading the government into the ongoing talks on limiting strategic arms. Biologists and chemists led the campaign against biological weapons. The horrors of modern weaponry, cannot therefore fairly be blamed on scientists alone.

Nonetheless, however ethical and responsible individual scientists may be, the public expectation that on issues of science policy their scientific advisors can deliver Wisdom is as futile as the notion they can deliver Truth. For "scientific decisions," even at their most scientific, are in many cases decisions based on values, and in this sense they are personal judgments, open to argument and alternative viewpoints.

Barry Commoner, the Washington University biologist, has well described the interpenetration of fact and values in such public policy choices in these words: In decisions about pesticides, "the *scientific* questions are, how much DDT do you need to protect the elm tree? and How many robins will that kill? After that is determined, all scientific relevance stops, and the question becomes, Which do you favor—the song of a bird, or the shade of an elm tree?"[17]

Scientific advisors can provide political informaion; they cannot substitute for political decision-making. A pluralistic society contains many competing notions about tradeoffs and cost-benefits; some enjoy the robin's song, some the shade of the elm tree. Laying upon the conscience of the scientist endless and unspecific demands for accountability and responsibility is an evasion of, not a means of dealing with, such choices.

But to a public that knows only enough about science to feel that at any moment it can die from it, scolding them for their incomprehension accomplishes very little. For the bewildered citizenry, it is frustratingly, frighteningly unsatisfactory to feel that the scientists themselves, who presumably know all of the inner mysteries of the universe, do not have any reliable answers to the big questions either.

To recapitulate, then, the present position of basic science—an activity rooted in the traditions of privateness, autonomy, and human service but in fact now carried on in both governmental and private institutions and to a considerable degree for governmental purposes—is a study in contradictions.

On the one hand, it is both substantially indentured and substantially free. It has now become essentially a Federal government program—funded by it and focussed by it on governmentally and publicly determined priority fields. And yet science is not the helpless victim of government. The power and importance of their knowledge is now so great that the scientists—within the framework of broad governmental priorities—can, from their working base in the universities, be about as free and independent as they wish to be. Paradoxically, basic science is both the part of the Third Sector most heavily subsidized by government and the part most able to protect itself *vis à vis* government.

On the other hand, the fundamental vulnerability of science in the American pluralistic system may lie in its relationship to the general population. Here its position is ambiguous and on balance deteriorating. It is worshipfully, ignorantly trusted and at the same time deeply, fearfully distrusted. If science were unimportant, it might be left alone. But as war is too important to be left to the generals, so science is now felt to be too important to be left to the scientists. Which means that undue expectations are placed upon science for certainty and guidance, while at the same time values and procedures from the political realm incompatible with those of science itself—such as openness and equality—are pressed upon it. Indeed, the relationship between science and the citizenry embodies the dilemma of elitism versus the idea of participatory democracy in its most intractable form.

In another time it might have been possible for these "two cultures" simply to ignore one another and to co-exist separately and indefinitely. But not now and especially not in the United States.

Yet how can they in fact be brought together? Various ideas are already being tried—a federally sponsored program of education to raise the public's level of "scientific literacy"; the creation of a Congressional Office of Technology Assessment to try to evaluate in advance the impacts and hazards of new discoveries; the establishment of a "science court" to "adjudicate" the issues of public policy arising out of scientific advances. They all, unfortunately, present overwhelming practical and theoretical difficulties. Yet these and other attempts to narrow if not close the existing breach of understanding must be encouraged, if only because the hazards to both science and the public interest of not trying are plainly intolerable.

5 ▶▶▶▶

The Health System— Getting Better, Going Broke

HEALTH-RELATED INSTITUTIONS—from medical schools, hospitals, insurance companies, research laboratories, and homes for the elderly to drug companies, various government bureaus, and the American Medical Association—are as massive an "industry" as education in all its aspects. They are also just as diverse, as decentralized in their control, and as wracked by the forces of economic, social, and political change. They are another of the great nonsystems of institutions which constitute much of the American system, overlapping, uncoordinated, fragmented, unplanned, and competitive.

But the contrasts between education and the health field are as striking as the similarities. Educational opportunity has long been considered an "entitlement" for Americans; access to health services has only recently reached that status. Public appetite for education may be on the wane, but that for health services still seems ascendant. If the most urgent problem of higher education is now the "management of decline," that of medicine and health services is the control of excess—excessive hospitalization, excessive resort to drugs and surgery, and especially excessive increase in costs.

Education has long since seen public institutions become predominant in scale and policy influence; but in the health field, private forces continue to hold a very strong position. Education,

particularly higher education, has a long record of political amateurism and ineffectiveness; but the private forces in health have
an equally long record of powerful, often decisive, lobbying influence.

In higher education, the parallel operation of privately and
publicly controlled elements is considered to be a matter of great
significance, and the distinctive characteristics of each are greatly
emphasized. In health, there is an even greater mixture of privately and publicly governed institutions. There are 112 accred-
ited medical schools, for example, of which 64 are public and 48
private. Of the nation's 7271 hospitals, 3622 are private "voluntary" nonprofit institutions, 2653 are governmental, and 996 are
"proprietary," (private profit-making) institutions. Of the 20,185
existing nursing homes for the elderly, 7 percent are governmental, 18 percent private nonprofit, and 75 percent proprietary.[1] The National Institutes of Health and many of their related
centers of biomedical research are governmental; the pharmaceutical and medical equipment industries are private and profit-
making. Health insurance is provided partly by the nonprofit
Blue Cross and Blue Shield plans, partly by profit-making insurance companies, and partly by government. The U.S. Public
Health Service and the medical programs of the Veterans Administration are governmental; but the vast majority of physicians
are private practitioners.

Thus the sharpest distinction between the field of health and
the other major institutionalized subsectors of the Third Sector is
that to an unusual degree it involves relationships among the
three major sectors—government, the private profit-making sector, and the private nonprofit sector—including the pharmaceutical and equipment industries; the health insurance industry; voluntary, proprietary, and governmental hospitals and special care
facilities; the organized private practitioners; and, most recently,
the swelling "health bureaucracy" and organized groups of consumers.

It has been the continuous interplay, and the shifting balance of
power, among these various elements which has governed the
rate and direction of the evolution of the health system. For a
crucial quarter century between the two world wars, nonevolu-

tion was its most prominent and troubling characteristic; but for most of the past 40 years, it has been in process of extraordinarily rapid and fundamental change. The great issue of the earlier part of the century, namely whether government should be allowed a major role, has been resolved, decisively and irreversibly. But the massive entrance of public funds has now thrown the system into a new crisis which turns on the question, once government intervention is accepted, of how it should best intervene to achieve efficiency as well as equity and to ensure freedom as well as access.

The Advent of Modern Medicine

Through the nineteenth century, with only limited exceptions, American medicine was a private affair, and to a considerable extent a private business. In that prescientific time, care was provided mainly in the home or the doctor's office rather than in a hospital. The health system was on the whole sketchy and generally of poor quality. The many existing small proprietary medical schools were of wildly uneven standards. They at least had the virtue, however, of turning out a large number of practitioners to meet the needs of a rapidly growing and spreading population.

Then with the turn of the century it appeared that a whole new era might be opening. Important biomedical discoveries had been made in Europe as well as great advances in the scientific training of doctors. In the United States Dr. Walter Reed and his associates had proved that a particular variety of mosquito transmitted yellow fever, which led to its virtual eradication. Major Bailey Ashford established the relationship of widespread anemia to hookworm and developed an inexpensive cure, which the Rockefeller philanthropies then undertook to apply throughout the American South. State and municipal boards of health became more vigorous in campaigns to improve sanitation, inspect milk, and chlorinate water. In 1912 the old Marine Hospital Service was converted into the U.S. Public Health Service, and the Federal government began to concern itself with a wider range of social welfare matters, including the general health of mothers and children. The American Medical Association (AMA) became increasingly devoted to the improvement of standards of medical training, and with the publication of the famous Flexner report in 1910, which had been financed by one of the philanthropic foundations created by Andrew Carnegie, reforms were rapidly instituted to bring American medical teaching up to the levels of the better European centers. Prestigious groups of doctors, and indeed the AMA itself, were in the vanguard of those seeking to reform medical education and to increase the accessibility of the health-care system. In 1917 a committee of the AMA published a memorable report endorsing the development of programs of health insurance for all income groups throughout the country. It was, in brief, a progressive and hopeful time and it revealed the existence both within the medical profession and the public at large of a deep interest in both the social and the scientific elements of health care.

As it turned out, however, although scientific and educational advances continued, the hopes for progress in dealing with the social and economic issues were abruptly snuffed out. The 1917 AMA report on health insurance for example was to be the last reformist and nondoctrinaire position taken by that organization on a matter of public policy for the next several decades.

The time and place when American medicine took an abrupt right turn in the direction of profits and politics can be established quite precisely: It was at the annual meeting of the AMA in 1920, held in New Orleans. The issue was a public policy proposal favoring the development of compulsory comprehensive health insurance. It had been developed by a prominent group of economists, labor leaders, lawyers, historians and physicians, including the then president of the AMA, Dr. Alexander Lambert. Though it was generally expected to carry the day, the proposal instead went down to heavy defeat. The vote marked the end to the leadership of organized American medicine by an elite group of medical educators and socially responsible practitioners and the transfer of control to a more conservative and self-interested group. Their perspective was essentially that of the individual practitioner. Their single-minded purpose was to improve his economic position and to protect his freedom from social or governmental controls of any kind.

They were encouraged about the possibility of using the AMA as an instrument to advance these interests by the fact that its membership had leapt from some 8000 in 1900 to more than 80,000 by 1920, and its growing political muscle had been demonstrated in a number of instances in the intervening years. Their mentality was that of the medieval guild, and once they were in control the organization moved quickly to set in place the essential elements of an effective professional monopoly. These classic requirements are essentially three: The power to restrict the supply of the service or commodity in question; the capability to maintain discipline and unity among the members; and the capacity to wage effective propaganda and political warfare against any public or governmental threats which might arise.

The power of the AMA to choke off the influx of new practitioners was already well established by 1920. As early as 1904 it had begun efforts to eliminate the get-rich-quick proprietary medical schools by creating a Council on Medical Education to encourage medical schools generally to raise standards. The publication of the Flexner report in 1910, as one of its side-effects, greatly strengthened the regulatory authority of the AMA because the reforms it proposed to weed out low-quality schools and incompetent doctors could be accomplished only by introducing an institutional accreditation process and the licensing or certification of individual practitioners. Both approaches were in fact used, and the AMA became the instrument for putting them into effect. Its Council on Medical Education defined the essentials for an approved school and became the accrediting agency. The licensing of physicians was a responsibility of the individual states, but their statutes were patterned on the recommendations of the AMA, and the state licensing boards worked in intimate collaboration with the state medical societies. As a result, within a decade after the publication of the Flexner report, one-third of the proprietary medical schools had been forced to go out of business and the annual number of medical graduates had been cut in half.[2]

The achievement of organizational solidarity came somewhat later but was fully effective by the end of the 1920s. Some feel the AMA's transformation into a monolithic, militantly conservative organization was a reflection of the antiprogressive political atmosphere following the war; others speculate that with the advent of scientific medicine the energies of the more social-minded and intellectual elements of the profession became absorbed in the laboratory and in full-time teaching with the result that they increasingly disengaged from the organization's affairs.

Whatever the causal factors, the observable fact was that the AMA became increasingly inhospitable to democratic participation. Its internal procedures were, on the contrary, conducive to the imposition of control by a minority of the members working in collaboration with the full-time professional staff in Chicago. To achieve a position of power it was necessary for a member to make a very long climb up the hierarchy, from the county medical society to the district and state society to the House of Delegates and finally to the Board of Trustees. Only a few members were prepared to devote themselves to that arduous process and, as events were to demonstrate, they were mostly practitioners whose interests were primarily economic and political rather than professional. The result was that from the 1920s onward the Board of Trustees was composed of an inner group of elderly members chosen largely from political stalwarts of the state societies devoted to the defense of the status quo. The Board of Trustees, although technically responsible to the House of Delegates, functioned with virtually no supervision and with broad authority over the organization's funds and policies. The governance structure combined with these procedures atrophied effective membership participation and enabled the inner circle to dominate the institution thereafter.

There was in any event no great disposition on the part of the mass of the members, who began to benefit handsomely from the AMA's monopolistic policies, to challenge the power structure. But whenever an occasional outbreak of dissension occurred, the organization had highly effective means of bringing "erring" members into line. Membership after 1900 had become imperative for all doctors, since if they did not join one of the county or district societies the doors of hospitals would be barred to them. Anyone inclined to challenge some headquarters policy might find his hospital privileges withdrawn. Other local doctors might boycott referrals to him, and if he persisted in his disobedience, he could find himself hauled up before the state licensing board—composed largely of AMA regulars—for disciplinary action. The combination of internal procedures making it possible for an organized few to impose its will on a disorganized and passive majority, plus the availability of a variety of means, ranging from the mild to the drastic, to put down internal dissent made the AMA into a particularly strong political instrument. And by the 1930s, politics had become its principal preoccupation.

The third essential requirement if the AMA was to be fully successful in its monopolistic program was to have the defensive and offensive capability to deal with whatever threats or opportunities might come along. This it found in the person of Dr. Morris Fishbein. He had joined AMA shortly after his graduation from medical school in 1912 and served the organization for the next 36 years. He turned out to be a natural genius at political and propaganda warfare—skillful and relentless. From his editorial platform of the AMA *Journal* and through his many books, articles and newspaper columns, he defined the public policy positions of organized medicine, shaped public opinion in support of them, and assembled the money, coalitions, and power to bring about the necessary legislative action.

With such devastating weaponry, the AMA during the interwar years tyrannized the politics of health in the United States. The trademarks of its program were militancy, constancy in pursuit of strategic objectives, and alert tactical accommodation and maneuverability.

AMA Dominance and Defiance

One of the AMA's most successful sustained campaigns was to control the supply of doctors. For 40 years, from the 1920s until well into the 1960s, it was able to keep the number of physicians per 100,000 of the U.S. population below the ratio which had been obtained by the first years of the century. During the 1920s the number of medical schools was steadily reduced, and with the advent of the Depression, the restrictive policy was given fresh impetus. The schools that remained were increasingly pressured to keep enrollments down, which with great docility and for many years they did. The results were that by 1972 the United States was forced to find half the net annual additions to its supply of doctors by raiding have-not countries like India and Iran of their medical graduates in order to fill vacancies in U.S. hospitals and clinics.[3]

To further cut down the competition to its members, the AMA battled unrelentingly against the licensing of osteopaths, chiropractors, and optometrists. In a particularly cruel aspect of its policy it also barred blacks from membership. New graduates from the few existing black medical schools found it almost impossible to locate a non-black hospital which would accept them for internship, and the black hospitals were few in number and mostly nonaccredited. Once they were in practice, black doctors found that because they were not AMA members, their access to the best local hospitals was blocked and they were also cut off from the usual channels for keeping up with medical progress. They were not able to participate in the activities of the local medical society or to take postgraduate refresher courses at nearby university hospitals. The racist and discriminatory policies of the medical societies remained in effect in some instances until well into the 1950s.

A second long campaign of the AMA—namely to repel various proposals for health insurance and group rather than solo practice—encountered greater difficulties. The two ideas tended to appear in tandem in public discussion as methods to ease the cost burdens and improve the quality of medical services. For the AMA, one of the most troublesome aspects of these recurrent initiatives was the fact that they were sponsored by some of the most eminent members of the medical profession. For example, a Committee on the Costs of Medical Care, funded by a group of private foundations, was created in 1927. It was headed by Dr. Ray Lyman Wilbur, then president of Stanford University and a former president of the AMA. Over the following five years,

the committee produced a 26-volume report on the problems of
the American health system. Its recommendations, which anticipated virtually all the major changes which have occurred since,
included the following: That medical service should be furnished
largely by organized groups of physicians, dentists, nurses, phar-
macists, and other associated personnel; that hospitals should be
developed into comprehensive community medical centers, with
branches and outlying medical stations where needed; and that
the costs of medical care be placed on a group payment basis,
through the use of insurance, taxation, or both.

Dr. Fishbein branded the report as "an incitement to revolution" and described the suggested group practice pre-payment
plans as "medical soviets."[4] The AMA counterattacked with all its
power and the report was shelved.

Only five years after it had been laid to rest another group of
leading physicians, called the Committee of 430, put forward a set
of still more sweeping proposals. It recommended that the American medical care system should give greater emphasis to preventive medicine and that government should play a much greater
role in subsidizing care for the needy and in financing medical education and research.

The AMA instantly and ferociously accused the Committee of
proposing to turn the control of medical schools over to the Federal government, of encouraging government to assume a dominant position over medical research, and of putting "hospitals
promptly into the practice of medicine." Doctor Fishbein through
the *Journal* charged that "the tender of government funds to such
institutions for the care of an ill-defined group called the medi-
cally indigent" could appeal only to "unthinking physicians." He
went on to impugn the motives as well as the judgment of the
members of the committee:

> Obviously some of these men must have signed merely after seeing
> the names of those who signed previously and because it looked like
> a "good" list. There appear also the names of some members of the
> House of Delegates which voted against some of the very proposi-
> tions which these members here support. Most conspicuous on the
> list are the names of those deans and heads of departments in medi-
> cal schools who may have signed because they saw a possibility of
> getting government money for clinics and dispensaries.

Such careless participation in propaganda as has here occurred is lamentable, to say the least. Certainly the unthinking endorsers of the Committee's principles and proposals owe to the medical profession some prompt disclaimers.[5]

Again, the AMA prevailed. The dissident group wilted under its pressures and gradually disintegrated. But it had at least served as a reminder of the continued existence of a substantial body of opinion within the medical profession opposed to the basic assumptions of the AMA's individualistic, medicine-for-money concept.

The aggressiveness of Fishbein's rhetoric was remarkably successful not only in smothering criticism within the profession but also in silencing public objection. The flat refusal of the AMA to consider any change in the American health system for many years was based on the constantly repeated assertion that the system as it existed was the best in the world. The credibility with which this contention was accepted by public and politicians was quite extraordinary in view of the fact that it was demonstrably untrue. In the words of one respected medical historian, Julius Richmond, now Assistant Secretary of HEW for health, "the very improvements in health for which the AMA took credit had little to do with the fee-for-service practice of medicine. Thus infant mortality probably was reduced as much or more as a consequence of the introduction of pasteurization of milk in 1913, the advent of public health practices, immunization for several infectious diseases, and improved standards of living, than as a result of the work of the individual practitioner."[6]

The power of the AMA over medical policy continued even through the early years of the reform-minded New Deal. There was moment in 1934, for example, in conjunction with the planning for the new social security system, when it seemed that proposals for health insurance might be included. Harry Hopkins was of the opinion that "with one bold stroke we could carry the American people with us, not only for unemployment insurance but for sickness and health insurance."[7] But staff proposals to this end were killed by AMA influence before President Roosevelt sent the proposed legislation to Congress.

Nonetheless profound changes were taking place in medical

practice, institutional development, and public attitudes, and these steadily and quietly were eroding the AMA's sovereignty. One of the earliest and clearest indications occurred in the hospital field. With the advent of scientific medicine, hospitals rather than the home or the doctor's office had become the principal locus for treatment. By the 1930s the number of hospitals had increased greatly and they gradually became conscious of themselves as an industry with its own interests and needs, particularly the need to strengthen the long-range financial viability of its member institutions. With their encouragement and collaboration hospitalization insurance programs began to develop for the benefit of special groups such as teachers, firemen, policemen, and nurses. The hospitals then took the further step of encouraging these plans for their surrounding communities in general.

The leaders of the AMA began to take worried note, and Dr. Fishbein set about to discredit the plans. If they continued to spawn, he warned in numerous editorials in the AMA *Journal* in the early 1930s, lay influence would "define" standards of treatment, local medical societies would lose control, and hospitals— not doctors—would become the "preferred creditors" in the payment of medical bills. Moreover, he predicted the plans could only lead to compulsory health insurance.

But despite the opposition of the AMA, hospital-sponsored Blue Cross plans flourished, and their subscribers together with the American Hospital Association came to constitute a political force too formidable to be dismissed. At this point, the board of the AMA became conciliatory. Joining forces with the hospitals it first devised a way to turn the existing insurance plans to the advantage of its members, and then proceeded, in collaboration with the hospitals, to extend the plans. Later, in 1939, after Senator Robert Wagner of New York had submitted the first of a series of bills to create a national system of prepaid medical care, the AMA brought forward an alternative approach—privately controlled medical insurance plans in which doctors would be in absolute policy control, in which free choice of physicians was assured, and in which the fee-for-service principle was observed. These Blue Shield plans, operating in parallel with the Blue Cross plans, prospered and within twenty years had more than 50 million subscribers.

Although organized medicine had been strongly opposed to the insurance approach at first, in the end the Blues were turned into a bonanza for the practitioners and for the hospitals alike. The privately based plans imposed no external quality controls on the services provided. The hospitals and doctors were free to set their own fees. And as hospital costs and physicians fees rose, the increases were simply passed through the Blues to the consumers in the form of increased premiums. The plans were in effect collection agencies for virtually whatever bills the providers chose to submit. In addition to the financial benefits, they also produced an important political dividend for organized medicine by dampening for a time at least public pressures for more extenisve changes in the health care system.

But if the AMA was flexible and opportunistic in adapting its policies to the advent of hospital and medical insurance, it was ideologically rigid and obstinate in opposing the group practice idea, which often accompanied insurance proposals. It regarded group practice as a direct menace to the position of the individual practitioner who made up the bulk of its membership, and its obsessiveness on the matter led it from brutal efforts of suppression to eventual criminal acts of conspiracy.

The assault on a small cooperative formed in Elk City, Oklahoma, in 1929 was typical of the strong-arm methods used by the various echelons of organized medicine to put down the threat. The cooperative had been organized under the leadership of Dr. Michael Shadid, one of the early heroes of the group practice movement. It was immediately tarred as "unethical" by the local medical society, whose members announced at the same time that they would never take a patient to its proposed hospital. Dr. Shadid shortly found himself "omitted" from membership in the society and was threatened by a petition to the state board of medical examiners to revoke his license. He found he could not get malpractice insurance, Fishbein's *Journal* refused to accept his advertisements for physicians, and the Oklahoma medical societies gathered a political war chest with which they persuaded a state legislative commission to investigate him for "subversive activities." It took him and his beleaguered cooperative more than twenty years of litigation to break the siege.

The case of the Group Health Association of Washington,

D.C., finally forced the AMA to end this kind of harassment. When the GHA was first formed the local medical society denounced it as a "socialistically inspired plot" to introduce European compulsory health insurance into America. Thereafter a sustained attack of boycotts, ostracism, and economic threats was mounted against it. The Department of Justice warned the society that legal action would be taken if it did not desist. It did not, and in late 1938 a grand jury indicted the AMA, three affiliates, and Dr. Fishbein himself on charges of criminal conspiracy. The evidence submitted by the prosecution included examples of physicans expelled from the local medical society for working with the GHA and barred from local hospitals even in emergency cases. Fishbein's *Journal* cried that the medical profession was being persecuted. But the jury handed down a verdict of guilty. On appeal the verdict was affirmed first by the U.S. Court of Appeals and eventually by the Supreme Court itself.

Although it had done its best, or worst, the AMA could not turn back the tide of group practice. By the mid 1930s such plans began to be established in all parts of the country, backed in many cases by industry, trade unions, and local government. In the West, the huge construction company of the late Henry J. Kaiser began a medical program to provide services to its crews working on dam and irrigation projects in remote locations. Known as the Kaiser-Permanente Plan, it has grown since World War II into the largest group-practice health-care program in the United States, enrolling more than 3 million subscribers in the western states and Hawaii and operating its own chain of modern clinics and hospitals. In the East another major program developed, called the Health Insurance Plan of Greater New York, backed by Mayor LaGuardia and influential unions. In the South, the United Mine Workers organized a group health program for its members in Appalachia. In the Midwest, a Labor-Health Institute was organized in St. Louis with strong political and trade union backing.

Local and state medical societies and the AMA fought them in the press, in the courts, and in the legislatures. But they survived and in time dramatically demonstrated the possibilities of cutting costs and improving health care by emphasizing preventive care rather than the episodic treatment of disease and by assembling groups of specialists to deal with the needs of the "whole patient."

By the outbreak of World War II, therefore, the AMA was fighting on more and more fronts and had become increasingly politicized and propagandistic. One of these fronts involved clashes with the voluntary associations organized to combat specific diseases. President Franklin Roosevelt in the late 1930s, for example, had helped create a national foundation to lead an attack on polio. After these March of Dimes campaigns had led to the development of the Salk vaccine, a national immunization effort was launched, which the AMA denounced as another example of "creeping socialism and a violation of the principles of free enterprise."[8] In due course, the Heart Association, the Cancer Society, and groups organized around the problems of arthritis, muscular distrophy, diabetes, kidney disorders, and other afflictions produced for the AMA a succession of other aggravations.

Even more upsetting to the organization was what was to become an unending stream of proposals emerging from government to extend and increase access to health services. To protect the turf of the private practitioner, the AMA felt obliged to maintain a constant watch to ensure that the U.S. Public Health service was kept in a weak and ineffective condition. Numerous efforts were made to expand governmental programs of maternal and child health care, which the AMA in its familiarly shrill and tedious rhetoric called "wasteful and extravagant . . . tending to promote communism."[9] After them appeared still more plans and projects to improve school health services, establish cancer clinics, and for other purposes which the AMA regarded as equally pernicious.

Yet its grip was slipping. It could still delay and deflect but it could not block the immense social, economic, and political forces at work. World War II strengthened many of these and accelerated the evolutionary process. Many newly licensed physicians no longer considered it mandatory to join the AMA and a growing number of previous members began to drift away. Though it still claimed to speak for all of medicine, the organization in fact came to represent only about half of the licensed practitioners. As medical specialization increased, a number of other medical "colleges" and "academies" were created and began to contest the role of the AMA as the exclusive voice of organized medicine.

Of special importance, and despite the AMA's determined opposition, the number of doctors in group practice continued gradually to increase. In the early 1930s it had been less than 15 percent of the total; by the 1950s it was beginning to approach 40 percent. This in turn spawned such new organizations as the American Public Health Association and the Group Health Association, which then began to speak out on medical issues with a distinctly different point of view. Most crucial of all perhaps was the increasing influence of organized medical "consumers"— including members of group health programs, subscribers to various hospitalization and medical insurance programs, trade union members, and members of social action organizations pressing for health policy reforms. Allied with these "consumers" on certain issues were the organized hospitals, the Blues, and even the commercial insurance carriers, which had entered the health insurance business by the hundreds in the wake of the immense success of Blue Cross and Blue Shield.

The Bursting of the Dam

The years of the Second World War intensified the pressures for change in the health system as in many other areas, and almost as soon as the war ended, the various forces demanding that long-neglected problems be given attention came into their own. This is to say, the view came to be politically predominant that increased government initiative and expenditure was necessary to correct what were seen as the major deficiencies of an excessively private, *laissez-faire* health system. And yet the forces in support of that essentially private system were still powerful, so powerful in fact that the reformers had to be careful to avoid direct confrontation with them. Thus, their initial efforts were focussed on two of the most elemental and least controversial objectives— more and better hospitals, and the mounting of a large-scale scientific attack on the causes of major diseases—and they succeeded. In 1947 the Congress passed the Hill-Burton Act to provide Federal assistance to build and equip local hospitals throughout the country. Over the following twenty years, nearly $4 billion was spent on this enterprise. Three years later, legislation enlarging the National Institutes of Health (NIH) was enacted. To support their research, $117 million was appropriated the first year; by 1965 the level had shot to $1.5 billion annually; by 1979 it had reached $2.7 billion.

Both of these important breakthroughs were tailored with great political skill. To appease the interests of organized medicine, the hospitals, and the health insurers, the hospital grants were given with no strings attached in regard to the cost and quality of care provided and with no requirement that the expansion of any hospital be coordinated with regional plans for the balanced distribution of health facilities. The NIH legislation was designed with equal sensitivity to the medical profession, the medical educators, and the voluntary health associations such as the Cancer Society and the Heart Association. Thus the funds provided supported not broad research on health but work in fields of particular interest to the powerful medical specialties and on diseases around which the major private groups had been organized.*

Both the hospital construction and the biomedical research programs have distributed large amounts of public funds with minimal accountability on the part of the recipients. Hospitals became newer and more numerous, free to pursue with government money their individual ambitions for expansion. But they were still controlled in their medical practices by local private physicians. They thus constituted, in effect, publicly financed workshops in which the doctors, without external restraint, were free to ply their trade for personal profit. Likewise, the medical schools and medical researchers were receiving a swelling volume of research funds essentially on their own terms.

The health system as a result was providing more and more technologically advanced care, and in increasingly elegant facilities, for those able to pay for it. These included the wealthy plus

* One indication of the decisive power of medical politics in the program was the fact that the legislation bars the responsible full-time officials of NIH from making any research grant without the approval of the relevant part-time "advisory" committee representing the institutions which benefit from such grants.

certain groups of organized consumers, particularly the white collar employees of large corporations and the members of a number of trade unions. But for other large elements of the population, including blacks, the poor, those living in remote rural areas, and the elderly, it was inaccessible—financially and often geographically. Even for many of those covered by the mushrooming health and hospitalization insurance plans, their coverage was frequently very thin, exposing them to crushing medical bills in the event of major illness.

By the early 1960s the demand for governmental action to ameliorate these problems of access, equity, and financial protection—which had always been the most unmanageable and controversial in the American experience—had become politically irresistible. Not only underprivileged groups of various kinds, but indeed most Americans, including the majority of conservatives as well as liberals, had come to believe that adequate medical care was a right—an "entitlement," not a privilege. Although the old forces led by the AMA threw all of their waning strength into the battle, Congress took a series of sweeping actions.

By 1963, it took steps for the first time to increase the output of health professionals in a major way, breaking the historic resistance of organized medicine; and over the following decade it financed a 50 percent increase in the number of physicians and an 80 percent increase in the number of registered nurses. In 1965, it acted to remove the financial barriers to health care for the elderly and the poor by creating two comprehensive public insurance plans called Medicaid and Medicare. As a result, by 1979 more than 90 percent of the nation's population—or some 200 million people—were covered by some type of health insurance, private or public, comprehensive or partial.*

With passage of these two measures, it could be fairly said that the United States had decisively shifted away from a predomi-

* However, only about 33 million, or 15% of the total population, have dental coverage. The problem of dental care, though it affects virtually the entire American population, oddly enough, has not generated the same kind of pressure for access and for insurance protection. The reasons for this in the opinion of some knowledgeable persons have to do with the factor of fear—in the case of medical care the fear of disability and death if it were unavailable and fear of catastrophic costs in the event of major illness. Dental problems, though common, painful, and sometimes expensive, are not generally regarded as present-

nantly private, market-based health system by the introduction of major governmental programs, funds, and influence. The resulting arrangements were untidy, fragmented and competitive. But they added up to a system with major virtues: The United States has become the world leader in biomedical research and in medical technology. Medical education is of excellent technical quality and continuously improving. The number of doctors and other health professionals by world standards is high and increasing. The proportion of women and minority members is also increasing. The American system had always provided wide freedom of individual choice for those able to pay, but now, because of Medicare and Medicaid, health services have become more equitably available to previously underserved groups. As regards the poor, in the late 1960s they saw doctors much less often than more affluent individuals; by the mid 1970s they were seeing them just as often and, by some figures, even more often. The 1976 annual report of the Robert Wood Johnson Foundation, which specializes in problems of the health system, reported that in 1975 low-income persons visited their physicians six times a year compared to a national average of five visits and that the inequity in the availability of doctors due to poverty "had been largely eliminated." Blacks, a group with generally low income and a generally high incidence of illness, were by 1975 for the first time seeing physicains as frequently as whites.

These are not inconsiderable attributes, and it is to be noted that both private and governmental contributions have been important in bringing them about. Still, a number of major problems remain to be solved: over-hospitalization, excessive surgery, and excessive use of drugs and medication; the excessive specialization of medical graduates and the need for more primary-care practitioners; the mislocation and duplication of health-care facili-

---

ing the same degree of health or financial risk and historically have not been the focus of the kind of massive and urgent demands for relief through changes in public policy. Another factor in the relative neglect of dental problems has been the lower status and lesser influence of the dental profession as compared to the medical profession.

Within the past 20 years, however, public policy has begun to give more emphasis to the training of dentists and dental specialists and to scientific research on dental problems. Also, dental care has increasingly become a "negotiable benefit" in agreements between employers and various trade unions, so that the coverage of dental insurance is now growing and in all likelihood will expand further in years ahead.

ties and the maldistribution of doctors, now heavily concentrated in the affluent neighborhoods of urban areas and only sparsely available in poor neighborhoods and rural districts.

The most sweeping and urgent issue, however, and that on which most public discussion now centers, is that of the runaway escalation of medical costs. In the decade preceding Medicare and Medicaid health-care expenditures increased at an average annual rate of 8 percent a year; but since then, the rate of increase has averaged about 12 percent per year. These programs have achieved their objective of widening access to medical care but they have done so at immense, unanticipated, unacceptable, and seemingly uncontrollable expense. In part the reason is that the programs simply coupled the nozzle of public money to the existing plumbing of the rickety private- and public-health-services structure. The immediate result was that it sprang leaks at every joint. In that first year of operation they cost $5.2 billion of Federal funds; by 1979 their cost to the Federal government was running over $40 billion annually. These increases inflamed public opinion, not only because they greatly exceeded the general rate of inflation but also because they were accompanied by scandalous examples of extravagance, cheating, and organized corruption. A Senate committee concluded in 1976 on the basis of a study of Medicaid operations in eight cities across the nation that from a quarter to as much as half of the $15 billion per year then being spent on the program was being wasted through fraud, poor quality of care, and provision of services to ineligible persons.[10]

The Carter Administration has sought to fix a good part of the blame for the hyperinflation of costs on the medical profession itself. Thus the Chairman of the Federal Trade Commission, Michael Pertschuk, testified on March 22, 1978, before a subcommittee of the House Commerce Committee that doctors control almost all the nation's 69 Blue Shield plans and dominate the groups that set fees and other policies affecting consumers. That same day the President's Council on Wage and Price Stability said that doctors' incomes were rising at a faster rate than the incomes of any other occupational group and that on the average their fees were "unjustifiably high by established economic standards." Jack Meyer, Assistant Director of the Council, said "we are not saying that doctors are greedier than anyone else" but he added that the nation's medical care system put doctors in the position of being able to determine the demand for their services as well as to set fees unfettered by constraints of supply and demand. He went on to charge that "anti-competitive practices"—such as discouragement of price competition among physicians by medical societies in the 1940s and 1950s—are also "partially responsible for the high levels of prevailing fees."

There is unfortunately considerable current data as well as much historical evidence to support the charge of profiteering by some private physicians. But in the intricate economics of the American health system, government health insurance and the rapacity of certain elements of the medical profession are only two of several factors driving the upward price spiral. Another is the "over medicalized mentality" of Americans, which both diminishes the individual's sense of responsibility for maintaining his own health and at the same time creates an almost unlimited demand for medicines, drugs, and the services of doctors and hospitals. A fourth is the reality of continuous and rapid scientific and technological development, which makes possible treatment of greater and greater sophistication, but only at greatly increased costs for facilities and instrumentation. A fifth and very important element is the mismanagement and the proliferation of hospitals. From 1950 to 1976 the consumer price index rose about 125 percent; medical care costs increased by 240 percent; but hospital costs leapt by more than 1000 percent. Among the reasons were overbuilding and underutilization, duplication of equipment and facilities, and uncoordinated and competitive programs of individual hospital expansion.

A sixth element in the price rise—one strongly emphasized by the health economists—is the effect of "third party" payment arrangements (the payment by public or private insurance programs of hospital and doctors bills). More specifically they criticize the practice, widely adopted under both Medicare and Medicaid, of reimbursing hospitals on a cost-plus basis, as well as the dual price system, followed by Medicare and most other forms of health insurance, under which the hospital is charged directly for most of a patient's care, requiring the patient himself to pay out-of-pocket only a small fraction.

This fraction is not only small but has been decreasing. Thus between 1950 and 1965, hospital costs increased more than nine-fold while the net cost out-of-pocket to the patient only increased twofold.

One result of these financial arrangements is the elimination of incentive for the "providers"—the hospitals and the doctors—to economize. The physician is free to prescribe maximum treatment at maximum cost. The hospital administrator has no motive to deny requests for higher wages or more equipment. To get more money he need only spend more.

At the same time, the dual price system distorts reality for the consumer and makes him indifferent, so the economists argue, to the cost of treatment recommended by his physician, however exorbitant, since it is the insurance company or the government that pays.

The net economic effect, whether one emphasizes "cost-plus" reimbursement or the dual price system, is to generate excess demand and to remove virtually all internal cost restraints on the system. The resulting inflationary spiral is made even more steep by the fact of heavy tax subsidies under existing law to individuals, unions, and employers which encourage excessive insurance—which in turn lifts the limits to further cost increases.

The absence of cost control is of course not mere happenstance. Partly it has its roots in the American medical ethos, partly it is due to the ignorance and indifference of the "consumers," and partly it is the product of the combined influence of the providers—the organized individual medical practitioners, the hospitals, the health insurance plans (whose policies are greatly influenced by the doctors and the hospitals), and the pharmaceutical companies (which are heavily dependent upon the patronage and cooperation of hospitals and of the individual physicians)—all of whom benefit handsomely from it.

The 1970s—Coping and Groping

Successive administrations since the early 1970s have struggled to cope with these various problems. The Nixon years were a time when climbing health care costs had already become serious but when the momentum of demands for further expansion of health services remained powerful. In the Congress, several measures were enacted to try to do something about deteriorating hospital standards and the random growth of health facilities. In addition, Senator Edward Kennedy began an effort to extend and consolidate the benefits of Medicare and Medicaid by the creation of a comprehensive national insurance program. His position seemed to have considerable public and political support and many observers predicted with assurance that the United States would adopt such a program before 1980.

President Nixon, while resisting this Congressional drive, sought to deal with the emerging crisis costs by a double strategy—clamping a lid on them and at the same time seeking to reduce the economic pressures underlying them. He imposed blanket price controls and he proposed the development of a nationwide network of Health Maintenance Organizations (HMOs) which would offer comprehensive medical services to members making fixed regular payments. The objective was to force the existing health care "providers" to reduce their charges by creating an alternative, competitive health care structure.

Neither part of the strategy succeeded. Price controls suppressed increases for a time, but they were lifted in 1974, producing an immediate explosion of "catch-up" increases. Congress in 1973 authorized Federal assistance for HMOs but the legislation was so limited and so laxly drawn that it produced many promotional ventures and widespread profiteering, but not much else. The brief term of President Ford was an inactive period in health policy, and thus far the achievements of the Carter Administration in this field have been undistinguished. It has dealt with the conflicting pressures for extension of the health care system and for control of health care costs simply by accommodating both. HEW Secretary Califano, until his ouster by the President in July 1979, steadily proclaimed the need for still greater access to health care for the poor and underserved, greater protection against the costs of catastrophic illness, the extension of counselling and preventive services, greater support for HMOs, and greater Federal authority to plan, coordinate, and redistribute health facilities. He called, therefore, not only for national health insurance—which by conservative estimates would add at least $25 billion per year to the Federal budget—but for a sweeping new health services program of unspecified cost to go along with it.[11] Meanwhile, from the White House, the President has just as regularly asserted the primacy of inflation control over other domestic objectives of government and presented himself as the steadfast defender of budgetary austerity.

To judge only by developments, or nondevelopments, on the Washington scene as the 1970s approached their end, it appeared that health policy was enveloped in confusion and trapped in a deadlocked political debate.

In fact, however, although it could not be perceived in Washington, the nation was beginning to sort out and reassess some of the experiments and ideas that had seemed so full of promise in the first years of the 1970s. For example, enthusiasm for group practice HMOs had visibly begun to sag. Despite increasing government subsidy and even the imposition of a legal requirement in 1976 that all business firms with 25 or more employees offer HMO coverage as an alternative to conventional health insurance, only 6 million Americans had become members by 1979, and more than half of those were subscribers to the Kaiser Health Plan, which was established long before HMO legislation was enacted. The theory of the HMO, with its encouragement of preventative care and its incentives to both providers and consumers to control costs, remained attractive. But on the basis of initial experience it seemed increasingly doubtful that HMOs could ever become a major factor in the health care system.

Likewise the chances for national health insurance had clearly begun to fade. The brutal impacts of sustained inflation had produced an unpredented cost consciousness on the part of the public in evaluating all proposed government programs. In addition, some of the principal trade union backers of Senator Kennedy's proposal had had a change of mind. In the opinion of Peter F. Drucker, a leading business analyst, most union leaders—and even more, their staff advisors—began to see "health care benefits as the *only* area of potential union gain in years ahead, considering the resistance to wage increases and higher taxes, and freedom to bargain on health care benefits as essential to the very survival of the American trade union movement."[12]

Moreover, in contrast to the logjam over health policy in Washington, many interesting new developments were beginning to occur all over the country. The capacity of American society to generate fresh ideas in this vital field was still quite obviously in splendid health.

In an earlier time, the breakup of the exploitive medical monopoly engineered by the AMA was led by private foundations, trade unions, and corporations—not the doctors, hospitals, or medical schools. In the 1930s and 1940s, group health care, the Wilbur Committee, the Kaiser Health Plan, and Blue Cross were among their great achievements. Again today, creative initiatives are appearing spontaneously and in unexpected places in response to specific community needs, on the basis of private leadership and initiative, and quite often with the support of coalitions of strange bedfellows. Business corporations are increasingly employing medical directors who, in cooperation with union representatives, are monitoring and exercising effective pressure on the level of local hospital costs. Blue Cross/Blue Shield, long dominated by the hospitals and the medical profession, has more recently taken powerful leadership in helping reduce unnecessary surgery and excessive, expensive routine hospital tests. Private citizen groups have launched a mushrooming hospice movement to encourage families to care for terminally ill individuals at home rather than in the cold, institutional environment of a hospital. Doctors themselves are setting up an increasing number of Independent Physicians Associations (IPAs) which are winning favor because they provide some of the benefits of group practice HMOs but in addition allow for the individual to choose his own physician and maintain control of standards of treatment in the hands of medical professionals.

Aaron Wildavsky, former head of the Russell Sage Foundation, has written that in the United States "health policy is pathological because we are neurotic [on the matter] and insist on making our government psychotic."[13] Surely the American people have long had contradictory and unrealistic expectations of the health care system. But it may not be quite fair or accurate to lay the blame for the present failures of government so heavily on the public. Indeed, at a time when political leadership and the official health bureaucracy seem, in Wildavsky's vocabulary, increasingly schizophrenic and cataleptic, a kind of consensus on the major issues of health care policy has begun to emerge on the part of the country as a whole. Its major features include the following:

Continuing support for the goals of a greater access, equity, and individual financial protection;

Acceptance of the continuing need for a strong role for government in guiding the general development of the system, forcing or inducing certain necessary further changes and protecting it against the predators which will infest it;

A reviving interest in quality of care and in the preservation of individual choice, suggesting that bureaucratization and governmentalization of the system have begun to produce a significant counteraction; and

A strongly increasing sense that, given the totality of needs of American society, the spiraling costs of health care have to be brought under forcible restraint and that governmental programs must in the future be far more carefully conceived and far more effectively and efficiently administered than in the past.

Some of the elements of this emerging consensus fit readily together. Others obviously do not and will have to be reconciled by slowing down certain changes, accelerating others, altering some priorities and accepting trade-offs.

The process at work is one far more subtle, dynamic, and creative than the old dogmas in the field of health care—whether fee-for-service medicine or socialized medicine—can comprehend. But it is vigorously under way. The emerging shape of the American health system can still not be forecast with confidence. Decisions on major policy alternatives are yet to be hammered out on the anvil of politics. The end result probably will look something like the egalitarian, governmentalized model of recent issue, but it will also undoubtedly reflect important other features, still undiscernable.

No more instructive example could be imagined of the infinite capacities of a pluralistic system in adapting to the continuously changing requirements of a great democracy than the American health system. The long story of its slow, digressive, and still incomplete evolution can of course be read in different ways. It can be interpreted simply as the consistent triumph of private vested interests—whether of the medical profession or of the owners of private proprietary hospitals or of the insurance companies—over the public interest and egalitarian principles. Or it can be interpreted as proof that the major institutions in a free society, though they are not necessarily corrupt or exploitive, are inherently biased in favor of the status quo and as a result, even in a matter as universally and vitally important to the citizenry as health services, are sufficiently strong to delay for decades major and strongly desired reforms.

Or the story can be interpreted as evidence that American society, for whatever reasons—historical, economic, even geographical—is not sufficiently politicized or sophisticated to be able on a purely democratic basis to shape a coherent "system" of health services. In this view the interplay of interest groups and other political and economic factors operates acceptably when the issue involves a piecemeal matter like building a local hospital. But there is not sufficiently broad leadership or ideological coherence in the society to make it possible on the basis of popular decision to bring into existence a balanced, fair, and coordinated total system.

Or the story can be interpreted in more positive terms—that American society (admittedly with many delays, digressions, and errors and with much parochialism) has long since achieved very advanced medical care in technical and scientific terms and has now begun to make real progress in the direction of a more adequate and more equitable health system; and that it has in the process accomplished something else of equal importance—it has enabled the nation to develop its own awareness, understanding, and competence out of the experience of participating in that untidy, inefficient, but profoundly democratic exercise to deal with the still more complex issues now upcoming.

6 ►►►►

Culture and the Arts—
Economics, Aesthetics, and
the Role of the State

FOR THE NATION'S private health, scientific, and educational institutions to become increasingly dependent upon government raises difficult, indeed grave, questions of public policy.
For its cultural institutions to be drifting in the same direction
raises similar but somewhat different issues, partly because their
degree of dependency is not yet so great and partly because the
arts are more vulnerable to deformation and suffocation by the
subtle, even the unintended, pressures of patrons, especially government patrons, upon them.

As of now, the most threatening and immediate danger they
feel they face is financial; but as the volume of government funding increases, as it almost certainly will in the years to come, economic concerns may rapidly be displaced by political ones.

The Prologue of the Past

The new American republic may have been conceived in liberty and dedicated to the proposition that all men are created
equal, but it took its ideas about culture directly from the privileged classes of Europe. To think about art was to borrow the

seventeenth-century continental distinction between the "fine" and the "decorative" (or "minor") arts. The legacy of the royal European academies and conservatories, and of the patronage traditions of the titled and the wealthy, firmly linked art in revolutionary America with ideas of high culture, educated taste, and elite society.

In the nineteenth century the nation's preoccupations gradually shifted from political development to economic development—and the personal fortunes acquired in that process paved the way for the cultural development which followed. The wealthy have been the leaders, the patrons, and the tastemakers of American high culture from then down to the present. They have provided the funds and the prestige on which the nation's symphony orchestras, opera companies, and ballet corps have been built.* Their art collections formed the core around which the major museums have been developed. The principal exception has been the theatre, which until recent decades was commercially profitable and self-supporting. These patrons financed those activities which appealed to their taste, and what is commonly accepted as "culture" and "excellence" has been defined by their standards.

In the first half of the twentieth century, the pattern of the previous century was modified first by the inclusion in 1917 of tax incentives for charitable giving in the new Federal income tax law, and second, by the expenditures of the Works Progress Administration (WPA) after 1933 to alleviate unemployment among musicians, artists, actors, and writers. By the former, the support of the rich for the arts was encouraged and institutionalized; by the latter the wall against Federal funding of the arts was massively, although fortuitously and only temporarily, breached. Some $45 million was spent in the years 1936–39 by the Federal Theatre Project, for example, to employ some 13,000 actors and

* A more precise picture of the successive stages of wealthy support is given by William Wright in his lively piece, "The Sound of Money: The Plight of our Symphony Orchestras" in *Town and Country*, October 1976: "The solitary backer gave way to a group of wealthy backers, usually rich blue bloods who regarded the orchestra as a cultural *cosa nostra*; as the old guard got tired of giving or ran out of money to give, it gave way to new money that in turn gave way to large corporations that were as eager to show off their civic responsibility as the parvenues were to parade their bank accounts."

.directors to give theatrical performances throughout the country; but then the Congress for political reasons cut off the funds.

Oddly enough, and despite the interest and generosity of many wealthy individuals in giving to the arts, the major philanthropic foundations and business corporations, controlled by the same social class, gave little to them until very recent years.

The years following World War II were a time of general prosperity, increasing leisure, rising levels of education, and rapidly increasing expenditures for recreational and cultural activities. Americans took more piano lessons, joined more art classes, invested in more records and hi-fi equipment, bought more books, saw more plays, and went more often to museums than ever before. The number of symphony orchestras, opera companies, theatre groups, and dance companies in the United States multiplied.*

At the same time they were going more often to the movies, watching more TV, taking more vacations, and purchasing more fishing tackle and photographic equipment. Some kind of major shift in tastes and habits was quite dramatically underway, but there were puzzling inconsistencies in the trends. Without doubt, there was a great increase in the volume and geographical dispersion of cultural activity. In every part of the country, colleges were sponsoring arts festivals, new museums and art centers were being built, libraries and churches were putting on concerts, and businesses were buying paintings and sculpture to decorate their offices. Yet the great mass of the population apparently still wanted popular culture and participatory culture.†

The evidence of the bottom line was incontrovertible: The temples of high culture remained impoverished, while the purveyors of recreation and entertainment were rolling in profits. By the late 1950s the disparities had indeed become so great, and the

---

*The pace of increase continues. Between 1968 and 1978, according to the National Endowment for the Arts, the number of major opera companies grew from 27 to 45; professional symphony orchestras from 58 to 110; professional dance companies from 10 to 70; and legitimate theatre companies from 12 to 50.

†Nonprofit arts activity in the United States constitutes only about one-eighth of all such activity inclusively defined—high and popular, commercial and noncommercial. The self-sustaining commercial arts—from broadcasting, motion pictures and publishing to rock music and advertising—are far greater in scale and receive 85% of the $11 billion annual total of arts expenditures.[1]

difficulties of established arts organizations so serious, that the United States for the first time in its history was forced to confront directly the problem of subsidizing high culture as an issue of major public policy.

The European Background

What was happening on the American scene had its precedents and parallels in Western Europe, where all those industrialized, democratic societies—in the context of their own long and varied traditions of cultural development—were also struggling to cope with the impact of new economic and political forces upon the arts, and with new and discordant concepts of the role and nature of art itself. It is instructive to compare three concrete cases: France, Great Britain, and Sweden.[2]

In France, since the seventeenth century, the state has taken a strong hand in subsidizing, guiding, and "radiating" the nation's cultural development. Napoleon I signed the decree regulating the operation of the *Comédie Française* during the winter he occupied Moscow. From the late nineteenth century until World War II, not so much because of as in spite of official interest in culture, the country enjoyed a flourish of artistic brilliance.*

But by the late 1940s French cultural life had lost much of its luster. When General de Gaulle became President of the Fifth Republic in 1958, one of his first acts as part of a broad effort to restore the "grandeur" of France was to create a new Ministry of Culture. Its approach was essentially to attempt to refurbish the museums and reinvigorate the traditional culture—opera, classical theatre, and chamber music; but over the following decade that stale objective became manifestly unachievable. Many new trends in painting, music, architecture, and other art forms were appearing along with various expressions of the underground and

---

* That brilliance, in the opinion of some French social critics was largely a result of rebellion against the rigidity of government policy. "It banished the giants of Impressionism and left them to eat out of garbage cans in Montmartre while academic nonentities were banqueting at the *Beaux Arts*," according to French writer Gerard Bonnot. "They were driven to innovation by their passionate determination to destroy the sterile official prototypes."[3]

the counterculture, and there was an epidemic spread of interest in popular culture, especially among the young. In the face of general resistance by artists, and general indifference on the part of the public, to the venerated forms of "official culture," an agonized accommodation was made: a new policy was announced in 1969 representing a major break with the monolithic past. No longer would there be a single authorized cultural standard. Rather, the role of the state would henceforth be "to promote the unrestricted expansion of diverse expressions of creativity."[4]

To implement the new policy, government expenditures for the arts have now substantially increased. France has been compelled to opt for evolution—but under continued strong state tutelage and at heavy public expense.

In Britain, in sharp contrast to the French tradition, patronage of the arts remained predominantly in private hands through World War II. Since then, central government subsidy has been provided—on a modest scale—through the Arts Council created in 1945. It currently spends about $50 million annually. Another example of British political inventiveness, it operates as a kind of nongovernmental instrumentality. The state provides the funds but takes elaborate measures to ensure that it does not dictate how they are to be spent. The Council, which relies heavily on the participation of artists and other private citizens in its advisory panels, is given full freedom in allocating its grants. The intent is to seek to draw forth other funds, private and local, through its outlays and to keep the central government's role secondary. Likewise, the Council holds to a posture of passivity and planlessness by relying on localities and on various private arts organizations to take the initiative in promoting new lines of development such as touring theatres, film festivals, and "Community Arts" which combine aspects of performance art with social and welfare activities. The increasing number of these initiatives, including those of various regional arts councils and associations, are putting increasing strain on the Council's past practice of allocating a considerable portion of its budget to such familiar national institutions as the Old Vic and Sadler's Wells Ballet. They are at the same time driving the Council relentlessly in the direction of decentralization of grant-making authority and of greater recognition of amateur and participatory art forms.

If France and Britain are being pressed somewhat reluctantly toward the "democratization" of culture, Sweden is leading the charge up that hill, or into that valley. There, broad subsidy of the arts by the central government did not begin until 1961, producing as its first result a vigorous and sustained national debate about the proper relationship between the arts and the state. This culminated in 1975 in the enactment of a new cultural policy.[5] Because tens of thousands of citizens from all parts of the country participated in its formulation, the report on which it is based constitutes what is probably the most representative statement in existence of the thinking of a modern society—in this case, an advanced Welfare State society—on the issues involved. Its content and conclusions can only be shocking to all believers in the classical or bourgeois conception of culture.

The report proceeds on the assumption that the state should exercise comprehensive and primary responsibility for providing society's cultural needs. The broad policy goals which are laid down are not aesthetic but social—"to contribute toward creating a better social environment and promoting increased equality."

No reference is made to the notion of the importance of excellence in art for its own sake. The values which underlie the document are functional and idealistic—social justice, communication, community-building, and individual development. It is couched in managerial language; planning, priorities, coordination, and the like. Following is its presentation of the "sub-goal" of decentralization:

> State support of cultural activity has long been concentrated on institutions in the larger cities. . . . It is an economically just demand that the state support the building up of independent regional cultural activity. . . . Cultural policy may thus from this point of view, be seen as a part of the policy for regional support, in the same way as the placement of industry in such areas is.

The conclusions of the report regarding "Society's Responsibility" reflect the same general ideological flavor.

Most of the production and distribution of culture today is in private hands. . . . Private culture activity, because of the demand for profitability, must be carried on with other goals than those society has for its cultural policy. . . . If profitability alone is decisive for what is to be produced and how the production is to be spread, this may lead to cultural poverty and superficiality. . . . The state's activities in the future should be aimed to a greater extent at offering alternatives to the private cultural activity in various sectors.

Although there is clear recognition of the dangers of commercial influence, little attention is given to the possibilities of political interference with artistic freedom. The hope seems to be that the countervailing effect of various interests and sources of financial support—municipal and county authorities, adult education organizations, trade unions, the press, and an increasingly educated public—will provide adequate insurance against such hazards.

To carry out the policy, the government provides ample funding along with strong centralized direction. The contrasts as well as the commonality of these European cases are striking: Each country seeks to find its own policy solutions in terms of its own history and national characteristics. Great contrasts are apparent among them regarding the proper role of the state and the emphasis to be given social or aesthetic objectives. But in all there is increasing acceptance of new tastes and standards, of the demand for wider opportunities for participation in arts activities, and of the need for increased central government funding as a condition of healthy national cultural development.

The American Way

In the American effort to come to grips with its particular requirements and objectives in cultural policy, there are both clear differences and some strong resemblances to what is taking place in Europe. Perhaps the most distinctive feature of the American response to the plight of the arts, which began to take form in the mid 1950s, was the leading role played by private elements in defining the premises of a new policy and in setting its general directions. To a number of influential leaders of society and distinguished professionals in the arts, the boom in popular culture and the impending bankruptcy for the institutions of high culture was seen as a call to action—to capitalize on the rise of interest in recreation and amateur arts to win new audiences for the established professional forms, and thereby to save the old institutions by gaining a wider base of support for them.

The first major institution to respond to the call was the Ford Foundation. Beginning in 1957, it launched a program of support to arts organizations which over the following twenty years provided them with nearly $300 million of new resources. This effort of unprecedented scale by private philanthropy focussed primarily on the performing arts—theatre, music, and dance—rather than on the visual arts, professional artists and arts organizations, and avocational artists and educational institutions. It was intended to develop their long-term capacity to sustain themselves on an independent, private basis. No definitive assessment of the program has yet been made, but without question it has profoundly changed the artistic landscape of the country. Dozens of national and regional theatre and ballet companies and symphony orchestras are now far stronger and more fully developed than they could have been without Ford assistance.

While many might disagree with the Foundation's choice of priorities, none could disagree with its consistency and courage in attempting to do what a private institution uniquely has the freedom and capacity to do—to set its own goals and to make discriminating choices, thereby contributing a distinctive quality and coloration to the tapestry of national activity in any major field.

At the same time that Ford was launching its program, a number of forces, both cultural and political, were converging to demand that the arts be given status as a responsibility of government, especially of the Federal government. The time was the crest of the Cold War, and many of the supportive arguments were consequently geopolitical and nationalistic: It was backward of the United States not to subsidize culture as generously as West Germany and France, for example; we could not compete in the global "battle for men's minds" without a stronger show of governmental interest in the arts; for the government to recognize the arts officially would give them dignity and "prove to the world" that Americans are culturally serious; and so on. In parallel, the bread-and-butter case was insistently put forth: Without more government subsidy, Culture simply could not survive.

Some voices were raised against the whole idea: Russell Lynes of *Harper's* magazine argued that the less the arts have to do with politics, "the healthier they will be, the more respected, the more important to Americans, and the more productive." He quoted the painter John Sloan to the same effect: "Sure it would be good to have a Ministry of Fine Arts. Then we'd know where the enemy is."[6] But these were dismissed by the emergent arts lobby as aberrant expressions of isolationism or philistinism, and the road to governmental involvement was little by little opened. The milestones along that road were the following:

> *1959:* Nelson Rockefeller, who had long been interested in the arts and who as Coordinator of Inter-American affairs during World War II had directed extensive official cultural programs with Latin America, became Governor of New York. He successfully pushed for legislation in his first year to create a State Arts Council and to provide substantial funding for it.
>
> *1962:* President John F. Kennedy named August Heckscher, scion of an eminent New York family, to the newly created post of Special Consultant on the Arts to prepare a report on the role of government in the arts, a document which helped lay the basis for subsequent legislative action.
>
> *1964:* Under President Lyndon Johnson, Congress authorized a $15 million grant for construction of a national cultural center as a memorial to the late President Kennedy. It also voted to establish the Advisory Council on the Arts, created by executive order by President Kennedy shortly before his assassination, on a more permanent basis.
>
> *1965:* A panel of prominent leaders in the arts assembled by a private foundation, the Rockefeller Brothers Fund, at the instigation of John D. Rockefeller 3d, issued an important report on the problems and prospects of the performing arts in the United States. It had a powerful effect because for the first time it gave blue-ribbon respectability to the idea of government funding. Later that same year the Congress ap-

proved a three-year program providing for the first time for direct Federal support of the arts through the creation of a National Endowment for the Arts.

The aim of the panel was to improve the financing of professional arts organizations from both private and especially government sources. But its dread was that this additional financial support and these vast new audiences might expose the arts to vulgarization. "We must never allow the central focus on quality," it asserted, "to weaken or shift. Popularization in any realm often leads to a reduction of standards. . . . Democratization carries with it a peril for the arts, even as it does for education."[7] But it was careful to avoid castigation of commercialization as a factor tending in this same direction. It was tolerant toward amateurism, but only if it contributed to the audience for and appreciation of the professional arts.

The legislation creating the National Endowment, and the programs which it has subsequently developed, on the other hand, embrace a far broader range of objectives and the accommodation of a wider range of influences and values than those of the Rockefeller panel. The Endowment is in fact a fascinating assemblage of conceptual and political compromises reflecting actual complexities of contemporary American ideas.

It is, for example, an "independent" agency of government, but not too independent. Its policies and programs are formulated with the advice of a National Council on the Arts made up of 26 private citizens appointed by the President. But it is also subject to specific directives from the President and to designated appropriations from the Congress.

Its programs and policies are capacious enough to include the old elite and the new populists, the professionals and the amateurs, and both high and popular culture. Its National Advisory Council is composed principally—but not quite exclusively—of the high culture Establishment; and in many of the Endowment's statements the theme of "excellence"—artists "of the highest talent," organizations "representing the highest quality"—is repeated, perhaps not with the obsessiveness of the Rockefeller panel but still insistently.

On the other hand, "the arts" as defined by the Endowment include not only the classical forms but also folk art, photography, industrial design, costume design, television, and radio. In addition to "arts exposure" programs to build audiences for high culture, there are crafts programs for prison inmates, the handicapped, and the elderly. Indeed there are offerings which permit almost everyone to witness or to join in cultural activity of some kind, from urban ethnics and ghetto dwellers to those in the smallest rural communities and the backwoods of Appalachia.[8]

By the diversity of its programs, the Endowment has broadened its constituency throughout the country. It has sagaciously headed off fears of domination from Washington by distributing block grants to the Arts Councils in every state, and it has placed heavy stress on matching grants to induce expanded private, state, and municipal contributions, thereby keeping the Federal share of funding to a minium.

The overall result is a program that is eclectic, diverse, and responsive, and one for which almost everyone has some enthusiasm and some criticism. The elitists are pleased that it has made a brave effort to hold to standards of quality in its grant-making, but they fear the growing attention given the amateurs and the "artsy-craftsy" advocates. The off-beat and avant-garde elements of the cultural community suspect the Endowment's heart is still with the old Establishment, but they are satisfied that they have been able to win at least a piece of the action. In private philanthropy there are those who deplore what they regard as too great a diffusion in the Endowment's grant-making, charging that it does little more than sprinkle dew on every leaf without watering, and deepening, any roots. But even they are impressed by the fact that the Endowment has been able in a particularly harsh political environment to persuade the Congress and three successive Presidents to increase its annual budget from $2.5 million in 1966 to more than $120 million in 1978, a 48-fold increase in the span of twelve years.*

In the past few decades the United States for the first time has

---

* In the same period, state and local government support has also increased, but not quite at the same rate. In 1965 Federal support of $5 million was one-fourth of the amount provided by state and local governments that year; in 1970 Federal support of $27 million

moved to the first rank in world terms in almost every major art form. It is to be noted that the sharp increase in government funding in more recent years has not thus far imposed any apparent constraint on innovativeness, tastes, or tendencies, nor has it lowered "the peaks of excellence."

The Problems in Prospect

That we are off to a good beginning is reassuring. But it is only a small and recent beginning. Between now and the end of the century the challenges American cultural policy will confront are likely to become much more difficult. The most fundamental of these will be in the basic philosophy of fund distribution.

Embedded in the Endowment's program and procedures are some assumptions which, though never avowed, constitute a philosophy, or the fragments of a philosophy, of governmental operation. The visible indications are the following:

–To a considerable extent it uses its funds, by its own expenditure and through grants to State Arts Councils, for the direct subsidy of selected arts institutions.

–In arriving at its choices it relies heavily on the advice of experts and leaders in the arts.

To many, this seems simple common sense: money is limited, choices are inevitable, and if they are to be made intelligently, the guidance of professionals rather than amateurs obviously should be sought.

But there are those who describe what takes place both at the national and state levels in quite other terms—namely that it has

was nearly one-half of the total state and local support; in 1975, Federal support of $157 million was well over one-half of the amount provided by lower levels of government.[9]

In addition to the funds provided to the arts through NEA, the Federal government supports the National Gallery of Art, the many components of the Smithsonian Institution, and spends an estimated $75 million of the appropriation of CETA (the Comprehensive Education and Training Act) for artists, cultural workers and supportive staff for arts institutions.

To keep these numbers in perspective, however, it should be recalled that the outlays of government in other nonprofit areas make its appropriations for the arts minuscule by comparison. In 1975, for example, government at all levels provided some $300 million to the arts, while it spent $85 billion—250 times as much—on education.

become a system of centrally directed and value-biased intervention, in that grants are made to certain preferred institutions and
art forms in order to accomplish certain centrally chosen objectives.

The whole approach which the NEA has so far relied upon is
likely to be under increasing attack in the years ahead because it
is considered by many to be objectionable on two related
grounds. The first is economic. Reliance on market forces, individual "consumer" choices, should wherever possible be the governing principle in distributing subsidies, not centralized allocations, which are distorting and ultimately wasteful. The second
ground is equity. The present approach is thought to be discriminatory because it is unduly influenced by an elite "peer group" of
experts and art leaders who are biased in favor of certain art forms
and institutions. The clearest expression to date of this alternative
viewpoint is contained in a report issued in 1975 by the Joint
Committee on the Arts of the California State Legislature.[10]

The Committee, after lengthy study, recognized the important
personal and social values to which the arts contribute, but it
rejected the idea that government should support the arts for
their own sake. In its view, government funding was justified essentially in order to equalize the citizens' access to the arts and
because the arts have been badly discriminated against in the past
in comparison to athletics, for example, on which public funds in
California have long been lavished.

In the distribution of any public subsidy, however, the Committee strongly urged that individual preferences be the allocative
mechanism, not centralized governmental decisions. It therefore
favored aiding arts organizations indirectly, by such devices as
voucher systems to lower ticket prices, thereby allowing individual purchasers to decide freely which artists and art forms they
preferred. To the extent that aid had to be given directly to artists
and arts organizations, the Committee recommended that it be
done by maximum decentralization to localities and to "millions
of citizens," explaining that "by allowing people to decide for
themselves what they want aesthetically, we recognize their
sovereignty, their self-responsibility, and their right to self-
determination."

The Committee was also highly skeptical of the practice of

allowing experts and arts-organization professionals to dominate decision-making, both because of potential conflicts of interest and because of their biases regarding "deserving" and "underserving" art. Moreover, the Committee observed, distribution of direct government subsidies on the basis of the advice of specialized panels means inevitably "that the rich get richer, the powerful more powerful, and the wasteful more wasteful."

By shifting to reliance upon market forces, the Committee recognized and was fully prepared to accept the fact that some art forms and arts institutions might thereby well disappear. "Like all else in life," it said, "the arts change and it is crucial to their nature that they do so. . . . When most people are attracted to one art form rather than another, events must follow their natural course and the other art form must die or fall to its natural level. . . . If government interferes with that process through arbitrary incursions into the marketplace—and the spending of tax funds taken coercively is certainly an arbitrary incursion—it would be trying to keep the dinosaur alive in the age of the mastodon." As regards the argument that government should support the arts because otherwise "the arts will die," the Committee observed that "the proponents mean certain arts institutions will die. If we believe that the arts satisfy a basic human need, we cannot believe they will cease to exist. They may transform themselves into forms that we cannot even imagine now, but that is natural and necessary; some forms of art as we have known them may cease to exist. . . . But while the arts speak to a real human need, they will survive. . . . Besides it is not the arts as such that are in economic trouble but the arts of live performance, the museums and the traditional arts inherited from nineteenth century Europe."

The Committee thus posed in raw and brutal terms a number of issues which are normally evaded or obscured. By extension, its opinions constituted a charge that the present policies of the NEA and the state councils are in large part undemocratic; inequitable both as regards institutions, individuals, and tastes; and dangerously intrusive into the natural evolutionary forces in the endlessly changing and basically subjective realm of art. Moreover, it concluded that to continue such policies can only beget unending and unlimited pork barrel politics.

It is appropriate that these views should have been posed by a representative political body from California—the most populous state in the nation, a leading center of activity in the newer and popular art forms, and a seedbed of many of the newer trends in American lifestyles, personal values, and politics. In the Committee's emphasis on the personal and subjective values of art, its antitraditionalism, its stress on equality, democracy, and participation, and its great skepticism of government and bureaucracy, it represents a distinctly contemporary and American perspective.

The NEA, even in its first decade, has traveled a long way toward accommodating some of the values reflected in the California report, and it is possible that within another decade it will accommodate most of them. Conversely, it is possible that the California approach represents so sharp a break with past practice, and so great a threat to important interests and contrary viewpoints, that it will generate overpowering resistance and be rejected as such. But whatever the outcome, it poses the ultimate issues on which the philosophical debate will turn.

Four Upcoming Tests

The arguments over basic values and concepts will go on. However, at the operational level American cultural policy must in years ahead seek to meet four practical tests: It will have to respond to the demands for both continuity and change—probably great change—in tastes and cultural conceptions; it will have to provide funds on an "adequate" scale; it will have to develop more rational and explicit criteria for setting its priorities and for channeling its funds in order to accomplish its stated objectives; and, as the volume of official fundings grows, it will have to keep tendencies toward bureaucratization and politicization under control. The prospects are that it will be considerably more effective in dealing with some of these problems than with others.

As to the first test, the new governmental patronage is likely to be more open and hospitable to diverse tendencies than private patronage has been in the past. Foundations and individual donors have often imposed their preferences rather arbitrarily and narrowly on the arts and on arts organizations. The American government as patron will feel obliged to be less restrictive. This is already evident in the growing diversity of the Endowment's program. Indeed, if one is to judge by the history of state-supported higher education, the problem is less likely to be exclusiveness than indiscriminate responsiveness. In that field there has been such willingness to organize new courses—from poultry husbandry to driver education—that they have almost crowded such subjects as logic, ethics, and literature out of the curriculum. Whether support for the classical forms of culture—from grand opera to ballet and chamber music—will in a similar fashion tend to be steadily downgraded in the Endowment's priorities as the influence of new pressure groups increases remains to be seen.

As regards the second test, namely the provision of "adequate" funding, the prospects are problematical. Although there is scattered evidence that cultural organizations are generally under financial stress, there is no precise, or even reasonably precise, measure of how serious their predicament in fact is. In the cultural field, one of the most highly developed art forms is that of dramatizing appeals for money. Superstar performers do it between the acts from center stage and on television, board chairmen at press conferences solemnly announce the imminent cancellation of the symphony's season, and the arts columnists of the metropolitan newspapers cry alarm—creating the impression that cultural institutions generally are facing catastrophe.

The evidence, limited as it is, does not support so bleak an estimate. First off, by the NEA's own figures the number of cultural institutions continues to multiply—which would seem to suggest growing, not declining, total support. Second, a few of the long-established institutions, such as the Metropolitan Opera, may indeed be on the brink of bankruptcy—and some others which are badly managed or badly overextended may also be in crisis. However the Ford Foundation, which has gathered the most comprehensive data to date, takes a moderately hopeful view. In 1971 it examined the finances of 166 major performing arts organizations and projected that they would encounter an extremely serious "earnings gap" by 1980. But checking on actual trends over the following several years, the Foundation found that their costs had risen somewhat less rapidly than expected, their earned income more rapidly, and the remaining "gap" was consequently lower than anticipated.[11] Clearly, arts organizations on the whole are not in good shape, but it is difficult to make a factual case that they are in worse shape than most other nonprofit organizations.

What seems most likely is not their demise but their greater dependency on government. The old basis of financing the arts by earned income and private gifts has now clearly become inadequate, and in the future will almost certainly become even more so. Some possibilities, probably limited, exist for stimulating further private support. There are also possibilities of easing budgetary strains by better more efficient institutional management. But the likelihood is that costs will increasingly outstrip earnings and gifts, and the widening gap can be filled only by official government subsidy.

How much subsidy will be "necessary" and what level of budgetary allocation for the arts will be "adequate" are questions to which ultimately there is no scientific answer—only a political one. And therein lies great uncertainty. How much money the arts will get from government in the end will depend upon the size and political clout of their constituency. Until rather recently, advocates of the arts, despite their generally influential social position and their articulateness, were ineffective in persuading foundations, corporations, or the government to aid cultural institutions. But in the past 20 years this situation has begun to change dramatically. People in the arts—and those interested in them—have belatedly found their voices, and have made impressive gains in causing both private and official sources of funding to give the arts a higher priority. The prospects for future success, however, remain unclear.

The fact that the Congress has increased the annual budget of the National Endowment more than fortyfold in the span of 12 years is no guarantee that such a rate of increase can long be sustained. The arts lobby now talks of a further doubling of the present NEA appropriation to an annual level of $250 million by 1980. But this seems unlikely. Concern about government deficits has grown. The competition for government resources will intensify if the growth of the economy lags persistently, if inflation continues and if—as is highly likely—the number of powerful claimants multiplies.*

But the volume will nevertheless grow, giving the program increasing visibility and necessitating the development of more refined social and economic criteria to justify various forms of subvention and to improve the "efficiency" of arts subsidies in accomplishing their intended objectives.

Dick Netzer, an economist at New York University, has made a brave pioneering attempt, despite the weaknesses of available data, to subject the policies of funding agencies to critical analysis in order to identify some defensible principles for giving public money to the arts and to assess the results of the money that has already been given. Thus far the blurry assumption has been generally accepted that increased funding for the arts would necessarily have beneficial results and that subsidies given for a particular purpose necessarily served that purpose. Netzer's researches, however, suggest that from an economist's point of view at least a number of the arguments advanced to justify public subsidy are open to serious question and that a good many existing subsidy programs, however well intended, have in fact been little more than shots in the dark made in ignorance of their potential effects and side effects. In some instances government funds have simply displaced or dried up private ones; in others, the main effect has been to greatly increase the personal income of already wealthy star performers, without net benefit to needy institutions or to new talent; and in a few they have had no detectible benefits at all.

For example, the first of the stated objectives of the NEA is "to make the arts more widely available to millions of Americans," and it has distributed a good portion of its funds in pursuit of this purpose. Netzer's evidence indicates that the expenditures have been successful in improving the geographical distribution of ar-

* Some of them, including proponents of greater assistance for the poor and for racial minorities, have already begun to argue in sharper tones that the only reason public subsidy for the arts is now being sought is that the upper class, which used to enjoy them as its special preserve, can no longer support them. So the ordinary taxpayer is now, in their view, invited to contribute to the amusements of the rich, on the theory that such amusements will somehow also be good for him.

tistic performances. But the attempt to broaden audiences through subsidy to include a greater proportion of younger, less educated, and less affluent persons has generally been a failure.

But if the NEA has only half-achieved its primary objective, it has overachieved a nonobjective; artists' earnings have increased as one of the principal effects of a number of its grants. They have made it possible for theatre companies to increase wages far more rapidly than they have increased in the rest of the economy; by increasing the number of performances of opera companies very substantially, they have increased the average annual earnings per artist much more than average annual earnings elsewhere in the economy; likewise, public subsidies to symphony orchestras seem to have had little other effect than to boost substantially the average annual salary of musicians.

Arts advocates are not hospitable to probing questions which seem to get in the way of their crusade for more money. As Netzer describes the process of policy formation in this field, those involved "are, and should be, creative and idiosyncratic individuals, not inclined to rigorous policy analysis. . . . As a consequence arts policy to date has been highly subjective and erratic, shifting with the attitudes and personal preferences of individual presidents, governors, and legislators—attitudes and preferences that are shaped in turn by the advice and importuning of those artists and advocates of the arts who have access to the key decision makers."

This may have been good enough when the amounts involved were chicken feed. But no longer. As the appropriations grow, so will the need for the Netzers. The rising volume of government subsidy which is in prospect for the arts means that the government portion of their funding will become greater in relation to private support and increasingly vital to institutional survival— thereby increasing the chances that the American subsidy system will fail to pass its fourth and final test, namely that of keeping bureaucratization and politicization in check.

Although the National Endowment for the Arts has in its first years been an agency not only well run but run with flair, this happy situation must almost inevitably erode. Programs in the arts confront any bureaucracy with a maximum of the kinds of decisions for which it has the maximum distaste, namely those which require discriminating choices to be made on the basis of nonobjective, nonquantifable criteria. Unless the whole practice of direct institutional grants is abandoned, which is unlikely, the logic of modern management will tend to drive the Endowment, and state arts councils as well, in the direction of fixed formulae in the allocation of funds—formulae relating to geography, population, audience size, and ratios of subsidy to institutional earnings.* Likewise, the tendency will be to retreat from funding the arts and artists as such, because of their controversiality and unquantifiability, and toward the more comfortable areas of research about the arts, of arts education, and of "outreach" programs. This trend will of course be powerfully encouraged by the great organized power of the educationists, who are at present acutely hungry for more jobs, grants, and contracts.

The prospects for politicization are not less worrisome than those for bureaucratization. At the high ideological level, there would seem to be little possibility, whatever degree of financial dependence on government funding develops, that any single political viewpoint will be enforced upon the arts. The tradition of assertive diversity in the American body politic provides bulwarks against that danger. But three other kinds of political intrusion are possible—the crude, the subtle, and the populistic.

The first derives from what might be called Archie Bunker or superpatriotic politics. This kind of demand for conformity has occurred repeatedly in the past; the Federal Theatre Project in New Deal days was prevented by the government from raising the curtain on one of its shows because it criticized Mussolini's Italy. Later the entire project was summarily demolished by a House Committee on grounds that it was un-American. In 1946 the State Department organized an exhibition of modern paintings to be circulated in Europe. When a member of the House Appropriations Committee criticized some of the pictures as "weird" and "unnatural," the Department promptly ordered the exhibition home. Later it sold the paintings as "war surplus." In the McCarthy era, the infamous investigatory team of Roy M. Cohn

* In New York State, to take a concrete instance, the legislature already requires the Arts Council to distribute "arts services" on the basis of 75¢ per capita per county.[12]

and G. David Shine reported that U.S. Information Service libraries overseas contained many publications they regarded as "subversive" (including such magazines as the *Nation* and the *New Republic*) and successfully demanded they be withdrawn.[13] With the end of the Cold War, this pattern of primitive censorship may have ended. Or it may not.

The second and more subtle form of intrusion on the arts could be the advent of what in European countries is called an "official culture." It is the result of an insidious process by which government standards and tastes progressively penetrate the cultural atmosphere. It is not forced upon the arts but rather is almost invited, reflecting an eager and willing conformity to official preferences by artists and arts organizations seeking funds or status.

In the United States there are some signs that the way is opening for the coming of this sort of "official culture," but there are also signs that it will be resisted. The arts, ever since Jacqueline Kennedy, have become politically chic. Leaders of the arts world are increasingly drawn to Washington to bask in the cultural glamor of the nation's capital, to consort with prominent public figures, and to press their claims for public funding. In such an atmosphere it is considered poor form to recall that at the time the legislation establishing the NEA was being discussed much reservation was expressed, particularly by musical organizations, about the wisdom of the whole idea. Indeed it was not until 1970, five years after the establishment of the NEA, that symphony organizations for the first time were willing to apply for grants. But little is heard of the possible dangers of public money on the part of arts organizations today—a tribute either to the skill and soundness of NEA policies in the intervening period or perhaps to the soothing effect of money and the growing need for it which has now developed. In any event the resistance that was aroused when organized government subsidy was being proposed has now noticeably subsided.

And yet sporadic expressions of dissent from the prevailing uncritical enthusiasm in arts circles for public funding continue to be heard, suggesting that there may be more concern about the issue of freedom than is visible on the surface of current discussion. For example Joseph Papp, the noted theatrical director and producer, attacked a prominent advocate of the establishment of an American national theatre, Hilton Kramer of the *New York Times,* in these words:

> Perhaps he prefers the Comédie Francaise with its stilted revivals and its complete disconnection with contemporary France and French life, not to mention its super-unionized seniority system which serves efficiently to deny young actors the opportunity of advancement. Or is he asking us to emulate the Swedish National Theater, which so recently lost its prime director, Ingmar Bergman, without the slightest protest or a call for a general strike; a theater which now has instituted an "improved" socialistic method of selecting plays by a vote of the entire theater work force? . . . What national theater in the entire world today has made more exciting contributions to the art of the theater than any one of the high-quality non-governmental theaters in England and the United States?[14]

Kramer himself has expressed worry about the effects of a cultural "welfare program" on the quality of American art:

> As I listen to some of the complaints that are made about our current "support system," I sometimes wonder if what is being called for may be something like a welfare program for artists (if not for the arts). What this would mean in practice, I think, is this: that no one evincing either a modicum of talent or the intention to cultivate talent for some esthetic purpose would be—or could be—denied a place on the public rolls. The life of art would, under such a program, be transformed into a life of social dependency, and one can easily imagine the size of the bureaucracy needed to keep it going. For some people, perhaps a program of this sort would have all the characteristics of a Utopian paradise. For myself, I must admit it sounds like a perfect nightmare, especially as we have no reason to believe on the basis of the current expansion in the artist-ranks that an increase in numbers brings with it an increase in quality or genius. If anything the very opposite may be true.[15]

Even W. McNeil Lowry, the Grand Almoner of the Arts during his splendid career with the Ford Foundation and a leading figure in the group that helped bring the NEA into being, now seems concerned about the passivity with which private supporters of the arts are tagging along after government. He is concerned that even though Federal and state funds for the arts are far smaller than those provided from private sources, many private and corporate foundations have allowed their grant-making to be shaped to conform to Federal or state initiatives. "The tail is effectively wagging the dog," Lowry writes, "but this is less the responsibility of the National Endowment than of those who overreact to its presence in the field."[16]

The case of the Corporation for Public Broadcasting can be taken as another sign that even if Americans may not be able to resist entirely the subtle deformation of the arts by the growing presence of official subsidies, they will rise up against flagrant government transgressions. In that instance, the Nixon Administration made a determined effort to establish partisan control over the Corporation's programming by the full use of its powers of appointment and of funding. But sufficient public resistance developed to block the attempt until the Nixon Administration became so preoccupied with certain more urgent problems that it abandoned its attack.[17]

On balance, therefore, though the arts are vulnerable to official blandishments, there does seem to be considerable reason to believe—whatever degree of "official culture" may in time develop—that in the American tradition it will not be able to smother out the great existing diversity of tastes and tendencies and it will continuously encounter much private skepticism and, on occasion, antagonism.

In the end, therefore, the most probable pattern of official intrusion upon the arts is the third, the populistic—plain old-fashioned pork barrel and vote-seeking politics.

The first major manifestation of this occurred with the advent of the Carter Administration in 1977. Nancy Hanks, the Republican appointee who had given brilliant leadership for eight years to the Endowment for the Arts was replaced by a Democrat, Livingston Biddle; Republican Ronald Berman was replaced as head of the Endowment for the Humanities by Democrat Joseph Duffey.

In both actions, the hand of Senator Claiborne Pell, Democrat of Rhode Island, and the most powerful figure in Washington for the arts and humanities, was clearly visible. Biddle was the Senator's long-time aide and close friend; Berman, on the other hand, had publicly disagreed with Pell about NEH policy on a number of occasions and the Senator exerted himself vigorously to ensure Biddle's appointment and to block Berman's reappointment.*

The *New York Times* commented solemnly that "A specter is haunting the arts and the humanities in the United States today— the specter of a catastrophic shift of government policy in cultural affairs. . . . No one knows exactly what changes await us, but few knowledgeable people doubt that change on a significant scale is on the way, and many fear that it will be change of the most baleful sort—that indeed, a new era marked by an aggressive politicization of Federal cultural policy is now imminent."[18]

Some of the rhetoric of protest was overblown, but there was also no question that more than the names and party labels of the heads of the Endowments had changed. Senator Pell, in his backing of Biddle and in his opposition to Berman, acted out of a strong conviction that the Endowments had to give much stronger emphasis to disseminating the arts and the humanities, to reaching out to the widest possible audience. The specifications drafted by the White House in its search for a new head for the NEH clearly reflected the same point of view: "the Ivy League, academic and scholarly establishments" were to be given less heed, and the new chairman "should probably be familiar to organized labor, ethnic organizations, community and junior college organizations, and principal educational broadcasters."[19]

As soon as the appointments were announced, a strong and unexpected blast of criticism came from Michael Straight, who had served as deputy to Hanks at the NEA and was serving as Acting Director at the time. He charged that "the cancer of political interference" by vested interest pressure groups, Congress, and the Carter Administration "had begun to undermine the credibility of the Endowments" and that President Carter had downgraded them into "minor political satrapies." Regarding the

---

* In so doing, he at the same time rendered Berman a considerable service, transforming his public image from that of journeyman bureaucrat, ideologically close to Richard Nixon who appointed him, to noble defender of excellence and academic independence and innocent victim of a political vendetta.

appointment of Biddle, Straight conceded his abilities and good credentials, but asked, "If the appointment of the Staff Director of the Pell Oversight Committee isn't political, what is? Why didn't they look for someone of national stature who would be known and respected by both political parties?" About Duffey, Straight asserted that "he has no credentials in the academic world; his credentials are that when he ran for the Senate in Connecticut, he came out for Carter."[20]

To those who had hitherto had predominant influence in the policies of the Endowments, the "elitists," the shift was dismaying. One of them, Robert Brustein, former dean of the Yale School of Drama, hurried to Washington to talk with the principal figures involved. "It seems to me," he told Senator Pell,

> that as a politician you are too preoccupied with the political justification of art and learning, and the way you try to do that is by speading them throughout the land like jam. As a result, you are giving a lot of thought to how to disseminate ideas to large numbers of people, but you don't seem too interested in how those ideas get formulated in the first place. What you are talking about, finally, is not the humanities, but a government sponsored form of adult education. You're too involved with how to make knowledge popular, and not enough with how this knowledge is developed. The question that interests me is, what can the Endowment do to help sustain a philosopher while he thinks?

But the Senator was not persuaded of the error of his ways, and Brustein later wrote:

> Flying back to my own city on that overcast afternoon, enjoying a misted view of Washington's great monuments and public buildings, I reflected on the Endowments and their increasingly cloudy future. It was true enough, as has been charged, that these agencies were being "politicized" but the politicization went much deeper than the intervention of pressure groups, vested interests and meddling politicians. It was the very politics of consensus American democracy that was now beginning to influence the policies and appointments of these important Federal agencies. Once fully professional and oriented toward the artist and the scholar, the Endowments were now preparing to spread their relatively meager moneys among educationalists, audiences and amateurs as well, on

the essentially political assumption that any resources generated by the people should benefit all the people immediately and simultaneously.[21]

Whether one shares Brustein's view or Pell's, there is little doubt that what the Senator advocates is in fact the direction of events, led even more by what is happening at the state than at the Federal level. David Dempsey, a writer on the arts, describes the projects now supported by the New York State Council on the Arts, the largest of its kind:

in Westchester, where I live, Council funds treated us to a fiddlers' contest, and in my local community, to a demonstration of Colonial drop spindling and ditty bag making. Folks in Albany who feel the need for inspiration can pick up the telephone and "Dial-a-Poem." New York City hobbyists might want to drop in at Aunt Len's Doll and Toy Museum. Landmarks are restored and archeological sites preserved. In recent years, too, the Council has helped fund five zoos, three botanical gardens, 11 science and natural history museums, an aquarium, a planetarium and a rare coin collection. All have high visibility, many are going broke, and not a few enjoy the benefits of geographical dispersal. The Council got out of the zoo business this year when the state legislature appropriated separate funds for this activity through the Parks and Recreation Department. Animals, however, are still eligible as long as they are stuffed: the American Museum of Natural History received $563,000 for 1978, about 20 percent less than the Metropolitan Museum of Art.[22]

Call this "populism" or "democratization" or whatever, it is the kind of "politicization" that seems almost certain eventually to dominate official arts policy in the United States because the legislature is the source of funding, and in the words of Livingston Biddle, "the voice of the constituent is the one most clearly heard by Congress."

This then is a time of multiple and uncomfortable quandaries in cultural policy. Art itself is in profound transition—in forms, standards, public tastes, and even definition. Moreover, the arts in industrialized, egalitarian societies are economically sick from the inherent, irreversible disease of stationary productivity and the ravages of persistent inflation. Their advocates generally believe that selective survival cannot be left simply to the Darwinian vicissitudes of the market, and yet the old forms of private subsidy are increasingly inadequate. The United States, like all the advanced Western nations before it, has therefore now turned decisively down a slippery road toward governmental subvention. As the record of all history testifies, this can be very hazardous to their health. But so is slow starvation, which under contemporary circumstances may be the only realistic alternative.

7 ▶▶▶▶

Social-Action Movements—
the Twilight Zone of Politics

CULTURAL CENTERS, like colleges, hospitals, churches, and research laboratories, constitute the established, highly structured "hard" portion of the Third Sector. The "soft" part, though it lacks such institutional crust, is equally large and in its fashion equally significant. It consists of that great amorphous body of groups and associations devoted to causes and to change—civil rights, environmental protection, women's liberation, anti-abortion, and tens of thousands of others—collectively called the social-action movements.

Important distinctions exist between the "hard" and "soft" elements in form, procedures, and objectives. The former are generally older, larger, better housed, professionally staffed, and better financed. They are concerned primarily with the provision of services and the performance of specialized functions—education, care of the ill, research, assistance to the needy, the performance of religious rites, and the presentation of artistic events. The latter, the social-action movements, are less structured, dependent largely on volunteer staff, minimally funded, and sometimes temporary in existence.

But whatever their form or procedures, they are devoted essentially to the advancement of some belief or the achievement of some reform. By definition they are not part of government, and characteristically they do not aspire to govern. They seek rather to press their values and claims on other groups and upon society in general. By the nature of their objectives, therefore, they normally exist in a state of tension, even conflict, with government and other elements of society.

These distinctions are more clear in concept than in practice. Nonprofit organizations do not break neatly into two distinct segments along the "hard" and "soft" boundary: rather they are arranged as points along a spectrum according to the particular mix of service orientation and reformism which gives each its distinctive personality. Many of these points along the spectrum, moreover, are moving points: a given institution, such as a church, may be aroused by some public issue to a high degree of activism for a time, returning to its normal religious preoccupations once the issue subsides. Social-action movements also tend to have life cycles, or career patterns. Some are born out of circumstances of mass excitement or unrest, carry on their efforts for a period, and subsequently disappear, having achieved their mission or having lost their motivation and following. Some begin as ardent reformers, evolve into more formal structure, and eventually become sedate operating entities, fulfilling their cause in the performance of a conventional function. Some are absorbed, or more often their programs are absorbed, by the existing political parties, and subsequently by government.

Despite the shadings and the amorphousness, however, the distinction is fundamental: the service-oriented institutions adjoin and relate to the administrative agencies of government and to some extent to service elements of the profit-making sector (proprietary hospitals, for example, and textbook publishers); the social-action movements adjoin and relate primarily to social forces and politics. Indeed, in democratic systems they constitute the soil from which new social demands and discontents, new perspectives and directions, commonly emerge, particularly those to which the established parties and political organs of government for one reason or another are resistant. They are factors of surveillance and stimulation operating on government and other institutions, vehicles for the formulation and transmission of new norms and ideas into the conventional social, economic, and political matrix. Some advocates of the movements have seen them as

knights on white chargers or as avenging angels. Oliver Wendell
Holmes Sr. used a rather different metaphor. In conceding their
usefulness, he once observed that reformers, interfering as they
did with vested rights and time hallowed interests, perform an office comparable to that of nature's scavengers for the removal of
material nuisances. In an oration in 1863 in Boston he said "It is
not the butterfly, but the beetle, which God employs for this duty.
. . . not the bird of paradise and the nightingale, but the fowl of
dark plumage and unmelodious voice."

The Successive Surges of American Reformism

America from the start has been a hotbed of social, economic,
religious, and political reformism, the impulse being manifested
in an unending rhythm of periods of intensive concern followed
by ebb or consolidation, followed in turn by resurgence. By some
process of contagion and interaction not yet fully understood,
reform movements seem to rise in parallel and quite often to sub-
side in parallel, thus building up the crests and deepening the
troughs of their undulating intensity. The revolution, the Civil
War, Populism, Progressivism, and the New Deal have been
among the earlier surges. The years since the end of World War
II have seen the eruption of a combination of powerful thrusts of
dissent and demands for change. The most notable of these have
been the civil rights movement, the anti-Vietnam War movement, the student rebellion, the environmental movement, the
consumer protection movement, the women's liberation movement, and the movement for greater responsiveness and accountability of institutions, both governmental and corporate. Each of
these has attracted hundreds of thousands, in some cases millions,
of adherents, and their practical achievements can only serve as
encouragement and stimulus to the maintenance of the tradition
by the reformers of the future.

In the 1950s, American blacks, assisted and supported by liberal whites, began an assault on established patterns of racial discrimination. Their strategy was to work partly through the courts
and partly through public demonstrations and organized protests

of various kinds. The results have been major legislation outlawing discrimination in education, employment, access to public facilities, and political participation. Although their economic position remains inferior, millions of blacks have become effectively enfranchised, and their voting power is now a significant factor in elections in many parts of the country.

In the case of the Vietnam War, protest activities beginning in the early 1960s eventually reached such scale and intensity, and evoked such a response among many elements of the American population, that fundamental policy changes were forced upon reluctant military and diplomatic leaders, and President Lyndon Johnson was driven from office.

Closely linked to the antiwar movement was a student revolt—deriving partly from conditions within the universities and partly from the fact that many students felt threatened by the military draft—which forced faculty and administrators of institutions across the country, theretofore entombed in complacency, to re-examine many basic questions of educational structure, policy, and governance procedures.

The social-action movements in the United States in the 1950s and 1960s were also in some respects youth movements in the European tradition. And in this regard some of the parallels are disquieting.

Here for example is the description by historian Hans Kohn of the German youth movement in the period before World War I:

it was not in any sense economic; it represented groups of younger persons in a highly prosperous society who took no part in economic life but who, as the sons and daughters of the well-to-do, were relatively carefree. It was an "idealistic movement," inspired by philosophy and poetry and manifesting itself through these media. It reflected the desire for a new way of life, for greater liberty, sincerity and beauty as opposed to the materialism, conventionalism and insincerity of Wilhelmine society. Traditions of the romanticists . . . were revived and folk song, folk dancing and folklore again came to the fore. A new stream of enthusiasm began to undermine the hard nationalistic utilitarianism of the older generation. The revolt of youth against parents, school and traditional authority was colored by religious or mythical enthusiasm and was often marked

by vague irrationalism. . . . Politically and socially the youth movement had no clear or definite aims. It had no alternative to offer for
the existing order which it disliked; it fought against all established
authority.

But Kohn pointed out, "it longed for a new authority, for a real
Führer instead of established bureaucratic leadership."

After the World War with the intensification and acceleration of
social and political unrest, the youth movements grew in number
and at the same time began to lose their character as movements of
individualistic revolt. . . . In the postwar states where new forms
of one-party dictatorship had been established—the Soviet Union,
Fascist Italy, National Socialist Germany—the new rulers depended on youth to effect the transition from the old order to the
new. The youth movements became official or semi-official organizations and very often the most faithful support of the new regime.

Kohn concludes, "in a sense National Socialism can be considered a product of the German youth movements, from which it
inherited its irrationalism, and its vague nationalistic sentimen-
talism."

Kohn's description of what took place in Germany fifty years
ago, and the consequences to which it led, should be sobering to
those who are inclined to believe that youthful enthusiasm and
idealism necessarily lead to positive social and political results.[1]

During the 1960s, though temporarily obscured by national
emotion over Vietnam and by dispute over the style and tactics of
the student rebellion, a number of older but quiescent reformist
efforts were rekindled—such as consumerism, conservationism,
and women's liberation.

Ralph Nader, beginning with an attack on the automobile manufacturers for selling products he called "unsafe at any speed," ac-
tivated a new consumer protection drive which has now resulted
in more effective enforcement of preexisting laws and in new legislation imposing severe restrictions on makers and distributors of
consumer goods.

At about the same time, sparked by a bestselling book by Ra-
chel Carson, *The Silent Spring*, about the dangerous effects of
pesticides, the old conservation movement which had been doz-

ing for half a century reemerged as a drive in behalf of environmental protection. By massive public demonstrations combined with well-organized legal and lobbying activities, it has already achieved passage of a National Environmental Protection Act which radically changes policy in this field. The economic decisions of every kind of institution now have to take into account the hitherto uncounted "external" costs of their environmental impacts. States and localities, following the Federal lead, are now enacting similar and in some cases even more stringent environmental laws. The economic recession of the mid 1970s somewhat slowed but has not reversed the trend.

Later in getting underway, but now spreading, has been a fresh campaign for women's liberation. The concrete results can already be seen in changes in the employment practices of government agencies and private firms and in the number of women elected to public office.

Each of these movements has brought about specific changes in policies and practices which are of great importance. Together, they have also had a pervasive effect on national values and sensibilities. The civil rights movement, which began with the blacks, has generated concern for the legal rights of all minorities and with questions of economic and social justice in general. The antiwar movement has led to a broader reexamination, which is still underway, of the moral constraints by which diplomatic and military policy should be guided, and of the proper role of the Congress in the shaping and control of foreign policy. The environmental movement has led to reexamination of fundamental notions of economic growth and of the necessary balance between material and the nonmaterial ingredients in defining "the good life." The women's movement has led to a penetrating reexamination of interpersonal relationships, of marriage and divorce, and of family structure.

All, including consumerism, have generated interest in the accountability and responsiveness of institutions in general to new social needs and changing values. This in turn has led to demands for breaking down secrecy of procedures, for greater public access to decision-making processes, and for higher ethical standards in the conduct of public officials and of the leaders of all institutions.

Watergate, the disgrace of Richard Nixon, and the ongoing exposure of corporate scandals are direct consequences of this new atmosphere.

Virtually everything—from personal lifestyles to foreign policy—has been touched by the movements and by the new awarenesses they have created. And virtually everything about them—their methods, their aims, and their results—remains enveloped in controversy. A French commentator, Jean-François Revel, in his book *Without Marx or Jesus* applauds them and sees their importance as not only national but global: "One of the most striking features of the past decade is that the only new revolutionary stirrings in the world have had their origin in the United States. From America has come the sole revolutionary innovation which can be described as truly original. I mean the complex of new oppositional phenomena designated by the term 'dissent.' "[2]

Eric Hoffer on the other hand, like a number of conservative American writers, saw the antiwar movement of the 1960s as a contemptible spectacle of draft evaders "performing for the media." When the "free speech" movement exploded on the Berkeley campus in 1964, he was "outraged by the sight of history made by juvenile delinquents." As events of that traumatic period evolved, he became horrified at "the thought of a world run by self-important, self-indulgent, self-righteous, violent and clownish punks."[3]

In historical terms, however, such movements are indisputably a distinguishing element of the American political and social tradition. Despite their organizational fluidity and fluctuation, there has been great continuity in their concerns and objectives. The present-day movements all have their direct forebears, most going back to the nineteenth century and some even earlier. They have typically been more idealistic and moralistic than ideological, and religious and intellectual figures have consistently been prominent in their leadership. The movements have often been interlinked through the simultaneous or sequential involvement of highly motivated individuals in several of them. Thus many women prominent in the early suffrage groups were also active Abolitionists and members of the Temperance movement. More recently, Northern students who went South to organize Negroes in Alabama and Mississippi later returned home to become active in the student revolt and the antiwar movement and still later to work for consumerism or environmentalism.

Quite often, by their zeal and tactical ingenuity in maneuvering their frail organizational craft, they have been able to overcome the great government armadas ranged against them. For purposes of the present argument, it is particularly important to note that their objectives—at least since the founding of the republic—have been overwhelmingly reformist, not revolutionary. Though they have sometimes closely skirted the borders of legality and frequently of respectability, they have seldom been violent or subversive. They have typically been a part of the democratic process, an often unloved part but a part of "the system" nonetheless.

The Scrabble for Funding

That social-action movements have flourished in the United States is a remarkable tribute to their esprit and dedication, for they have generally had great difficulty in raising funds; and the more activist and controversial the group, the more severe its funding problems have been.

The first consequence of the hard scrabble for money to which they seem to be condemned is that they are obliged to live frugally. On the whole, and relative to established service institutions, their costs are very low. Their facilities are simple, their staffs are largely volunteer, and even their full-time workers are usually paid at a level which makes them quasi-volunteers.

Many are shoestring operations to a degree not widely appreciated. For example, one-third of the environmental organizations in the country operate on a budget of less than $500 a year, half on less than $1000.[4] In the early 1960s, at the moment when the Port Huron Statement had been drafted and Students for a Democratic Society chapters were being formed and becoming active on campuses throughout the country, the organization consisted of two full-time staff members, one operating from a cubicle in Atlanta and the other from a rented room in Greenwich Village in

New York City. An unknown lawyer, Thurgood Marshall, and one assistant planned the strategy and initiated the litigation which was eventually to bring about a total change in the interpretation by the courts of the constitutional rights of racial minorities. The Congress of Racial Equality (CORE), one of the most influential of the groups which in the 1950s began to shake the underpinnings of segregation in the U.S., had a staff in its first years of a handful of persons paid meager salaries, plus some youthful volunteers. Ralph Nader's hall bedroom and the table in the back of a delicatessen in the nation's capital from which he has conducted a good part of his activities are a familiar part of the legend which surrounds that folk hero.

The search for funding by the movements has necessarily been unending—and where they have managed to find it, and where they have failed, constitutes a commentary on themselves and on American society in general.

On the whole, they obtain little or nothing from the great established elements of the economic system, nor from the major mechanisms for raising charitable contributions. Corporations and their philanthropic foundations, with few exceptions, exclude the social-action movements from their grant-making. The trade unions, with the exception of the United Automobile Workers and one or two others, have been almost as unhelpful. Likewise, the United Funds across the country distribute the vast sums they collect almost exclusively to service institutions of various kinds, not to activist groups.[5]

Throughout American history, reform movements of many kinds have had a strong moral or religious basis, and this continuing tradition is reflected in the fact that churches and church-related organizations have played a significant role in the funding of the civil rights movement, the antiwar movement, and various efforts in behalf of corporate responsibility. The mainline Protestant churches have been the leaders. The Catholic church has contributed selectively, as in the case of its support for the work of Cesar Chavez; the evangelical Protestant churches, not greatly involved in the past, appear more recently to have begun to be increasingly sympathetic to certain activist groups.[6]

The record of the private foundations is mixed, and mostly indifferent. Of the 30,000 or more in the United States, only a few dozen have given assistance to the social-action movements. Most of these have been small family foundations—Stern, Field, Taconic, New World, New York, Ottinger, Norman, Haymarket, DJB, Vanguard, the Rockefeller Family Fund, and a few others. Their gifts tend to be relatively small, but they have been given to a broad range of groups, including some of the most controversial. Quite often their help has been offered at an early stage when the needs of an organization for "venture capital" have been most acute.[7] Only a very few of the large private foundations have been forthcoming. These include the Rockefeller Brothers Fund, which has supported civil rights, environmental, and anti-apartheid organizations; the Carnegie Corporation is a rarity among the big foundations for having made a grant to any Ralph Nader organization; and the Ford Foundation, which has assisted a range of civil rights and environmental groups and has been the major private supporter of the public interest law movement.*

The social-action movements as regards their private funding are thus in a peculiar and weak situation. Their own membership and constituencies tend to be the young and disadvantaged whose capacity to give—except in the form of volunteered services—is severely limited. But contributions of time and effort are not considered to be tax-deductible gifts. Moreover, the so-called "tax incentives" for charitable giving which are now embedded in the Internal Revenue Code are so extravagantly discriminatory as between poor and rich donors that for the social-action movements they are effectively meaningless as a help in soliciting individual gifts.†

The tax system as a whole is of no assistance in enabling them to be self-supporting through the contributions of their own members. Rather, it condemns them to dependence on baronial benefactors. But, to make the Catch 22 complete, the barons with few exceptions, are indifferent.

* The extreme caution of the large foundations in funding social reform is the more surprising in view of the exceptional success of a number of their grants to some of the movements. For a careful listing of these, see the study of Sarah Carey, "Foundations and the Powerless," done for the Filer Commission in 1975.[8]
† A fuller treatment of this fundamental problem, and some possible solutions to it, will be found in chapter 9.

It is hardly surprising, then, that reformist groups are compelled to rely largely on their own resources—of dedication, ingenuity, sweat, and sacrifice. Given their role, this is almost inevitable and quite possibly proper. But however right or wrong in theory, the preoccupying fact to most of today's movements is that their financial survival is becoming increasingly problematic.

Like those of other nonprofit institutions, their costs are going up sharply, not only because of general inflation but also because many of the organizations, formed in the last ten to fifteen years, are now at the point when they have to begin to pay salaries approximating market rates to their staff. The freshness of the early years has now somewhat faded and the passion cooled. The highly motivated volunteer workers of the earlier period have now gone on to regular employment in law firms, government, or business and have been succeeded by an equally competent but less fiery generation whose motivation is strong but whose salary expectations are much higher. The impact of the replacement of the amateurs by professionals on organizational costs has often been dramatic.

At the same time, their income from private sources is generally down and will in all probability decline further. Only a few of the "name" organizations have ever been able to solicit contributions and memberships successfully from the general public by mass mailings and the media, and their returns from such efforts are now markedly off.*

The smaller foundations which have given money to the social-action movements are rarely sources of support for the long haul. Their preference and practice is to give start-up funding and then to move out and on. The few larger foundations which have made grants in the past have now lost much of their limited interest; and Ford, overwhelmingly the principal single source of private foundation support, has now slashed the level of all its programs, including those in behalf of activist groups. Where foundation funding continues, it tends increasingly to be concentrated on a

* Common Cause, organized in 1970 by John Gardner, former Secretary of HEW, is, however, an exception. Perhaps because of its spectacular series of successful reform efforts in recent years—in exposing the finances of the Nixon reelection campaign in 1972, in leading the fight for public financing of Presidential elections, and in helping break the seniority system in Congress—its basic constituency of supporters has remained rather stable.

small number of the better organized, more expert, and more research- or service-oriented groups.

Jeremy Stone, director of the Federation of American Scientists, suggests an interesting further explanation of why the social-action movements currently are in difficulty. He points out that the Nixon and Ford Administrations were, in retrospect, a period of great prosperity for public-interest groups of the left. Such groups, however, face a twin disaster, in his view, with the election of a liberal President. "Right-wing Presidents considerably incense the left, as the left wing Presidents incense the right. As things stand, Jimmy Carter is a bonanza to those right-wing mail operations that have been making it on the Panama Canal and the strategic arms limitations talks. Meanwhile the liberal groups—that want to defend him on just such initiatives—find the public saying, 'leave it to Jimmy.' "[9]

As a result of the scissors effect of steeply rising costs and sagging income, activist organizations are now energetically, even desperately, seeking to find new ways to sustain themselves.

Public-interest law provides an important example of the attempt to do so on the basis of earned income. Some older organizations, such as the Legal Aid Society, the National Association for the Advancement of Colored People (NAACP), and the American Civil Liberties Union have long been active in providing private legal assistance to the poor and to minorities. In more recent years, their activity has spread from legal aid to class action and other litigation relating to environment, women's rights, access to the media, health, and many other issues. They have also moved from efforts to improve legal representation of the disadvantaged to political initiatives for reform of governmental structure and procedures. This extension of the range of their activities, along with increased activism and controversiality, has had direct—and negative—funding implications. Newer public-interest law groups, which started with a primary interest in class-action litigation and broad legal reform, generally were launched with the initial assistance of a few foundations, large and small, plus the strategic gifts of a few wealthy individuals. But now foundation funding is shrinking, and the professional bar, which might seem to be a national source of support for *pro bono* legal activity, has in fact never been very enthusiastic about legal aid, and has been even less enthusiastic—and less generous—as regards public-interest law.

Thus the search for more permanent funding has had to concentrate on the possibilities for earned rather than donated income, specifically on the possibility of receiving fees for services rendered in successful litigation. But this has proven to be a course with many obstacles. First, the Internal Revenue Service in 1970 decided that class-action litigation was sufficiently different from traditional legal aid to suspend the tax exempt status of public-interest law groups. Subsequently they were permitted exemption but only on condition they did not accept fees for their work. Then in 1975, rulings were issued permitting the receipt of fees, but only if court-awarded and only to an amount totalling less than 50 percent of their costs.

During those years, Federal and state courts in a number of cases awarded such fees, arousing the hope that public-interest law groups in the future might become largely self-supporting on the basis of them. But that hope was struck down by the Supreme Court in the 1975 Alaska pipeline case, which ruled that such awards can be given only on the basis of specific statutory authorization.

The decision was a severe blow to both the morale and the funding of the public-interest law movement. To overcome its effects, several legislative proposals have been submitted in Congress to restore the authority of the courts to award fees in a number of specific areas, such as civil rights or environmental protection, and also to authorize the courts generally to award such fees in all public-interest cases. None has so far been enacted.

Earned fees are at least a possibility for public-interest law groups, but for the vast majority of social-action organizations this is not the case. Their efforts to reinforce their financial situation have accordingly been concentrated on the search for new ways to increase and stabilize the flow of individual gifts.

Ralph Nader has been the most persistent and ingenious of the social-action movement leaders in this quest. Two of the support mechanisms he favors are checkoffs and tithing.

The checkoff idea was first tried in the fall of 1970 in connection with the creation of Public Interest Research Groups (PIRGs) at a number of campuses across the country. The method of financing is for a majority of the students to petition the university to add a small amount to student activity fees for this special purpose. The added amount is refundable to any objector. Some 20 PIRGs are in operation, collecting a total of some $1.5 million annually. The main centers of interest are schools in New York, Minnesota, Massachusetts, Oregon, and California.

The relative success of this experiment led to exploration of the possibilities of instituting payroll deduction plans in offices and factories, comparable to those widely used to collect union dues and United Fund contributions, to fund local Business and Urban Research Groups (BURGs). This effort has not proven fruitful, however, and more recently Nader has urged that the checkoff idea be concentrated on companies that use "take-it-or-leave-it" contracts (insurance policies, leases). These companies would be required to offer every user or policyholder an opportunity to support a consumer organization in that particular field simply by checking a box on his contract or bill. The company would then automatically add a fixed amount to the individual's bill and forward it to the donee organization. The organization would then use the funds received to provide a consumer perspective about important decisions (such as a rate increase) and to ameliorate customer services. To date, however, no major corporation has volunteered, or been required, to institute such a checkoff system.

The second approach Nader advocates is a slightly modified version of an old fund-raising mechanism—tithing. He would like to see people entering a profession agree to give at least 1 percent of their income each year to a member-controlled group that would deal with social justice issues within their field—whether law, medicine, accounting or teaching. None of the established professions has yet joined up, although a few doctors and lawyers have begun to make individual contributions on a regular basis.

From the viewpoint of the social-action movements, such methods—which theoretically could gather very large sums of money—offer promise of freeing them from reliance on benefactions of a few wealthy individuals or foundations. They would also provide a relatively stable and broadly based constituency of individual supporters.[10] Nader himself entertains even more ambitious expectations of them. In his view, such mechanisms "for mobilizing large numbers of people in democratically-controlled structures" would fill a major vacuum—the lack of solidly based civic institutions. The absence of such institutions "has tilted our political-economic system in favor of organized and bureaucratic power." New funding mechanisms therefore could help transfer power to the powerless, which Nader believes is "the most basic issue in our society".[11]

Whether or not the social-action movements will be able to persuade state legislatures to establish checkoff systems or persuade the governing boards of the great professional organizations to institute tithing remains to be seen. Likewise, whether the movement will be able to bring about changes in the income tax system to provide greater incentives for low-income and youthful givers, or to win legislative approval for court-awarded fees in public interest cases depends ultimately on the degree of general voter support they enjoy. The present generation of reformers is acutely aware of the historical cycle of ebb and flow in public enthusiasm for reform and they are working hard to break it. But by the late 1970s there were many indications that the great burst of social activism which characterized the period from the mid 1950s to the early 1970s had begun to wane.

The Strange, Reversible Relationship with Government

Social-action movements by definition are gadflies on the rump of the great beast of the Establishment. It is not to be expected therefore that they would be embraced and assisted by those governmental and private institutions whose objectives, procedures, and behavior they seek to change.

The logic of this proposition is generally borne out by the actual record of their experience with private-sector institutions. But in their relationship with government, a curious and important reversibility can be observed: Until an activist movement crosses that invisible line which admits it to official acceptance, it faces endless legal obstacles and administrative disadvantages—and sometimes worse. But once it is on the other side, its efforts may suddenly begin to enjoy governmental support (financial and other) to an almost unimaginable degree.

The patterns of American government response in the period since World War II are reasonably clear. As regards the extremists, if a movement espouses violence (the Black Panthers, the Weathermen, or the bizarre Symbionese Liberation Army), it will bring down on itself vigorous, even violent, official reaction. In addition, members or sympathizers of an activist group not necessarily committed to violence, but who find themselves in an ambiguous or provocative situation which gets out of control, may encounter clubs or even gunfire, as in the riots in Chicago at the time of the 1968 Democratic Party convention and in the student antiwar demonstrations at Kent State in 1970.

In the civil rights struggle, even organizations committed to nonviolence sometimes encountered drastic official reaction, both at the local and national level. According to the records of the Student Nonviolent Coordinating Committee (SNCC), for example, its members in the summer of 1964 in the state of Mississippi endured more than 1000 arrests, 8 beatings, 35 shooting incidents, and 6 murders.[12]

The best-documented example of this kind at the Federal level, and the most disquieting, is the experience of the late Reverend Martin Luther King Jr. This black leader's commitment to nonviolence was not only a political tactic but a deeply held moral and social philosophy. His "Letter from a Birmingham Jail" written in 1963 is a classic statement in the Socratic and Gandhian tradition of the obligations of responsible dissenters to their society and to the law.[13] Yet, from the early 1960s until King's assassination in 1968, all of the arbitrary power and lawless habits that had accumulated in the FBI over the years were marshalled to destroy his reputation and the movement he led. The effort began with the indexing of King as "Communist" and the leaking of stories to the press, the Congress, and others that his organization, the Southern Christian Leadership Conference (SCLC), was subversive. After the huge civil rights march on Washington in 1963, the agency branded him as "the most dangerous and effective Negro in the country." It therefore decided to go beyond the collection of "legalistic proofs" to the use of other "imaginative tactics" to take King "off his pedestal" incuuding "placing a good-looking female plant in King's office." [14]

A memorandum in early 1964 from William Sullivan, assistant director of the FBI, to his chief, J. Edgar Hoover, pointed out that if the Bureau were successful

> the Negroes will be left without a national leader of sufficiently compelling personality to steer them in the proper direction. This is what could happen but need not happen if the right kind of a national Negro leader could at this time be gradually developed so as to overshadow Dr. King and be in the position to assume the role of the leadership of the Negro people when King had been completely discredited.

To the agency's dismay, however, and despite its diligent efforts, King's influence and prestige continued to soar. FBI agents were busy bugging his telephones, whispering stories to the Washington press corps about his alleged sexual activities, and inviting various influential persons to listen to tapes it had made of his private conversations. They were also active in trying to get the Ford Foundation and the National Science Foundation to cut off his funding, to discourage universities across the country from offering him honorary degrees, and to dissuade the Pope from granting him an audience. Nonetheless their target was named *Time* magazine's Man of the Year in 1964, and he was also offered the Nobel Peace Prize.

Clearly, it was felt, something more had to be done. In November of that year, shortly before he was to go to Oslo to receive the Nobel award, the agency went to the grotesque length of mailing an anonymous letter and a tape of some hotel room recordings to King and to his wife, Coretta. The letter said in part:

> King, there is only one thing left for you to do. You know what it is. You have just 34 days in which to do it. This exact number has been selected for a specific reason. It has definite practical significance. You are done. There is but one way out for you.

According to King's close associate Andrew Young, now Ambassador to the United Nations and former Democratic Congressman from Georgia, when King received the letter "he felt someone was trying to get him to commit suicide."

The "Threatening" Dissenters

This unedifying case was but one example of a general pattern of government behavior which developed in the troubled 1950s and 1960s. The nation's very sensitive security nerve was stung by civil disorders at home and military pressures abroad. Dissent even of a lawful and nonviolent kind was seen by government agencies as a threat to security and led to massive, institutionalized lawlessness by a number of government agencies in a virtual war against the dissenters. The agencies principally involved were the FBI, the CIA, the military intelligence services, the National Security Agency, and the Internal Revenue Service.

The FBI's treatment of Dr. King may have been unusually unsavory because of Director Hoover's personal animus toward him, but it was not uncharacteristic of the Bureau's methods. Hoover for many years had blackmailed Congressmen with derogatory personal information he had collected about them and which he used whenever necessary to retaliate against any critics. The FBI committed burglaries and gathered political intelligence at the request of various Presidents and engaged in covert operations to disrupt the activities of various political groups. It worked hand-in-glove with Senator Joseph McCarthy and the House Un-American Activities Committee in their general attack on dissent and nonconformity. Its COINTELPRO program established in 1956 "to disrupt the Communist Party and related organizations" became a screen for a wide-ranging campaign in the following years against civil rights, antiwar, and other groups of generally liberal orientation.

The CIA, beginning in the early 1950s developed an equally wide-ranging and illegal program of surveillance, infiltration, and disruption of law-abiding dissenters considered to be "threatening." In 1952 it began secretly to open, read, photograph, and reseal hundreds of thousands of first-class private letters. It financed major academic research centers in the U.S.; it carried on a nationwide program of surveillance of American citizens which included burglaries, wiretapping, and bugging. By the 1960s, it was infiltrating and disrupting various student groups and activist organizations and manipulating a number of nonprofit institutions through control of their funding. Between 1963 and 1966, the Senate Select Committee on Intelligence Activities found the agency "had been involved in nearly one half of all the grants by American charitable foundations exclusive of Ford, Rockefeller and Carnegie organizations."[15]

The Internal Revenue Service was a latecomer to the war against domestic dissent, but it became a full and active collaborator after 1969. In July of that year it created a Special Services Staff (SSS) to investigate and collect intelligence on "ideological, militant, subversive, radical and similar type organizations" and on "non-violent" people such as those who "organize and attend rock festivals, which attract youths and narcotics." Ultimately, the SSS compiled 11,458 dossiers on such cases as former Mayor Lindsay of New York and the entire University of North Carolina.

In 1975, IRS Commissioner Donald Alexander testified to a Senate committee that the agency maintained a computerized list of 465,000 citizens, predominantly "liberals, radicals, anti-war activists and blacks," about whom it compiled extensive information "unrelated to enforcement of the tax laws."*[16]

A series of Congressional inquiries, plus the Rockefeller Commission created by President Ford, plus the Watergate revelations, have produced tens of thousands of pages of richly detailed documentation of the violations of law and of individual rights by government agencies which occurred over at least a quarter cen-

* An excessively benign evaluation of the IRS during this period is contained in a Filer Commission study by David Ginsburg et al., members of a prominent Washington law firm, which along with other legal business handles tax matters before the IRS for its clients. It concluded that "the Service has not been totally immune to improper political or partisan influences, but that on the whole its resistance to such influences—even from the White House—seems to be unusually strong. Perfection cannot realistically be expected of any government agency in the face of powerful Congressional or White House pressures. However, apart from the aberrations of the early Cold War era which affected the Service equally with the rest of the nation, the instances in which the Service may fairly be regarded as having succumbed to partisan or ideological bias appear to be few."[17]

tury. In the words of one goup of scholars who carefully examined the data, these "were not isolated incidents of zealous agents exceeding their authority in the field, however frequently such may occur. Rather, the abuses were ongoing, bureaucratic programs, often continuing over decades, involving hundreds of officials and aimed at thousands of citizens, and ordered and approved at the highest level of the executive branch of government."[18]

Such improper actions were not effectively controlled within the Executive Branch, and neither the courts nor the Congress were able or willing to exercise effective restraint and oversight.

For our purposes the most pertinent fact about this deplorable pattern of governmental behavior, at least in recent decades, is that it is triggered by what has been called "the security obsession"[19] and that once triggered it is directed in large part against law-abiding private groups operating at or near the edge of what officials consider to be dissent of a "radical" character—which in fact has included most of the prominent reformists of recent times operating within the framework of their constitutional rights.

The Moderate but "Controversial" Reformers

Social-action organizations of a more moderate and domestically oriented character, while they have not been faced with physical violence by the police or intrusions by the FBI, CIA, and others, have nevertheless been subject to consistent prejudice by governmental agencies in administrative actions and interpretations. The Internal Revenue Service has been a focus of complaint, partly because of the vital importance of its rulings on tax exemption to the survival of nonprofit groups and partly because its behavior, at least in the view of a number of critics, has at various periods been hostile. For example, scores of black politicians and civil rights leaders from the South have formally charged the IRS with prejudice and harassment in the discriminatory use of tax audits against them.

An instructive example not of illegal conduct but of the more common problem of administrative delay and indecisiveness by the IRS, and of the destructive consequences for a nonprofit organization, is that of the efforts of the Project on Corporate Responsibility to obtain tax-exempt status. Organized in 1969, its first action was the solicitation of General Motors stockholders for proxies to elect public directors to the company's board, a campaign which generated great publicity and controversy. The Project at the same time applied to the IRS for tax exemption. The agency responded with a request that the Project divide itself into two parts, one to conduct research and disseminate information, which might be tax exempt, and the other to initiate shareholder actions, which would not be tax exempt. The Project complied, and reorganization on this basis was completed by 1972. The agency, notwithstanding, declined to issue a ruling. In May 1973, the Project therefore filed suit, and in December of that year, a Federal court declared the proposed research and information center to be exempt and ordered the IRS to issue a formal letter to that effect. This was finally done in March 1974. But by then it was too late. Without tax exemption, the enterprise, after five years of struggle, had not been able to win sufficient foundation and other support to survive and had expired.[20]

The Big Switch

So long as the social-action movements are adversaries and "outsiders," they are nonprofits without honor in their own country. But once they succeed in winning legal or political sanction, their objectives, and sometimes the organizations themselves, receive a massive boost from government. By its victory in the *Brown v. Board of Education* case in 1954, the NAACP in its fight against school desegregation was thereafter reinforced, not obstructed, by the full enforcement apparatus of the American legal system. Likewise, once legislation was enacted to extend voting rights, assure equal employment opportunity, and protect the environment, much of the work of the civil rights and environmental movements became a responsibility of government, backed by large professional staffs and millions of dollars of appropriations.

For example, the total funds available to environmental groups in 1969 are estimated to have been well under $5 million, and the outlays of the Federal government for environmental protection that year were minimal. But 12 months later, the newly established Environmental Protection Agency (EPA) had a staff of 5000 and a budget of $1.3 billion. By 1977, its staff had grown to 10,000 and its budget to $1.8 billion.

The effects upon the movements of having thus "won" in the big political casino vary. They do not after their victory voluntarily retire from the field and disappear. Indeed, it is increasingly the conviction of many that they must remain active and vigilant to keep the government agencies established by their efforts from being taken over by the interests or industries they were designed to regulate and that they must continue to press for what they see as ever-evolving needs for reform in their fields of concern.

But shifts in government policy and the creation of new government programs can cause some of the private groups responsible for such developments to wither and others to flourish. A number of civil rights organizations, for example, once they had achieved official "respectability," discovered that their chances of obtaining funding from the larger foundations somewhat improved.

But private foundations in general tend to be both slow to support reform efforts and, once the efforts appear to have succeeded, quick to abandon them. The Citizens Research Foundation, for example, whose work over many years contributed to passage of Federal campaign financing reforms in the mid 1970s, promptly found itself financially strapped once the legislation passed. Despite much work left for it to do, its foundation supporters had turned their attention to new matters.

If political success does not necessarily improve the capacity of activist groups to attract continuing private funding, it does greatly improve their opportunities for receiving substantial government funding, at least for research and service activities. There are exceptions: the ending of the American involvement in Vietnam has not brought about any increased encouragement or funding from governmental sources for antimilitary or pacifist groups generally. But in the consumer, environmental, and civil rights fields government has begun to reach out increasingly to utilize the skills of these private groups on a grant or contract basis.

Public-interest law again provides the clearest example. While this movement is encountering severe problems in financing its activist programs through philanthropic gifts and earned litigation fees in class-action suits, it finds a very different situation in the other area of its concern—the provision of legal services to the poor and the disadvantaged. There, it is both increasingly competed with by a proliferation of new government services and is itself increasingly funded by government to provide such services.

Throughout the Federal establishment and in many states, offices of Public Advisor, Public Advocate, Public Counsel, and Ombudsman have been created in recent years to inform affected groups about rule-making proceedings, to facilitate public testimony, and in some instances to argue substantive positions on behalf of the public in official agency proceedings.[21]

In addition, an increasing number of agencies are prepared to reimburse disadvantaged groups for their legal costs in participating in their various rule-making and adjudicatory proceedings. This provides public-interest law centers with a significant source of earned revenue. The practice by some Federal agencies of making block grants for their general support is another.

Table 1 indicates the volume and the various sources of funding in 1975 for these in-house and grant and contracting costs in a single major field, namely civil legal services for the poor.

It is estimated that for the period 1972–1975, the total funding of the 90 leading public-interest law centers—from the American Civil Liberties Union to the Native American Rights Fund—was $126 million. Of this, foundations provided $47 million; private gifts and memberships $48 million; and government funds $31 million. The private gifts were largely for legal services to the poor and disadvantaged, as were the government grants and contracts; foundation grants were the main support of the advocacy and reformist activities. But the latter are now in decline, while the government portion of the income of the centers continues to increase.

Indeed, the flow of government funds—not only to public-

TABLE 1.   FEDERAL FUNDING OF CIVIL LEGAL SERVICES FOR THE
POOR[a] (1975)

Source	Amount
HEALTH, EDUCATION AND WELFARE	
Community Services Act (Non-Office of Legal Services [OLS])	$2,427,915
Social Services (Title XX, Social Security Act)	11,721,137
Older Americans Act, Title III	1,513,322
HOUSING AND URBAN DEVELOPMENT	
Housing and Community Development Act	2,393,545
Model Cities	930,337
DEPARTMENT OF LABOR	
Comprehensive Employment and Training Act of 1973	4,078,176
Migrant	965,500
REVENUE SHARING	
City	1,085,458
County	1,589,181
State	787,947
Township	11,100
OTHER FEDERAL SOURCES	
Law Enforcement Assistance Act	2,512,458
ACTION	1,303,287
HEW, Community Services Administration (OLS)	63,115,290
Other	1,165,567
TOTAL FEDERAL FUNDING	$95,600,220

[a] Information provided by the National Legal Aid and Defender Association, Management Assistance Project. This Survey was compiled from responses to a questionnaire distributed to all known providers of civil legal services in the United States and its territories. Figures represent data received by Jan. 20, 1976. From *Balancing the Scales of Justice—Financing Public Interest Law in America*, Council for Public Interest Law (Washington, D.C.: 1976), p. 280.

interest law centers but to many social-action groups as well—to carry out studies, conduct information, education, and training programs, and provide counselling and other services, has become so substantial that they now find themselves faced with the question of how dependent on government funding they wish to become, and how much distortion or transformation in the nature of their programs—from advocacy and activism and toward a service orientation—they are prepared to accept.

Conclusions

The social-action movements are mavericks, very different in their aims, structure, and financing from the other elements of the Third Sector. Because their essential purpose is social change, their relationship with government and the established, conservative elements of society is inherently an abrasive one. Their efforts are impeded by heavy disadvantages of many kinds; the inbuilt warp of tax policies, the habitual biases of philanthropic foundations, and sometimes (as recent revelations of the extent of illegal behavior by the FBI, the CIA, and other agencies have now made indisputably clear) official hostility and harrassment.

Despite these problems, there has been in recent decades another resurgence of the long, strong American tradition of social activism. The many groups and loose associations which have sprung up have obtained their resources largely in the form of volunteered services, "sweat equity," provided by their members and adherents. A few wealthy individuals and a handful of foundations have also given some help.

With this slender outside support, and despite other handicaps, major, indeed heroic, successes have nonetheless been achieved. If their goals are legislated into public policy, much of the work of the movements is then taken over by government and vastly increased resources of paid staff and funding are provided. Some of them at that point even begin to benefit from and to become dependent on direct funding from government.

But the great majority of the groups—including all of the movements still in their militant, unaccepted phase—remain in a disadvantaged and difficult position. Indeed, their financial condition at present, in the wake of their recent triumphs, is best described as desperate because of the drying up of much of the church, philanthropic, and general public support on which they have depended. Thus, another of the many paradoxes of this precious and peculiar part of the Third Sector is that it dies as much from its victories as from its defeats.

III

REDRESSING THE BALANCE

8 ▶▶▶▶

The New Politics of Pluralism

EVEN A BRIEF scan of recent developments in these five key subsectors is sufficient to give a sense of the deep transformations now underway within the Third Sector and between the Third Sector and other major elements of the American pluralistic system. The currents and crosscurrents of new economic, social, and ideological forces are powerful and complex. The resulting changes are taking place at different speeds in different institutional categories. But if a single point can be identified as the dividing line between the past and the present, it would be the period of World War II.

Before the war, the terms of the old social compact between society and the private nonprofit sector on the whole still obtained. Those terms, as they had evolved over the previous century or more (including some which had medieval origins) were the following:

It was believed that government's role in promoting the general welfare should be limited. Much of that responsibility was considered to be in the private domain, and governmental encouragement for private "good works"—such as the founding of hospitals, colleges, and philanthropic foundations—was accepted as appropriate and beneficial.

Such encouragement was mostly broad and indirect—including legal privileges and tax exemption, and later, after enactment of the Federal income tax, inducements to private charitable giving.

Beyond that, government's posture was to be essentially passive. Enforcement of the requirements of the tax laws relating to nonprofit organizations was loose and minimal. Social regulation in its earlier forms generally exempted the nonprofits. It was assumed that they did not require detailed surveillance and that with little more than a benign attitude on the part of government they could fend for themselves.

The nonprofits were expected to refrain from direct political and lobbying activities—as well as from commercial enterprise—as the price of their privileges. On the other hand, government was not to trespass upon the freedom of education, science, medicine, and culture as well as religion. Wide trust was accorded nonprofit institutions, including associations of the liberal professions, to regulate themselves.

In effect, the compact was seen as a bilateral agreement between government, as the agent of society, and the responsible trustees and officers of the private organizations. The clients and constituencies of the organizations and the public at large were not regarded as having effective rights to be consulted independently or participate directly in decisions taken. Status, authority, closed procedures, and institutional privacy were accepted elements of the relationship.

Official regulation and subsidy was limited; the freedom of action of the private institutions was extensive. The Third Sector was fluid, self-directed, and largely autonomous, little encumbered by government. In the nonprofit area, as in the profit-making economy, the spirit and the practice was *laissez faire*.

The New Context

That whole pattern of relationships between government and the private elements of American society has now collapsed under the consequences of war, depression, and the advent of new social values and political ideas. For the Third Sector, the result has been a radical shift in its status and role and in its constraints and involvements. The whole context of its existence and operation has been altered, and it has been thrust into an agonizing transition, a process which is now far advanced but not yet quite complete.

The most obvious of these changes, and the most far-reaching, has been a vast enlargement of the responsibility placed upon government for the provision of services of various kinds and for the general advancement of the public welfare.

The public appetite for educational, health, welfare, and cultural services has proven to be very great and capable of apparently unlimited expansion, and the political affairs of the nation have to a considerable degree now become organized around the demands of various groups for special benefits.

As a corollary, the presumption has become well established that government can and should do all the things considered necessary to satisfy these demands—create its own staffs and facilities; fund the operations of private agencies; oversee, coordinate, and regulate. The Federal government is now even developing a growing program in behalf of "volunteerism," which raises some delicate problems of public–private relationships. Through AC-TION, it will now provide grants to create new "volunteer" organizations; it will provide program money if the organizations will do things the Federal government wants done, and it will pay those "volunteers" who cannot support themselves in doing volunteer work. The theory is that encouraging such "volunteering" encourages good citizenship and it is also "cost/benefit effective" from the government's point of view: volunteers are cheaper than civil servants. In the opinion of Mr. Harry Hogan, formerly assistant director of the Office of Policy and Planning of ACTION, the flow of private giving will also be increasingly manipulated to serve official purposes: "It is predictable . . . that our Federal Government will more and more impose various kinds of conditions on charitable contributions so as to direct gifts into the delivery of services which the Government wants accomplished."

Thirty-four Federal agencies already have express statutory authority to use volunteers and some two to three million volunteers are so involved. "The utilization of all talents, including talents and capabilities that cannot be reached through the market system but can be reached through volunteerism, is a social imperative," writes Mr. Hogan, the leading theoretician of this aspect of Federal expansionism.[1]

These developments have had a number of profound effects upon the Third Sector. The scale of the demands for services has overwhelmed the capabilities of private agencies. In turn, the gigantic expansion of governmental programs and agencies has reduced the private element, formerly substantial and even predominant in many fields, to a relatively secondary and sometimes dwarfed position—which in turn has constricted the autonomy of private agencies in many and sometimes unanticipated ways. The authors of the American Constitution from the outset recognized that power could be abused and they therefore provided safeguards against this possibility. But what they did not imagine, and what has now been made manifest, is the possibility of deformation of a political system not from the misuse of government but simply from its expansion. The predicament of the Third Sector, attempting to operate along the flank of the mountainous official presence, is a graphic example of this problem.

A second and equally significant effect of the advent of the full-blown welfare state upon the Third Sector is a change in the direction to which citizens now look for the fulfillment of their needs—to government rather than to themselves. Thus there has occurred an alteration in the preferred method of social action—toward the organizing of political pressure on government rather than initiatives of their own; a shift from the premise of self-reliance and responsibility to one of political right and entitlement; and the breakdown of constraints and discipline upon the scale of demands for services as the financing is shifted to more distant and seemingly cost-free sources at city hall, the state capital, or Washington.

It can of course be persuasively argued that these changes have been both inevitable and beneficial; that the old system of charity and self-help was not only hopelessly inadequate to the needs of a modern industrial society—as the scale of distress during the Great Depression demonstrated—but that it was also discriminatory and demeaning. Still it is indisputable that fundamental changes in the accepted definition of the proper role of the State in the fields in which the Third Sector functions have taken place, and these changes have deeply affected its position and its future prospects.

The crucial consequences of these events has been the dissolution of whatever boundaries may have existed in the past—except of course in the constitutionally reserved area of religion—between government and the Third Sector. Those boundaries throughout American history were more apparent than real, more conceptual than actual; but nevertheless, the degree of interpenetration and of dependence—even interdependence—which has now developed is unprecedented. The present and prospective condition is one of continuous and comprehensive contact, collaboration, competition, and mutual involvement.

The old era of *laissez-faire* pluralism is therefore beyond any doubt past. The new era is one of socialization and politicization, of complexity and interconnection. A time of planned, governmentalized, officially subsidized, and guided pluralism is upon us. Nonprofit institutions, as one element of a society in radical transition, will never again be the same in status, relative scale, function, or autonomy.

Most of the Third Sector—including all of its great institutionalized elements except the churches—must henceforth live within the embrace of, and to a significant degree as dependents and instruments of, government. That situation already and unmistakably obtains, and there is no plausible basis for supposing that it can be reversed—or indeed that either party to the relationship wishes to reverse it. The leaders of most of the major categories of Third Sector institutions want more government money, not less, and are fully prepared to accept the regulatory consequences. And government, recognizing the impossibility of carrying out its social programs purely through its own lumbering bureaucracy, desires to continue to make extensive use of their capabilities.

Coexistence is therefore the present and future actuality, and for the private nonprofit associates and beneficiaries of government, the problem is how to coexist with dignity and integrity despite an essentially inferior and vulnerable position.

Profit-making institutions have of course also been struck amidships by these same trends. In economic affairs, governmental programs and regulations have proliferated to compensate for the perceived inadequacies of the free market, and hybrid institutional arrangements have flourished, producing the so-called "mixed economy"—neither capitalistic or socialistic. The Third Sector is in that same troubled condition, but with some significant differences. The impact of Big Government upon the economy is widely discussed; the corresponding developments in the nonprofit sector are still almost totally unrecognized by politicians and the general public. Second, the Third Sector is very small—perhaps only a tenth as large in GNP terms—compared to the profit-making sector. It is therefore weaker and more open to governmental intrusion, cooptation, and domination. Third, the results for the ultimate character and quality of American life, if the Third Sector should slip largely under governmental direction, could be even greater than those which might come from a fully managed economy.

Under the circumstances, what is called for is not mere nostalgia for what is past, nor futile diatribes against the society for changing its beliefs and priorities. Rather, the problem—if one is at the same time prepared to accept as simplistic the idea of a sharp separation between the domains of government and the nonprofit sector, and to reject the total absorption of the Third Sector by government—is to try to define the modalities of a new social compact which within a framework of mutual and joint responsibility will respect and preserve the essential values of both.

This could not be easy even if only two parties were involved: to strike some new balance in a situation of serious and increasing imbalance is almost by definition unlikely. The Third Sector is small, it is weakened and fragile, it is heavily dependent on government for funding as well as other privileges, and it is now encased in governmental regulation. Moreover, the tides are running heavily against the values it has traditionally embodied: individual responsibility, private initiative, elitism, diversity, decentralization, and the precedence of commitment over efficiency. Egalitarianism, cost-effectiveness, coordination, and rational planning in the allocation of resources are the current watchwords.

But in addition, a third party must now be included in the process of devising an acceptable new social compact—namely the increasingly organized and assertive elements of the general citizenry and of the clienteles and constituencies of the nonprofit agencies. There is much public skepticism about the legitimacy and responsibility of all institutional leadership, governmental and private. There is an unwillingness to trust government, both politicians and the bureaucracy, to represent the interests of the population and an unwillingness to trust private elements and institutions to regulate themselves and protect the public interest. For government, the result is growing pressures from citizen advocacy and litigation groups for greater official accountability. And for the Third Sector, the result is growing insistence on openness of institutional decision-making procedures and on the right of public groups—patients, students, consumers, neighborhoods, etc.—to be consulted and to participate in institutional decisions affecting them.

The effects of these demands upon traditional concepts of institutional autonomy, the responsibility of governing boards and managerial authority, are very great. Nonprofit institutions and government as a consequence are now faced with the need to formulate a new trilateral social compact, which involves the people directly affected by their activities and decisions.

The Elements of a New Social Compact

Social compacts are not enacted or signed and sealed around a green baize table; they are deduced and deciphered from the swirl of history. To attempt to define the rights and responsibilities of the parties to a new compact between the Third Sector and American society is therefore an essay in speculation and interpretation. But taking into account the broad contextual changes which have occurred, plus the more specific developments in the various subsectors reviewed in the preceding chapters, a first tentative approximation of an emerging new social compact can perhaps now be drawn. In schematic form, it might look something like this:

A. *The rights and responsibilities of government.*

The right to exercise a general planning authority over total service systems, including both private and public elements.

To impose over duplicative and wasteful development of facilities and services.

To regulate Third Sector institutions on the same basis as other private institutions and to require their conformity to legislated social goals and norms, including openness of procedures, nondiscrimination in employment, etc.

To require reasonable accountability on the part of Third Sector institutions for funding provided by government.

On the other hand.

The responsibility to exercise more active concern for the general well-being of the Third Sector at a time when the older pattern of benign passivity is manifestly no longer sufficient.

To avoid damage to the Third Sector by unreasonable government competition and duplication of services and facilities.

To utilize private nonprofit institutions wherever appropriate and feasible rather than create competitive government facilities and operations.

To avoid drastic and unpredictable shifts in the level of government funding and the direction of government policies affecting Third Sector institutions.

To exercise self-restraint in the application and enforcement of accountability requirements on private nonprofit recipients of government funds.

To refrain from partisan, political, and ideological intrusion upon the integrity of Third Sector organizations.

To give full opportunity to the Third Sector for participation in the formulation of governmental plans, rules, and regulations affecting nonprofit institutions.

To protect and encourage the autonomy, diversity, and civil liberties of private nonprofit organizations in order, among other purposes, to control the excesses and improprieties of government itself.

B. *The rights and responsibilities of the Third Sector.*

The right of private nonprofit organizations to freely determine their own fields of activity, methodologies, and substantive approaches.

To choose whether or not to make themselves available for government utilization on a grant or contract basis.

To be free, if they are recipients of direct government funding, of unnecessarily burdensome bureaucratic requirements of reporting and accountability.

To be consulted and to participate in government rule-making and policy decisions in their fields of interest and competence.

To sue the government for redress of injury before administrative tribunals and, on appeal, to the courts.

To monitor and criticize government policies and procedures and to present their point of view at their initiative to both the legislative and executive branches.

To a generally fostering, encouraging, and protective attitude on the part of government.

On the other hand.

The responsibility to be accountable for the use made of government funding.

To conform to government social regulation.

To cooperate in government efforts to achieve a coordinated, cost-effective, and planned total service system.

To offer equitable access to their services and openness in their procedures.

C. *The rights and responsibilities of the public.*

The right to full information about the policies and plans of both governmental and private nonprofit agencies.

To be heard in planning, policy-making and rule-making procedures of both private and official agencies providing social services and of governmental regulatory agencies.

To engage in legal forms of social activism without governmental harassment, intimidation, or invasions of privacy.

To equitable access to the services of private nonprofit organizations.

To a governmental policy of tax incentives for private charitable giving that is not limited to the rich.

On the other hand.

The responsibility to support private nonprofit activity through individual contributions of time and money.

To exercise self-restraint in demanding the expansion of social services of all kinds, and to provide fully for the costs of the services demanded.

To refrain, in exercising the rights of social activism and

participation, from the kind of obstructionism and sheer li-
tigiousness which can paralyze the operation of any democratic system.

Such a first approximation of the ingredients of a contemporary
social compact contains some that is old and much that is new;
some that is conventional and familiar and some that may be
regarded as a sharp departure from the past; some that will be
given broad public endorsement and some that may still be
regarded as debatable.

Given the many possibilities of disagreement with this initial
formulation, a highly useful exercise for those concerned with the
future of American democratic pluralism might be to elaborate,
refine, revise, and test it.

Coexistence and Contradictions

Defining, or divining, the general terms of a new social compact is one thing. Interpreting and enforcing it, making the compact work, is another. Government and the Third Sector are now
destined, or condemned, to coexist, collaborate, and depend
upon one another permanently. And yet their interests and obligations, and their underlying values and goals are not identical
and in many instances are contradictory. Their extensive and continuous involvement with one another must inevitably be accompanied by tension, and sometimes by conflict.

The inherent dilemma, and the implicit battle-line that runs
between them, borders the concept of public accountability on
the one side and private institutional autonomy on the other.
From the governmental point of view, nonprofit organizations
must, as a condition of their privileges, conform to requirements
of the law; in addition, if they receive public money, government
has the right and the responsibility to ensure that it is spent only
for authorized purposes. But from the standpoint of private nonprofit organizations, the unilateral and unlimited nature of such
propositions must be qualified: government in enforcing the law
must not intrude upon their constitutional rights and freedoms;
and though they have become dependent on government fund-

ing, they must in essential respects remain independent. In effect, though they have now become in some degree responsible to government, they ultimately must remain responsible to themselves.

Both of these views are valid. The problem is not good versus evil but good versus good, a much more interesting and difficult one. The cases in which this dialectical contradiction becomes concrete typically do not take the form of great, clear, historic clashes but rather occur as incidents to the multitude of daily dealings between them—financial, regulatory, and contractual. To deal with the infinite variety of such disputes, and to resolve them on a reasonable basis, calls for a spirit of conciliation and compromise, the development of procedures for mutual accommodation, and the achievement of what the economist or administrator would call tradeoffs. Yet in the actual conduct of the huge workaday commerce between government and the Third Sector there are powerful tendencies and habits of mind on both sides which encourage intransigence and impasse.

In the world of the nonprofits, there is constantly present a great latent righteousness because most of the inhabitants feel they are serving some high moral purpose in behalf of the commonweal. As a result, educators, scientists, artists, and reformers can be readily aroused to assert the claims of their institutions in passionate and absolute terms. To educators, education is not only virtuous but the bedrock and precondition of democracy and therefore something which deserves an absolute priority in public policy. Scientists view the quest for knowledge as an activity not simply meritorious but as essential to human advancement and well-being whose needs must therefore be fully served and whose rights must in no degree be infringed upon. Those devoted to cultural activities see them as the core and very definition of civilization and insist that society has a primary responsibility to encourage creativity and generously nourish and sustain the arts. Likewise, doctors, religious leaders, and social activists all can express the value of the work to which they have committed their lives in the most ardent and uncompromising terms. Regulatory consistency, precedent, cost effectiveness, detachment, and moderation are not values they ordinarily hold to be of the highest importance.

The eloquence with which such viewpoints are expressed, often by individuals of the highest integrity and achievement, only adds to the difficulty. A particularly illuminating episode in this regard occurred a few years ago over the question of accountability and autonomy in the field of pure science. The protagonist of the scientific view was Jacob Bronowski. An eminent mathematician, lecturer, and author who had played a role during World War II in the Allied effort to mobilize the scientific community, he spoke not only with professional credentials but also from first-hand experience in dealing with officialdom and the military. In the postwar period, as he reflected on the problems of science and government, he became more and more deeply distressed, and in November 1970, in a speech before the British Society for Social Responsibility, he dropped a double bombshell. He proposed that all intellectual workers "must urgently dissociate themselves from the apparatus of government in general—and from government grants and contracts in particular." And at the same time he proposed that government continue to provide substantial direct as well as indirect financial assistance to science—but without the right to set research priorities or hold the recipient scientists accountable for the proper expenditure of the funds.

Subsequently printed as "The Disestablishment of Science" in the July 1971 issue of *Encounter* magazine, Bronowski's thesis was cast in terms of high principles of humanity and of integrity. He asserted that all of us experience a conflict of values between patriotism (which can implicate us in war) and our sense of universal humanity (which requires a commitment to peace). Intellectual workers, and especially scientists, he maintained, should be keenly aware that they belong to an international community and therefore their allegiance to humanity, not patriotism, should take precedence. Thus it is the role of scientists to act "as keepers of an international conscience." They, therefore, must disavow not only a direct part in war work but also any indirect part in it.

In effect, he declared, there is no way by which a scientist, with honor, can collaborate with and take directions from government. To take government money is to take war-machine money. "A scientist who accepts money from such a source," he wrote, "cannot be blind to the subtle conformity that it imposes on his own conduct and on those who work with him, including his students. The obligations that he silently incurs are dormant, but they are there, and he will be in a quandary whenever a government in trouble decides to make them explicit." Much the same is true, he argued, of the advisory function: "The scientist who joins a committee becomes a prisoner of the procedures by which governments everywhere are told only what they want to hear, and tell the public only what they want to have it believe. The machine is enveloped in secrecy, which is called 'security' and is used as freely to hoodwink the nation as to protect it." Bronowski therefore called for the disestablishment of science—and for scientists to refuse to accept money from governments. But the separation from the State would only be partial, and the scientists' rejection of its funding would only be tactical. For he conceded that science has to have, and government has an obligation to provide, public money for its support. By going on strike, scientists would quickly bring nations to realize that they could not function without science and they would therefore then submit to the turning over of funds to the scientists with no conditions whatsoever attached.

But how can the public be assured that this no-longer-tainted money will be spent wisely and in society's interest? By relying on the special ethos and morality of the scientific community—its openness, its disinterestedness, its principled pursuit of knowledge.[2]

Bronowski's thesis of the innate wickedness of government and the innate virtuousness of science provoked an immediate and critical response both from politicians and other scientists. Anthony Wedgwood Benn, a prominent British political figure who, among other high governmental posts, had previously served as Minister of Science and Technology, suggested that the disestablishment proposal envisaged the creation of a dictatorship of the scientists and that Bronowski himself "was emerging as a new authoritarian elitist." The problem, Benn held, was not how to avoid politics, but how science could be immersed in it in order to establish a democratic consensus.[3]

Edward Shils, an eminent sociologist, wrote that scientists, if they are willing to accept society's money, must also accept its responsibilities. "The upshot of all this is that scientists, whatever their scientific genius, are really no better than anyone else." To solve any of our painful problems—nuclear war, pollution, overpopulation—Shils wrote, "the cooperation of scientists, politicians, engineers, administrators, businessmen, labour leaders, social workers, academics, *et al.*, is unavoidable. . . . It is of the most profound importance for mankind, and for our national societies, that scientists engage in a continuous dialogue with all these others."[4]

Bronowski had sounded a heartfelt cry of anguish, but his policy prescription was both defeatist and contemptuous of democracy. It was therefore unacceptable even to most of his fellow scientists. But it truly reflected the sense of special virtue, and therefore the right to be exempted from the obligations laid upon ordinary mortals, which pervades many quarters of the nonprofit sector and in turn seriously obstructs cordial relationships with government.

A further factor contributing to the abrasiveness of the nonprofits in their dealings with government is their sense of weakness, of being at the mercy of government. It has often been observed that power corrupts; but it has less often been observed that powerlessness corrupts also. And it particularly corrupts the sense of confidence and the willingness to give as well as take in negotiations. To some extent, of course, the fragmentation and quarrelsomeness within the nonprofit sector itself, and the managerial and technical incompetence of many nonprofit organizations, is at the root of their sense of inadequacy. But whatever the cause, the result is a "last ditch" mentality which, from the viewpoint of government, adds rigidity to righteousness to the Third Sector's behavior in their dealings.

The Echelon of Encounters

Within government, different but equally destructive attitudes to an easy partnership with the nonprofits can be identified. Every day, in thousands of offices, innumerable transactions between government and the nonprofits occur, many incident to the

transfer of public money into private hands. These concern contract terms, audit findings, clearances and approvals, record keeping, and the endless other banalities which are involved in the
process of doing a great deal of business together.*

In this workaday commerce, the government representatives
are engaged in carrying out such impeccably proper tasks as ensuring accountability on the part of private agencies for their use
of public moneys and ensuring their compliance with applicable
regulations. But the inner dynamic of governmental bureaucracy
seems to ordain that items which begin as reasonable general
requirements inexorably develop into a degree of detailed scrutiny and a burden of paper work which would have seemed unimaginable when the process began. Thus the legal objective of
ending sexual discrimination in education ends with the elaboration of hundreds of pages of detailed regulations covering such
matters as the number of toilets, and the design of their seats, in
college athletic facilities. Whatever is worth doing becomes worth
overdoing.

The explanation is partly the inherent limitlessness of administrative logic. But it is partly an expression of the practical sense of
self-preservation of the members of the bureaucracy. They are
well aware that no rewards are given by Congress or the press for
reasonableness and restraint; there is only punishment for laxity.
Any error or omission, once detected, thus becomes a reason to
tighten restrictions upon grantees and contractors. No events
operate to loosen regulations; traffic on the administrative street
moves only one way. Moreover, the "plane of accountability"
gradually descends as responsibility for the administration of policy is passed down the chain of command to lower ranking and
more and more specialized auditors and compliance officers.

Whatever the causes, the effects are that compliance becomes
more and more burdensome for the "beneficiaries" of government
grants and contracts and the range of intrusions by government
more extensive. The end result is a system which by its sheer
mass and inertia is exhausting, immobilizing, and defeating. Jus-

---

* Most will involve amounts of money which by government standards are chicken-feed.
But, as Warren Weaver of the Rockefeller Foundation once observed, chicken-feed is very
important to chickens.

tice Holmes once wrote that justice is secreted in the interstices of legal procedure. Injustice, for the nonprofit organizations dependent on government, is secreted continuously in the interstices of administrative habits and procedure. That fact is an inbuilt disadvantage of them in their new intimacy with government.

They are equally disadvantaged at the level of direct negotiation about money and the basic terms of their collaboration. In such situations government has a strong, often decisive, bargaining advantage. If the official agency decides to withhold its funding, the private agency usually has no alternative sources of support to which it can turn. But if the private organization threatens to withhold its services, the government with only rare exceptions has other willing and available sources of supply. It negotiates from strength, the private organization often from desperation. The general effect over time is to undermine both the viability and the sense of autonomy of the latter.

In the echelon of encounters between Third Sector institutions and the executive branch of government, the highest are those which involve substantive issues of policy. In these contests over research priorities and program directions, which take place behind closed doors, the powerful and consolidated position of the Administration is pitted in most instances against the divided and disheveled ranks of the nonprofits. The government's position therefore normally prevails. Typically, its institutional concern, whatever the substantive matter at issue, is for its own interest and convenience; and its manner of dealing with the nonprofits is, in the common style of a predominant partner, frequently heavy-handed. The extraordinary degree to which the preoccupations of both the executive and legislative branches are essentially governmental—in the sense of government as a special interest—and the degree therefore to which their policy decisions are often negligent of, or detrimental to, the interests of the Third Sector, is a point which will be further developed in the following chapter. As regards the heavy-handedness of government, Charles L. Schultze, Chairman of the Council of Economic Advisors in the Carter Administration, took that as the theme of his 1976 Godkin

Lectures at Harvard University. "Whenever we seek to achieve some social purposes," he said, "we now characteristically do not re-structure things so that public goals become private incentives; we choose instead to remove the decision-making power from the private sector and turn it over to the public sector."[5] The Command-and-Control approach of a centralized bureaucracy, according to Schultze, has now become virtually the only operating mode of American government.

There are exceptions and variations; government is not always dominant, even in some situations where it should be. Private health organizations, for example, have been able to resist over an extended period the imposition of governmental cost and quality controls. Some major charitable organizations, if they have the right ethnic or religious connections, cannot be held strictly accountable by the authorities in instances of wastefulness or even misuse of public money. In basic research, an inner group of eminent scientists, working in close collaboration with government, was able for a number of years to confine the flow of public research funds largely to their own institutions. But these are exceptions.

The coexistence of government and the Third Sector is therefore inherently a difficult one. The frictions arising from the prickliness of the nonprofits and the bureaucratic excesses of government can perhaps be eased to some extent by better training and better procedures. But it is not to be expected that they will ever be eliminated, because they derive from the nature of two very different elements. Tension punctuated by conflict is probably a permanent fact of their relationship, which though aggravating is not necessarily unhealthy.

In any event, the heart of the difficulty is not that the wheels do not turn easily but rather that there is a fundamental imbalance in the position of the two parties. Individual private organizations on the whole are more dependent upon government than government is upon them. They tend as a result to be outgunned in specific negotiations, overpowered in closed-door policy disputes, and generally smothered in the governmental mass. From their point of view the balance is badly tilted toward government and destructive of fair and reasonable outcomes. Unless it can be redressed, they fear for their integrity and autonomy and even their life.

The Descent, or Ascent, into Politics

To a degree the Third Sector can find remedy and protection in the force of its evidence and arguments, in the respect which exists for the tradition it represents, and in some situations in appeal to the courts.

A reformulated social compact, in this dangerously unbalanced situation, can be useful in clarifying the present confusion of concepts and in providing a framework for dialogue and debate. But however perfect it may be in its accommodation of divergent values and forces, it cannot provide an iron-clad guarantee of the rights and freedom of the private parties. The differing interests of the private sector and government are in conflict at a number of points along a very extensive and ambiguous interface. They involve subtle and constantly changing questions of degree and circumstance. There are no clearly etched boundary lines, no fixed and absolute terms which can be frozen into a formal treaty, no pure and self enforcing principles, and no priesthoods to which the tasks of interpretation and enforcement can be entrusted.

No compact can provide more than a basis for the continuous adjustment of the formula for coexistence. It must ultimately be intepreted by the life processes of the society and, in the United States, enforced by the turbulent, strenuous methods of democracy itself—the endless tug and pull, the quarrels and coalitions, and the application of power as well as principle, politics as well as rationality.

The final arbiter in nearly all the major struggles can only be the political process in the broadest sense—the force of organized public understanding and concern in support of, or in opposition to, the goals and methods of the voluntary sector.

One has only to recall some of the larger issues to be faced in the several subsectors which have been examined in the preceding chapters to grasp how political they are.

In science, at what level will public support be forthcoming for military, space, energy, and biomedical research? And in what proportions will it be shared among these purposes? To what extent will the government be permitted, or required, to guide and control research fields such as recombinant DNA research? To what extent will the general public be permitted to share in such monitoring and control?

In the area of health, to what extent will public authority be permitted to change the geographical distribution of physicians and health facilities? To what extent will the poor and residents of remote areas be given access to health care? What balance will be accepted between expenditures for health care and for other social needs such as education and housing?

In education, to what extent will new types of educational services be funded to make use of the available physical facilities and supply of teachers? To what extent will major cutbacks be imposed? To what extent will the available funds be shared between public and private institutions? To what extent will church-related schools be financed with public funds? To what extent will special programs for minority and disadvantaged groups be continued?

In culture, to what extent will the professionals and the elites be permitted to control the distribution of funds, and to what extent will such control be dispersed and decentralized to the communities, trade unions, and other nonprofessionals? To what extent will the institutions of national and international prestige be given special preference, and to what extent will subsidies be distributed on the basis of geographical formulae and other "nondiscriminatory" considerations?

For the social-action movements, to what extent will they be given "standing" to pursue class-action suits in the courts? To be reimbursed for their legal costs in successful suits? To participate in administrative rule-making procedures? To what degree will they be protected against police and political harassment? Ultimately, to what extent will they be encouraged by a society believing it has need for more diversity and creative disturbance? Or, alternatively, to what extent will they be restricted by a society believing it has need for greater unity, stability, and conformity?

Because all these value-laden and interest-laden questions are

intrinsically political, and because they are of crucial importance
to the survival and significance of the Third Sector, it follows that
unless the Third Sector denies the role of countervailing power it
must become more mobilized and more politicized in order to
bring the force of its constituencies to bear on them.

To some this is an offensive prospect. For this hardy band of
true believers, education, science, culture, and the rest should be
above politics. Such activities represent the realm of the spirit, of
reason, and of disinterestedness, and involvement in the rough
and tumble of politics can only soil and demean them. According
to this view, politicization is not only distasteful but wrong.

However there are many more, especially among the leaders of
nonprofit institutions, who realize that the Third Sector must
defend its status, viewpoints, and interests along the crucial political battleline. Some do so wholeheartedly, even enthusiastically.
But many, while conceding the necessity, do so with much disquiet—a disquiet deeper than just the apprehension that grubby
self-interest and partisanship will begin to pervade the atmosphere of the Third Sector. Rather, the fear is that to put the fate
of private nonprofit institutions and all they represent in the
hands of politics is to place them at the mercy of a process which
is inherently unfair, which progressively will degrade them, and
in which in the end can only defeat them.

These somber concerns have substance and must be candidly
addressed. The belief that the push and pull of politics must be
inequitable in its results for nonprofit organizations derives from
the manifest differences in the financial strength, breadth of constituency, organizational sophistication, and popular appeal of the
various subelements of the Third Sector. Medicine clearly has
more political clout than welfare rights organizations; the major
religious denominations have more than Chicano groups; advocates of funds for cancer and heart research have more than
those interested in chamber music; and so on. Inevitably, therefore, in the political arena, some groups and causes will prevail
more than others, will get a greater share of the public money,
and will be better able to protect themselves against official transgressions. The more that politics and popularity predominate, the
more the differences between the strong and the weak in these

terms will widen: grand opera will tend to get less government subsidy and folk music more; science and "practical" courses in the universities will get more and the humanities less. To traditionalists and conservatives, this will be deplored as "populism" and vulgarization; by the New Left and the New Right, it will be attacked as "interest group pluralism." Whatever the terms by which it is denounced, it can hardly be denied that some nonprofit elements will do better than others in any political competition, and the problem of inequity which can result is real and serious. It is also one for which no very convincing solutions have been proposed.*

That the nonprofits cannot win in the political arena, and that the more they try the more they will degrade themselves, are apprehensions that also rest upon a body of plausible evidence. Government does generally command the high ground and the big battalions in any struggle with the Third Sector, and the nonprofits commonly lack the skills, the unity, and even the heart for such a struggle. Many of them, by their nature, are not political or politicizable creatures. Some are gentle humanitarian enterprises. Some are quietly scholarly. Some are devoted to aesthetic and spiritual purposes. Some are concerned essentially with esoteric and private, personal concerns, from bird watching to antiquarianism. They are mostly devotees, not advocates, pursuers of their various visions of truth, beauty, and duty. When their freedom to follow their own paths is challenged, they can be ferociously self-protective. But characteristically they are individualistic and separatist, not organizable as a movement; and in political terms, they are mostly inert, not activist. If their fate should depend on politics, how can they possibly prevail?

On the other hand, the great institutionalized elements of the Third Sector, including education, medicine, and science (and not

---

* One of the least convincing, and least palatable, is that of Theodore J. Lowi, presented in his study *The End of Liberalism*. After holding forth for 300 pages on the evils and injustices of pluralistic theory and oligopolistic political competition, he can think of no better remedy for the problems of democracy than less democracy. His proposals for "radical reform" consist of an appeal for stricter Supreme Court restraint upon the Congress, reliance upon the elaboration of more rigid and detailed administrative rules, fostering the creation of an independent senior civil service on the British model, and other such escapes from the untidy and plebian processes of citizen participation.[6]

excluding the churches) have shown they are capable of being effective, even happy, political warriors. Indeed among them politicization and mobilization are already well underway. New headquarters are clustering around Washington. Grand coalitions are
being formed. And even within subsectors, as in education, sub-
subsectors are organizing—the land-grant colleges, the private
colleges, the two-year community colleges, the religious colleges
and so on. The sense of embattlement grows, and the juices of
combativeness are flowing ever more freely. But among the
sounds given off as the groupings develop are screeches of friction
among the factions and a growing clamor of jurisdictional, sectarian, and other unedifying quarrels. Moreover, if one recalls the
depths to which the AMA sank during its long career of political
activism, there is ample reason to feel anxious about the corrosive
effect on the character of nonprofit groups as a result of their sustained immersion in politics.

To ignore, or to lightly dismiss, the defects and the dangers of
the political process as the final guardian and court of appeal for
the nonprofit sector would be naïve. But likewise, to dwell too
compulsively on the uncertainties, inefficiencies, and imperfec-
tions of democracy is to lose sight of important potentials in the
process and to fall victim to overly intellectualized pessimism.

The Potentials of Politicization

There are real grounds for fear about the fortunes of the Third
Sector as the United States heads into an increasingly secularized,
skeptical, and insecure future. But there are also plausible
grounds for believing that nonprofit institutions can play a major
and constructive role in the nation's social politics, and that by so
involving themselves they will at the same time renew and reinvigorate themselves. Indeed, the major political challenge they
now face may, in a Darwinian sense, be the best available means
of checking their decay and decline and the key to their eventual
adaptation and survival.

First, as to their positive political role, despite the inertness of
some and the narrow self-interestedness of others, there is not

necessarily reason to despair. Granted that the performance of higher education in the political sphere has often been amateurish, of the churches unseemly, and of medicine deplorable. But one branch of the Third Sector has been spectacularly successful in smiting the snout of the great beast of government most painfully when it poked improperly into private places; and, beyond such disciplinary and defensive action, it has brought about fundamental changes in the procedures and priorities of government. That branch consists of the social-action movements.

Despite their smallness in many cases, and their impecuniousness in almost all, they have been able to arouse strong public enthusiasm for their initiatives and have been able to mold diverse constituencies into effective political forces. The results of their efforts have been great; they have probably had as much impact on the policies and direction of the country in the past thirty years as any other element of American society.

For the Third Sector in its present underdog status, the social-action movements have therefore a very special and highly encouraging significance. They have been able to do for the whole sector what most of its other components have not been able to do for themselves—check and offset the dominance of government by superior organizational and tactical skills. They have also been able generally to maintain their idealism and breadth of social purpose. They have become forces for the accountability and responsiveness of government. At the same time they have served as scourge, equalizer, and sword for the weaker elements of the political system, such as nonprofit organizations, in their endless and otherwise hopeless struggle with the leviathan of the modern welfare state.*

With the help of the advocacy groups, the rest of the Third Sector may be able to make government restrain itself and on occasion even redirect itself. But it cannot depend on them for its

* This linkage between voluntarism and advocacy, particularly in correcting the drift of government toward unresponsiveness and injustice, was first recognized by Alexis de Tocqueville in his great book, *Democracy in America*, written a century and a half ago. "Among the laws that rule human societies there is one which seems to be more precise and clear than all others," he observed. "If men are to remain civilized or to become more so, the art of associating together must grow and improve in the same degree in which the equality of conditions is increased."

long-term survival as a significant force. Although the social-action movements have shown vigor and effectiveness in recent decades, they are not necessarily immune to the disease which historically has sooner or later stricken almost all reformist groups—their own bureaucratization, cooptation, or disintegration after a relatively brief active life. More fundamentally, the institutions of the Third Sector will over the long term be able to hold their position of significance only to the extent that they build and broaden their base of public support by responsiveness, service, and greater involvement of their clienteles and constituencies in their governance and operations.

It is failure in these areas, at least as much as the destructive tendencies of bureaucratized government itself, which menaces the Third Sector. For despite the glory of the values they express and the splendor of the democratic concepts they embody, the performance of a great many nonprofit institutions is mediocre or worse. The priorities, governance structures, and general orientation of many private nonprofit institutions are out of step with the times. Some are little more than pathetic examples of stultified elitism. Many are wasteful in managing their resources and incompetent in providing their services. And the great majority, fragmented and parochial, are simply incapable of addressing the larger and more complex issues facing American society in the fields in which they operate.

Unless this can be changed, unless the Third Sector can be brought to clean its own house, invigorate its operations, develop a broader and more creative outlook, and begin to relate itself more effectively to the evolving needs and demands of the American people, it is hard to see how its currently dangerous and worsening position vis-à-vis government can be redressed.

The causes of the sclerosis and inability to adapt, however, are very deep-seated. For at the heart of private nonprofit activity lies a series of extremely difficult contradictions. There is the contradiction of seeking to achieve efficient management and improved performance by institutions in which efficiency in the conventional sense is not the primary objective, in which "performance" is difficult to measure (even to define), and in which the "bottom line" is not necessarily at the bottom. And there is the contradiction of seeking to achieve greater representativeness and responsiveness by institutions many of which derive from, and depend heavily on, funding and volunteered services by the small, privileged, upper-class elements of the society.*

This preoccupation with internal concerns and isolation from the larger needs and values of the society characterizes many elements of the Third Sector and goes far to explain why its base of public support has weakened at the same time that its position relative to that of government has shriveled. If it is to rebuild that base of support, it must open itself up to outside ideas and concerns and improve its performance according to the priorities of those whom it serves. The more that nonprofit agencies reach out to involve the society in their plans and operations, the more they engage openly in social policy debates, the more they explain their actions candidly, and the more they open up their structures and procedures to wider participation, the more they will make themselves socially accountable, the more they will increase their relevance, and the more they will arouse the respect and enthusiasm of their constituencies. In that process they may find their own salvation. The challenge they face is therefore political in the broadest and most democratic sense. It is a grave challenge. And quite clearly, nothing less than the pressure of such an imperative outside challenge can bring about the changes which are necessary if the Third Sector is to save itself and be saved.

Major social institutions can of course respond to challenges or they can fail to respond. In this instance, there is some encouraging evidence that the Third Sector is beginning to react positively to its problems: the initiative of the United Ways to reexamine and overhaul their program priorities, governance structure, and

---

* Private foundations have in the past been an important source of the larger guiding ideas for the Third Sector—for example the Flexner proposals for the reform of medical education, the impetus given by Beardsley Ruml to the social sciences and to interdisciplinary studies of social problems, the leadership of Warren Weaver to the development of biophysical and biochemical sciences, and the sponsorship by John Gardner and James Perkins of major research and development programs for higher education. But the present generation of American foundation heads has on the whole been a dull and undistinguished lot, which has deprived the Third Sector of a much needed and formerly available stimulus.

relationships with various community groups; the developing effort among cultural institutions to improve their management, build new audiences and reach out to new funding sources, especially corporations; the ferment among educators to reexamine the role of their institutions as they face a long period of prospective decline; the new readiness on the part of at least some portions of the medical establishment to rise above self-interest and respond to neglected social needs; the growing understanding among scientists and scientific institutions of the necessity to protect the integrity of science against the interest of its financiers, especially the military; and so on. If the nonprofit sector as a whole can now be motivated, or forced, to adapt itself to its future opportunities by the imminent danger of its demise, it will enhance the prospects for survival of American democracy itself.

9 ▶▶▶▶

Proposals for Public Policy

GOVERNMENT IS A LARGE PART of the problem of the Third Sector; it can also be a large part of the solution. It is the biggest operating factor in fields of interest to private nonprofit organizations. It lays down the rules and regulations within which they operate. It is also a major source of their funding.

Their future, therefore, to a great extent lies in its hands. The attitudes of government toward the Third Sector, the structures and procedures of government for dealing with (or ignoring) it, and the policies of government affecting it are of central importance. Unfortunately, these policies as of now are a poisonous mixture of benign indifference and impulsive intrusion. They rest on the assumption that once certain tax and other legal privileges are accorded, the private nonprofit agencies, like the grass in the fields, will flourish on their own. No committee of the Congress, for example, concerns itself with the needs and well being of this entire sector. Both the House and Senate traditionally have dealt with its problems and needs on a fragmented and episodic basis, and nonprofit agencies have been discouraged from taking the initiative in coming forth with broad policy proposals in their areas of competence or to lobby for their viewpoints.

On those occasions when Congress has felt impelled to take a direct interest in them, it has most often done so in an investigatory and critical spirit. In the case of private philanthropic foundations, for example, the main instances of Congressional interest have all been of this character—from the Walsh Commission in 1913 to the Cox and Reece investigations of the mid-1950s, to the efforts of Representative Wright Patman in the 1960s. Such intermittent bursts of Congressional concern have in most instances produced rather little in the way of objective information and useful proposals for changes in public policy.

The executive branch, likewise, does not recognize that a Third Sector exists. There is no Federal official, high or low, whose responsibility is to keep informed of its condition and to deal with its overall problems. There are those concerned with hospitals, for example, and those with colleges. But such official interest is partial and piecemeal, and there are vast numbers of nonprofit organizations which are ignored entirely.

Historically, for reasons that are not entirely clear, volunteerism and the Third Sector in American life have not been regarded as a sector or "interest" in society requiring or deserving even the collection of information about it of the kind which is regularly published about agriculture, banking, commerce, and labor.

Much more than neglect, however, is entailed. Not only have nonprofit agencies been battered by changing economic and social conditions, but they have been equally injured by the inadvertent side-effects of all manner of governmental actions. The sheer magnitude of the many Federal programs in health, science, education, welfare, and the arts in comparison to parallel private activities is such that even the slightest modification of policies and priorities can have smashing impact on particular private institutions or categories of such institutions. These impacts, great and small, in fact occur every day as part of the endless stream of administrative, budgetary, and program decisions made by Federal agencies.

The following are a few examples among many in recent experience which have imposed heavy costs and serious upsets of various kinds on nonprofit organizations:

- A decision by the Secretary of HEW requiring special ramps and other facilities in public buildings for the benefit of the physically handicapped—which will cost nonprofit institutions hundreds of millions of dollars in construction costs to comply with.

- A decision by the Congress to extend the benefit coverage of the social security system and to raise employer taxes to finance these additional costs—which will increase the costs of labor-intensive nonprofit institutions by tens of millions of dollars per year.
- A decision by the Federal government through ACTION to provide payment to certain categories of volunteers—such as retired persons—in return for their "volunteer" services. This will be of benefit to some nonprofit agencies in increasing their supply of paid "volunteers" but will create immense problems and frictions for others which rely on volunteers in the unpaid categories.
- A decision by the Occupational Safety and Health Administration to revise the minimum safety standards for ladders, exits and catwalks in work places—which imposes millions of dollars in sudden, unanticipated compliance costs on nonprofit institutions.
- A decision by the Congress forbidding the Defense Department to finance research projects which do not have a direct military relevance or objective—which can interrupt basic research activities formerly supported out of military budgets in university laboratories across the country.

Decisions such as these, despite their fateful bearing upon the status and strength of the Third Sector, often neglect to take such possible consequences into account.

The habitual indifference of government to the existence of the Third Sector results in missed opportunities to make effective use of it and at the same time to reinforce it. A particularly instructive example, because of its scale, was the history of the Emergency Employment Act of 1976, which appropriated $4 billion to create some 800,000 jobs, nearly all with state and local governments. The possibility of creating jobs in private nonprofit agencies as well as units of government (even though many of the jobs would be in health, welfare, and educational activity) was not even considered until the last stages of debate over the bill. The breakthrough represented by the limited inclusion of positions not on government payrolls in this act has fortunately been followed by similar and more generous provisions in other legislation. For example, it is estimated that 15 to 20 percent of the $11 billion appropriation for the Comprehensive Employment and Training Act (CETA) of 1979 will be spent through private nonprofit agencies to provide jobs for unemployed young people.

As government funds—whether through grants, contracts, or matching money—are increasingly spent through such local organizations, another range of issues arises. These center on the degree to which the nonprofit groups are permitted to employ Federal funds flexibly to fit what they consider to be local requirements or whether they will be forced to abide by rigid, uniform, and detailed national requirements. Congressional debate on the Older Americans Act in 1977 focussed sharply on this question of the degree of control to be exercised by government over subsidized local "meals on wheels" groups feeding elderly citizens. In the 96th Congress the same issue will have to be faced in the broader context of Title XX of the Social Security Act authorizing Federal matching funds for the provision of various social services by local nonprofit organizations. Ultimate questions of political philosophy—centralization versus decentralization, and accountability versus autonomy—are involved and will be strongly contested.

Government, when it thinks of nonprofit institutions at all, as a rule thinks only of regulating them or of using them to carry out its purposes. On matters directly and indirectly affecting the Third Sector, the preoccupations of both the executive and legislative branches are totally governmental—the government's needs and convenience, the possibilities of action by government, and the budgetary and revenue requirements of government. This way of thinking is now so ingrained that even the most monumental manifestations of it—with their monumental negligence of the needs of the Third Sector—pass quite unrecognized as negligent.

For example, one of the major policy initiatives of the Nixon Administration—in response to growing discontent with the growth and centralization of government powers—was "revenue sharing." But such revenue was shared only with other units of government; it took the form of general undesignated grants of funds to states, cities, and counties for their allocation and expenditure. At the same time, direct Federal support to many local nonprofit groups was cut back, obliging them to look to local governments for assistance. The result was to strengthen government at all levels at the expense of the voluntary sector, and incidentally, to attenuate Federal responsibility for guarantees of minority rights and encouragement of citizen participation.[1]

This whole pattern of unmindfulness toward the Third Sector must be drastically changed. If its great potentialities for contribution to the national welfare are to be realized, the sector must begin to receive continuous and considerate government attention. It must become the object of active protection and affirmative reinforcement by government. It is a fragile and vital national resource, and unless there is such a far-reaching change in the attitude of government toward it, it will increasingly be deformed and damaged.

Structural and Procedural Reforms

Once such a shift in attitude can be brought about, the first steps to be taken are structural and procedural.

A. *The Congress should begin to pay regular attention to the Third Sector by establishing standing committees, or a joint committee, on the subject.*

In addition, the Congress should make more effective use of the General Accounting Office (GAO) as a source of information on developments and problems and as a watchdog over the policies and procedures of the executive branch which have significant impact on the well-being of nonprofit institutions. The GAO should continue to monitor the movement of government contract and grant funds into the private nonprofit sector, but it should begin to do so with a double purpose—to see whether contract terms, grant conditions, and accountability procedures assure proper use of public funds, and also to see whether they protect the private recipients against excessive red tape and other destructive requirements.

B. *A point of focus and responsibility must be established at the*

White House level for comprehensive and continuous attention to the needs and potentialities of the Third Sector.

This new special assistant to the President should serve as a liaison with and complaint bureau for the Third Sector. He should maintain contact and communication with all private nonprofit elements regarding their needs and concerns; maintain a continuous watch over the actions and proposals of those Federal agencies which may have significant impact on the private nonprofit sector; bring the viewpoint and needs of that sector to bear on decision-making processes while policy alternatives are still under consideration and open to modification; and generally take initiatives of whatever kind, including possible proposals for legislative action, to protect and preserve the sector's vitality and effectiveness.

The proposed presidential assistant should exercise influence upon all agencies of government to coordinate their policies toward private nonprofit agencies, and to consider carefully and in advance (possibly through the establishment of an impact-statement procedure) the consequences of their budgetary and legislative proposals, their actions and their administrative policy changes on the Third Sector.

He or she might also be responsible for presenting to the President an annual "State of the Third Sector" report on its condition, needs, and capabilities.

This analysis concentrates on needed changes at the Federal level. But nearly all the problems of Federal government–Third Sector relationships exist also at the state and local levels—where the rate of growth of activities and expenditures in recent years has been greatest. If there is a need for an ombudsman for the private sector in the executive branch of the Federal government, the need is equally great for a similar person or committee in the administration of every state and of every large metropolitan area in the country.

The situation perhaps suggests that the Federal ombudsman for the Third Sector might help stimulate the establishment of similar positions at lower government levels. It suggests equally that serious consideration might be given to offering Federal financial assistance directly or indirectly to states and major metropolitan

governments to encourage them to establish their own ombuds-
men.

C. *A permanent, top-level presidential advisory council on the
Third Sector must be created.*

The council should seek to reappraise the relationship between
the nonprofit sector and government not in terms of the needs
and priorities of government, and not in terms of the self-interest
of subgroups of the nonprofit sector, but in terms of the health
and diversity of the sector as a whole. Its composition is therefore
of vital importance if it is not to degenerate into a pressure group
to get more government money for the represented private agencies, or a governmental device to impose more conformity upon
and solicit more collaboration from the private sector. If foxes are
not to be set to guard the chickens, its governmental representation must therefore be from the White House level, and its
private members must not be chosen to "represent" various institutional groupings.*

Because of the lack of such a body in the past an atticful of neglected policy problems and proposals for improvements remains
to be considered. Among the more obvious and urgent of these
are the following:

1. *A general review and evaluation should be made of the principles and practices of government agencies in enforcing "accountability" on the part of private nonprofit agencies receiving public
funds.*

The conceptual and political problems of devising and policing
a proper balance between the rights and responsibilities of government and of Third Sector organizations in their increasingly
intimate and complex relationships have previously been discussed.

The most important recent effort to examine this thicket of dif-

---

* The Filer Commission as one of its major recommendations proposed the creation of a
national commission somewhat of this kind. But there were serious confusions in its concept regarding composition, function, and governmental location. The suggested commission was in fact set up in late 1976 within the Treasury Department and attached to the
IRS. When the Carter Administration took office, the new Secretary of the Treasury, W.
Michael Blumenthal, promptly disbanded it. Subsequently it was reconstituted on a less
formal basis as an advisory body to White House assistant Stuart Eizenstat. After a few
perfunctory and unproductive meetings it then became moribund.

ficulties was the work of the Commission on Government Procurement created by Congress in November 1969. This bipartisan body labored for three years collecting and analyzing documents and testimony and issued its four-volume report in December 1972. The commission concluded that there was need for much greater interagency coordination of procurement policies to correct extensive inconsistency and inefficiency. It proposed the establishment of a central Office of Federal Procurement Policy located in the executive branch to promote uniformity and simplification and to provide an effective forum where the interests and viewpoints of recipient private organizations could be considered. The commission also recommended changes in the present dispute-resolving process to increase the flexibility of the system, to reduce the need for protracted and expensive litigation, to encourage the negotiated settlement of disputes through informal administrative review conferences, to upgrade agency boards of contract appeals, and to allow claimants the option of direct access to the courts for the resolution of their claims.

In the period since the presentation of the commission's report, a special committee in the executive branch has been at work to modify existing policies and procedures accordingly, and some progress is being made—although at a rather stately pace.

The commission included members from the public as well as the legislative and executive branches, but its mandate and its perspective was to study and recommend methods to the Congress "to promote the economy, efficiency, and effectiveness" of procurement by the executive branch. Its viewpoint and its concerns therefore were essentially governmental.

Such attention as it gave to the needs and rights of private agencies was incidental to its principal purpose. Since the Commission ended its work, the great growth of Federal contract research centers has created new dilemmas in the definition and enforcement of accountability. The Medicare program, administered in considerable part through private voluntary agencies contracting with the Federal government, has created another range of problems. So has the proliferation of quasi-public organizations such as the Corporation for Public Broadcasting.

These problems of accountability are a major and distinctive feature of the mature welfare state; they are new and complex and they present important conceptual and practical issues. A fresh examination of them might help to extricate both parties from the present bog of red tape and endless quarrels in which they are now floundering.[2]

2. *A general review of the many devices now used to transfer public money to the private sector needs to be made—both from the point of view of their effectiveness in achieving governmental purposes and from the point of view of their effect upon the integrity and strength of the recipient institutions.*

One weakness of the ad hoc approach the government has used in its methods of transferring funds has been its encouragement of confusion and inconsistency. But its virtue has been to permit a wide range of experiments, some unfortunate but some very promising. The time has come to appraise these various approaches as a basis for achieving greater coherence and effectiveness.

For example, one interesting development has been the so-called block grant. It provides lump-sum support to selected categories of institutions without detailed performance requirements being placed on the recipients. In Great Britain this approach has been used in providing financial assistance to private universities and to various research centers. The government fixes the overall total of funding. The allocation of support to specific institutions is determined by a body of private citizens. In the United States block grants have been used in recent years to provide financial support for cities. They replace and lump together the funding which formerly flowed to a whole range of specific programs—Model Cities, urban renewal and neighborhood programs, water and sewer grants, neighborhood and senior citizen centers, and parks and recreational areas.

The British system of insulating universities and research centers from political influence and from bureaucratic impositions may not be fully applicable to the American situation, but its possible benefits and deficiencies deserve fuller examination than they have been given.

A second important innovation is the so-called voucher system. By it the government funds certain kinds of activites not by direct grants to "provider institutions" but to individual "consumers"—

students, concert goers, or patients. Proponents of the system contend that voucher systems not only decentralize allocation of resources but they also give consumers more freedom of choice. Among other benefits claimed for it, this system will produce an effective incentive for nonprofit organizations to conduct their affairs efficiently and imaginatively. Proponents of the system believe that adaptations of programs and procedures to changing public needs should not be handed down from distant bureaucrats. Instead, consumers should choose those nonprofit agencies which best fulfill their individual requirements. Allowing prospective clients to "vote with their feet," it is claimed, introduces the functional equivalent of marketplace and ballot-box discipline into the Third Sector. Some argue that consumer subsidies are the key to democratizing private nonprofit organizations and to dramatically increasing their accountability.

The voucher method, judging from experience to date, contains great potentialities but some hazards. There is a clear need for a full and systematic evaluation of the various voucher plans now in operation including food stamps and the huge "Basic Educational Opportunity Grants" program of HEW, in order to develop new public policy recommendations.*

A third important innovation which is increasingly being used in the United States is the establishment and funding by government of public foundations and endowments—which in turn, with extensive private participation both on their governing boards and in their operating procedures, make the suballocations of funds to particular institutions. The National Science Foundation and the National Endowments for the Arts and for the Humanities are prominent examples of the concept. The Endowments in particular present significant contrasts. That for the arts seems to have shown a flexibility, creativity, and flair most unusual for a government agency, while that for the humanities seems to have displayed both operational stodginess and considerable confusion regarding its role.

---

*Whether voucher systems will ever be given a fair test remains highly problematic. David Cohen and Eleanor Farrar, in a *Public Interest* article that appeared in the summer of 1977, have given a graphic account of the hostility toward them on the part of civil service unions, civil libertarians, and government administrators fearful of losing control of their budgets and turf.

A special public policy panel on this subject would face a rich opportunity for assembling, developing, and evaluating new ideas for governmental funding methods which could diffuse and decentralize responsibility for the execution of programs, better insulate recipient agencies from bureaucratic burdens and political influence, and encourage citizen participation and greater freedom of individual choice.

3. *A blueprint needs to be carefully drawn for the establishment of a new public foundation for the Third Sector to enable it to improve itself and to plan for its own future.*

The Third Sector, for all its difficulties, has never been able to overcome its fragmentation and diversity sufficiently to study its problems, identify its needs, and come forward with serious plans and proposals for its own protection and development. Paradoxically, governmental initiative is required to cause such action to happen.

The creation of a high-level private/public body is needed to stimulate and oversee the gathering of data about the condition and needs of the Third Sector, to commission policy-oriented research on its problems, and to initiate proposals for both private and public action to deal with them.

Ordinarily funding for such activity might be expected from private foundations. But they have been notoriously (and mysteriously) uninterested in supporting broad study and planning for the body of institutions receiving their grants—except under the spur of a Congressional inquiry.* At such times, they have rushed in with heavy financing for hastily devised schemes to deflect the threat. But once the investigation was over, their interest in the field promptly subsided.

Funds on the order of some $10 million a year are probably required. They might be taken from the "surplus" revenues currently generated by the audit fee imposed by the IRS on foundations for auditing and surveillance purposes. As a vehicle for the disbursement of these "surplus funds," a new public foundation

---

* The most recent attempt to develop a sustained research program of this kind was led by Kingman Brewster, then President of Yale University, and John Simon of the Yale Law School. The financial needs of their proposed center were estimated to be on the order of $5 million for the initial five years. But after two years of vigorous solicitation, the center, even with such prestigious leadership, had been able to raise less than $1 million.

for the private nonprofit sector might be established—which would operate somewhat in the fashion of the National Science Foundation or the National Endowment for the Arts with a mixed government–private board of trustees, with a small professional staff, and with review committees on grant applications made up of private citizens. It would be desirable for the private sector itself to contribute some proportion of matching funds to the new foundation's income each year, thereby reinforcing the position of the private element in the new foundation's policies and actions.

The Need for Political Leadership in Defining a National Policy

These suggested structural and procedural changes could create an awareness of the problems and possibilities of the Third Sector and could begin to provide information and ideas for changing its presently conflict-plagued relationship with government into something more productive.

But a still greater task remains—the need to develop a broad new strategy and a set of national goals to strengthen and invigorate the whole private nonprofit element of American pluralism. Nothing less than a new, explicit national policy in behalf of the Third Sector is called for. To achieve that, political leadership at the highest level will be required, because it is a matter touching fundamental issues of government role and responsibility and involving powerful and conflicting interests.

If President Carter or his successors were interested in providing such leadership, the following steps might be considered:

A. *To the maximum extent possible, every Federal agency should strive to carry out its responsibilities through the funding of private agencies, not through the expansion of its own bureaucracy.*

Government funding of Third Sector institutions has been increasing in recent years, but not rapidly enough. The position of private agencies relative to that of directly administered governmental programs continues to shrink; and important new opportunities for drawing upon private agencies in the execution of governmental objectives continue to be neglected.

It is impossible on the basis of present information to project with any degree of precision the magnitude of the Third Sector's overall financial needs for the decades immediately ahead. Some recent studies suggest that if a severe contraction of the number of nonprofit institutions and their total service capacity is to be avoided, government funding to the Third Sector over the next two decades will have to quadruple or quintiuple. But more precise and carefully developed estimates are very much needed.

The large increase in government funding that will be required to maintain a minimum "critical mass" of private nonprofit activity in the processes of American life can in principle come either from an expansion in the volume of direct supportive and rescue grants or from the increased use of private agencies on a contractual basis to carry out government research, training, and service programs which are now administered directly by government agencies. In political terms the latter is likely to be far more difficult to accomplish than the former. Turning resources in any major volume over to nongovernmental agencies would immediately threaten bureaucratic turf and legislative prerogatives. Official agencies will not readily agree to shrink their own staffs and become mere overseers of private contractors. Some legislators too are wary of delegating the implementation of public programs to private groups because they perceive it as a weakening of their control over the programs funded.*

* The practical problem involved here is reflected in the history of a Bureau of the Budget directive known as Circular A-76. First issued in 1955, it relates primarily to the provision of goods and services needed by government. The policy is bipartisan and has not shifted since 1955. But government, by and large, has ignored the policy since its inception— even though it is rhetorically reaffirmed by each new administration. On the whole, government does rely on private sector providers in obtaining goods. It does not build computers, for example, but buys them from private companies. In the service area, however— from cleaning and maintenance services for its buildings to the development of computer "software"—most of the $20 billion the government spends annually for such work is done in-house by government personnel. Less than half is obtained from the private sector by competitive contract.

John F. Judge, editor of the publication "Government Executive," believes there are two primary reasons why A-76 has been ineffectively applied. The first is the opposition of the Federal employee labor unions. "It is obvious that such organizations, now more than a million strong in membership, have a vested interest in furthering government growth in employment. It increases their membership. . . . and the second reason bears on the first—it is the power of these unions, as represented by their veto as citizens, brought to bear on the legislative branch."[3]

The union view is represented by a nationwide advertising campaign of the American

There are obviously many governmental functions which cannot be carried out except by government. But there are some
where it might be more efficient and effective to rely on private
agencies. To ensure fair consideration to this alternative, a rule
might be desirable which would place the burden of proof on government agencies to justify any decision to execute a new program through the enlargement of their own staff and facilities
rather than by contracting with a private agency. But because of
the powerful pressures within government, strong presidential
leadership surveillance would be necessary to establish and en-
force it.

Despite such difficulties, there are those who advocate an even
more aggressive approach to the need of redressing what they feel
is the extreme overgrowth of government. One of these, Peter
Drucker, has called for the "reprivatization" of a wide range of
functions now performed by official agencies and civil servants—
from school teaching to fire protection.[4] On the basis of the few
experiments which have been tried to date, the prospects for
wresting present and established functions away from government
cannot be called encouraging—not because the experiments have
failed but because of the massive opposition and controversy they
have aroused. In the late 1960s and early 1970s, for example, the
idea of "performance contracting" for teaching was tried in some
16 states. The contracting firms were not able to do better than
the public schools in raising academic achievement. But apparently they did not do worse. Nevertheless, the massed opposition of the public school interests rather quickly and effectively
suffocated the whole effort.

Rather than direct confrontation with the bureaucratic, political, and ideological forces in opposition, an approach more likely
to be successful both in serving the general welfare and the needs
of the Third Sector might be the creative development of new
kinds of institutions which can combine the capabilities of govern-

---

Federation of State, County and Municipal Employees (AFSCME), begun in 1977, on the
theme: "In Boss Tweed's day, they called it graft. Today, it's called contracting out." The
text of one such advertisement carried in various national magazines concluded: "Our
union represents the public workers who provide public services. We've heard contracting
out called 'progress' many times. . . . Unfortunately, it's usually more lucrative than old
fashioned patronage. And often just as corrupt."

ment and private organizations, profit and nonprofit, in new ways to carry out "domestic missions."[5]

There is already a rich variety of such inventions which have demonstrated the possibilities and the limitations, and which have proven the political feasibility of the approach. The most famous of all these government–private sector mixes was developed under the National Aeronautics and Space Administration (NASA) for project Apollo. Government facilities and funds, nonprofit organizations, and private corporations were combined in a well-coordinated and spectacularly successful effort of space exploration which at its peak in the mid 1960s involved some 20,000 different entities.

With the backing of the President and the leaders of Congress, a systematic attempt could be launched for the first time to explore this exciting and promising frontier.

The second new line of policy which must be laid down relates to tax incentives for charitable giving.

B. *The new goal must be to increase the volume of individual giving to charity by at least 100 percent and, equally important, to greatly broaden the base of such giving by offering incentives to middle and lower income taxpayers.*

The dollar contributions of individual American citizens to the support of nonprofit institutions now constitute a source of private financial assistance roughly equivalent to the funding provided by government. These gifts represent the indispensable element of Third Sector sustenance. Without this critical percentage of voluntary support, nonprofit agencies can be driven to become mere compliant adjuncts of the state. Moreover, without strong support of individual citizens, such institutions lose their meaning as vehicles for the expression of individual concern and responsibility for the general welfare.

The persistence of the practice of private giving in the United States is quite extraordinary in the face of the neglect, even the antagonism, that wittingly or unwittingly has been one of the major characteristics of public policy toward it. Among those who give to charity, 23 million taxpayers itemize their gifts in order to benefit from tax deductions, and another 75 million take the standard, unitemized deduction. In 1977 they collectively gave $26 billion to charity, quite apart from contributions in the form of volunteered services.

But there are nonetheless ominous weaknesses in the situation. At best, the present level of giving is inadequate to maintain the position and vigor of the Third Sector; relative to the steady increase in GNP, to the growth of costs of nonprofit institutions, and to the general growth of total national outlays for education, health, welfare, etc., it is steadily falling behind. And it is doomed to continued decline—in financial terms and in public esteem—so long as present tax incentives to giving are in effect, for they are manifestly inadequate on two counts: They do not produce a sufficiently large flow of gifts; and they are extravagantly discriminatory and inequitable. Private giving has diminished over the last decade and a half, whether measured as a percentage (in constant dollars) of gross national product or as a percentage of total personal income. The less than 1 percent of households with incomes over $50,000 per year give 21 percent of all gifts. Two-thirds of all gifts of appreciated property—the large gifts—go to some 20 blue-ribbon educational institutions.

Most specifically, the present incentives contain four built-in, reinforcing inequities:

1. As they are structured the incentives have the effect on the basis of present tax rates of giving a government subsidy of 14 percent to the charitable gifts of the taxpayer in the lowest bracket and of 70 percent to a taxpayer in the highest bracket. They are in this sense regressive, not progressive.

2. They double this bias in favor of the rich by the way in which unearned income—that is, capital gains—is treated. In general terms, a wealthy person by making his contributions in the form of appreciated property or securities can often make his gift at little or no net cost to himself, whereas the averge person, whose income is in the form of salary or wages, cannot do so.

3. Whatever little inducement the system offers the person of low or medium income is nullified by the standard deduction, which in effect, says to him, "it makes no difference whether you actually give anything to charity; you get the standard deduction anyway."

4. Finally, the whole system is upside down and backwards, because it ignores the fundamental fact that a poor man's gift to charity involves more of a sacrifice in the real sense of that term than that of a rich man. Yet the inducements to give are focussed on the man or woman for whom giving presents no real financial deprivation.

It is little wonder, then, that a good many Amerians, laboring under increasingly heavy and unfair tax burdens, regard these inducements as merely another "loophole," another scheme by which the wealthy avoid their fair share of taxes. And it is remarkable, as well as a most encouraging evidence of the strong charitable inclination of so many Americans, that large numbers of them, including many of very low income, continue to contribute to many causes and institutions despite the irrelevance to them of present tax incentives.

Nothing is more important, therefore, for the scale, diversity, and legitimacy of the Third Sector than to accomplish a radical transformation of the present tax provisions on which a large part of present giving practices rest—provisions that constitute a wall of discrimination against the participation of at least four-fifths of American taxpayers in the practice of private giving and which permanently condemn the Third Sector to inadequacy and public suspicion.

Any adequate formula for reform would have to satisfy the following five criteria:

1. It must meet the issue of equity head-on—and make it as painless for a poor man to give to charity as a rich man.
2. It must offer a sufficiently powerful attraction to draw millions more taxpayers—from every age, ethnic, and socioeconomic group—into the practice of charitable giving.
3. It must thereby generate a substantial increase in annual private giving—an immediate increase of at least 25 percent over present levels.
4. It should produce an increase in resources to the private sector at least equivalent to the resources diverted from government revenues.
5. It must not jeopardize the continued existence of those very

important cultural, educational, and scientific institutions which are particularly dependent on the gifts of wealthy taxpayers.

As a first, though partial, step in correcting some of the worst weaknesses of the present tax rules, some two dozen of the nation's largest charities, led by the United Way of America, moved in early 1978 to mobilize grass-roots support for a bill to make it possible for taxpayers who take the standard deducation to take an additional deduction against their taxable income for contributions to charity. In effect, the bill would restore some tax incentive for charitable giving to those three out of four taxpayers who currently take the standard deduction. This campaign was provoked by the package of tax proposals presented by the Carter Administration in late 1977, which, among other changes, sought to extend the standard deduction to some 84 percent of all taxpayers, at a probable cost to charity of $1.3 billion per year in contributions.

The treasury department vigorously opposed the proposal of the charities on grounds that it ran counter to "simplification" of the tax system, a theme of President Carter's general tax policy. In addition, the department claimed that permitting such deductions would create serious enforcement problems for the IRS. In the final package of tax compromises which the 95th Congress passed in 1978, the amendment proposed by the organized charities was dropped and the Administration's proposal to further erode the incentive for charitable giving by ordinary taxpayers was accepted. But the bill supported by the charities has been reintroduced in the 96th Congress and a broad campaign is underway to build support for it. The sponsors are highly optimistic that by 1980 it will be enacted. Even if this happens, it will be only one of several basic changes which are called for in the existing system of so-called tax incentives for charity. A more adequate possibility, which would largely meet the requirements of reform would be the following:

Every taxpayer should be offered, as an additional option under the Internal Revenue Code, the right to make a direct deduction from his Federal tax bill of perhaps $50 per year

($100 on a joint tax return) on presentation of documentation that he or she has in fact given that much or more to a bona fide charity.*

Such a proposal would, up to the limit of credit decided upon, equalize the incentive to both the poor and wealthy taxpayers. By making gifts within this limit cost free it would provide an extremely powerful incentive for charitable giving; and it would not stifle major giving by wealthy taxpayers because it would simply offer an additional option available to all taxpayers while not eliminating the present special incentives in the tax system for the rich to make large donations. It could add to the nourishment of the Third Sector by billions of dollars annually.

Bills proposing tax credits for one purpose or another have been presented regularly in the Congress for the past several years—to help parents pay parochial school fees, to help support the arts, and so on—without winning enough support even to get through the powerful House Ways and Means Committee. But in 1977, Democratic Senator Moynihan of New York and Republican Senator Packwood of Oregon introduced a bill offering tax credits of up to $500—calculated on the basis of 50 percent of tuition expenses up to $1000—covering all elementary and secondary schools as well as public and private colleges. Aimed directly at the restive middle-income taxpayers, it immediately gathered impressive public and then Congressional support. HEW Secretary Joseph A. Califano Jr. promptly warned President Carter that "We must move quickly if we are to seize the initiative on this very hot issue" and within a matter of days the Administration countered the bill with a plan to expand the Basic Educational Opportunity Grants program to include families with incomes up to $25,000 and to offer subsidized student loans to families with incomes up to $40,000. The plan was expected to cover an addi-

* What the exact dollar limit of such a tax credit should be can be determined only after more information is available on the total increase in private giving which is needed to ensure the overall strength and position of the private sector, and after further study has been made of the probable impacts of a tax credit on levels of giving and on government revenues. Justification for paralleling rather than replacing the present inequitable incentives is a practical and not theoretical one, because the large contributions of wealthy taxpayers to charity provide an important pace-setting function in fund-raising drives, and it would be seriously damaging to important categories of institutions abruptly to eliminate these incentives.

tional 3 million students and cost an additional estimated $1.5 billion annually.

The fundamental issues were clearly joined, and a major political storm ensued. The Moynihan-Packwood bill offered wide scope. It provided for payment of tuition costs at elementary and secondary schools as well as at private and public colleges and universities; it focussed on all those population groups which had not been the prime beneficiaries of the recent "income transfer" programs of government; and it offered a simple method of assistance: leaving the money in the taxpayer's pocket for him or her to spend rather than taking it in taxes, processing it through a government agency, and redistributing it selectively to preferred groups of recipients. The Carter counterproposal omitted any assistance to parents of children in private or parochial schools and concentrated exclusively on higher education; it enlarged the circle of recipients of existing Federal student aid progress to include the children of middle income taxpayers (but only under the threat of the Moynihan-Packwood proposal); and it envisaged an "administered," "targeted" program of collecting from all and redistributing according to politically determined priorities.

Around the Senators' proposal gathered the angry "working poor," the old conservatives, the parochial school lobby, and the anti-government and anti-"progressive" forces. But in addition it attracted many others—those concerned about the failures of public education, about the future of private colleges, about excessive bureaucracy, and about individual rights and individualism. Around the Carter plan gathered the public school lobby, the minorities, the "egalitarians," and the old liberals.

The charges levelled against the Senators' proposal were violent: it was elitist, it would destroy the public schools, it was unconstitutional (because of funds that would go to parochial schools), it was racist and reactionary.

The New York Times expressed a moderate version of the conventional liberal position in supporting the Administration plan: it was more "equitable," because it would allow the benefits to go only to the "needy"—in this case middle-income families; and it was more "efficient" because it would not allow any of the money to leak back into the hands of the well-to-do.[6] The newspaper did not bother to calculate the "inefficiency" of the Carter program in terms of the administrative, reporting, and corruption costs which might be involved; and its view of equity had to do strictly with financial need. Other conceptions such as the equity of maximizing educational choice, the importance of avoiding government monopoly of education, and the desirability of minimizing the weight of the harness of government on all citizens were ignored, evidently not even considered to be relevant.

In the end, the Moynihan-Packwood approach won considerable support but it was overcome by the political weight of the Administration. The Senate voted for credits for higher education but not for private schools; the House voted for both school and college credits; the two bodies could not agree and the Administration's plan was approved.

Encouraged by the response their proposal won, and angered by some of the arguments and tactics used against it, Moynihan and Packwood have resubmitted their bill in the 96th Congress. The debates which will be aroused will provide an important new reading on the American state of mind regarding the point of desirable balance to be struck in educational policy between excessive government and excessive *laissez faire*.

But viewed in a longer and broader context, the Moynihan-Packwood proposal is at most a partial and special-interest approach to the much more encompassing problem of maintaining the general strength of the entire Third Sector. Therefore the basic issues which it churned up in such heated form would rise and rise again until the concept of an across-the-board tax credit for charitable contributions was confronted.

If and when such a credit is enacted with the help of strong presidential and Congressional support, what might be some of the broader social benefits that could result?

First, some degree of public confidence in the reasonability and fairness of at least one aspect of the tax system might be restored. Second, the resulting democratization in the sources of charitable giving would be at least as important as the sheer increase in the volume of giving. The principle and the practice of personal contribution to nonprofit agencies and activities would receive significant stimulus among all elements of the population. These changes would make it as easy for the average taxpayer in the future, as it has been for the wealthy person until now, to give something to his library, church, or local hospital. It would make it realistically possible, for the first time, for the poor and the people of the ghettos to give real financial support to their own community organizations—which has some relevance to self-respect, dignity, self-responsibility, and social harmony. It would make it possible for young people with modest incomes to contribute to the YMCA, or Naderism, or CARE, or whatever civic cause or institution that inspires them—which has some relevance to the problems of alienation and cynicism, as well as to the prospects for social change. It would provide a significant and probably constitutional way for those interested in the survival of parochial schools to give tax-deductible help to them—a fact which has some relevance to the problems of building strong political support for legislative passage of such a proposal.

For those whose primary concern is the reduction of government deficits, this kind of proposal of course represents a threat. For it does constitute a new and more fundamental approach to the much-discussed matter of "revenue sharing." The kind of revenue sharing here contemplated envisages a redistribution of resources between the governmental sector and the private nonprofit sector, at .least to an amount of a few billion dollars. This "diversion" of revenue from the funds available for use by governmental agencies will not, of course, be helpful in balancing governmental budgets. But from the viewpoint of those who are seriously concerned about the degeneration of the Third Sector in American life, the public policy choice involved here goes beyond budget balancing to a consideration of the very nature of the kind of society—more pluralistic or more monolithic—Americans hope to achieve.

The third new line of policy which must be advanced relates to the freedom rather than the financing of nonprofit organizations. C. *The need is for sustained, affirmative action to protect nonprofit organizations from official harassment and to permit, indeed encourage, them to play their full part in the shaping of national policies and priorities.*

Historically, the participation of nonprofit organizations in the legislative process has been restricted on the theory that their tax-privileged status did not entitle them to the right of full access. From 1934 until 1976 an ambiguous provision of the Internal Revenue Code threatened them with loss of their tax exemption if they should devote more than an "insubstantial" portion of their funds to lobbying or "propaganda." It is arguable whether the provision has ever had great practical effect in deterring them from such activity. But in principle it was disciminatory, since business firms were freely permitted to lobby and propagandize and were allowed moreover to deduct from their taxes the cost of their legislative appearances and publicity programs in behalf of their interests as ordinary and necessary business expenses. Moreover, the provision, to the extent it was effective, deprived the legislative process, to that degree, of the full benefit of hearing the viewpoint of the nonprofit sector on a wide range of public policy questions on which it could be presumed to speak with special knowledge. It also crippled in some degree the ability of the private nonprofit sector to defend its own interests in the process of government policy formulation, a process which by the mid 1970s had become increasingly decisive in its fate and affairs.

After years of debate on the matter, the Congress in late 1976 passed an amendment to the Federal Tax Code setting out more liberal and specific boundaries for permissible lobbying activity by nonprofit organizations (other than churches and private foundations) and providing graduated penalties for any violations. The change effectively reestablished their rights of legislative participation and is a significant gain.

But as regards the civil liberties and protection of nonprofit organizations in a more fundamental sense—namely their freedom to dissent, to oppose objectionable government actions, and to monitor governmental performance—the progress being made is more problematic. For at least the past 30 years, in one of the sorriest episodes of American history, the Federal government under a succession of Presidents engaged in massive, sustained programs of illegal action in violation of the constitutional rights of law-abiding citizens and nonprofit organizations. Discussion of such improper surveillance, intrusion, and intimidation, in the words of Tom Wicker, columnist of the *New York Times* "was beclouded in vague, portentous rhetoric about 'national security,' 'national interest,' 'the powers of the Presidency' and leaving the latter no weaker than the incumbent had found them. Such talk, we now know, whether or not Presidents knew it, cloaked assassination attempts, black-bag jobs, outrageous tapping and bugging, and the political harassment of thousands of innocent Americans."[7]

Because of the mass and incontestability of the evidence uncovered by several Congressional investigations and by the Watergate prosecutions (and perhaps triggered by the shocking assertion of ex-President Nixon on national television earlier in the year that a President was "sovereign" and therefore above the law), the Carter Administration in August of 1977 announced plans to strengthen legislative as well as executive restrictions on the FBI and the CIA. These would include prohibitions against the CIA's domestic spying on Americans, the FBI's investigations of political organizations in the name of "domestic security," and programs of covert harassment of people and groups regarded by law enforcement officers as "controversial."

Vice President Mondale in announcing the plans asserted that "it would be short sighted to think reforms within the Executive Branch alone" could prevent such abuses. That "would imply that all of these abuses over several decades were caused by evil people and that all we have to do is change the cast of characters and the problem will be solved." But, he continued, "the problem is in fact power itself, if it is unchecked, unrestrained, and unaccountable." He therefore charged Congress "not to depend on our good will or that of any future executive, to do their job. They will have the tools to detect, expose and stop abuses by government agencies on their own"—a pertinent reminder that Congressional "oversight" in the past overlooked much more than it oversaw.

In the post Vietnam, post Watergate mood of official repentance, the time was propitious for enactment of such new formal protections. But a considerable body of unhappy national experience suggests that if and when another period of internal social tension and concern about external military threats recurs—as it very possibly might—all the powerful pressures for governmental lawlessness and the suppression of dissent will again be unleashed. And without active monitoring by the citizenry, the infinite ingenuity of certain elements of the apparatus of government will succeed in finding means to circumvent the regulations.

For the Third Sector, this is a vitally important concern, for private nonprofit agencies, including universities, scientific research centers, and social-action movements, tend to be precisely the focus of such governmental acts of intrusion and intimidation.

Only in a democratic society, determined to preserve the justice and adaptiveness of its own system, could a duty on the part of government to increase the restraints upon itself and to ease those upon its potential critics be invoked. But in the United States it remains appropriate and even realistic to do so.

The above recommendations for governmental action constitute *in toto* a program of self-denial and of self-restraint, of a redistribution of power in behalf of a principle of pluralism and of participatory democracy. They imply a reversal of the basic thrust of the modern state toward greater scale and more comprehensive responsibility, toward greater centralization and bureaucratization. They fly in the face of immense vested interests within American society and of conventional attitudes and assumptions. They therefore will not occur without the most determined and inspired political leadership backed by a people determined to preserve the character of its democratic system. Also, they will never occur if they do not begin to be instituted within the coming few years, for the preponderance of government is already so great and the onrushing pace of its further expansion is so rapid that the point of no return, if it is not already behind us, soon will be.

10 ▶▶▶▶

Prospects and Possibilities

WHAT ARE THE PROSPECTS, realistically, that such a considerable set of changes in public policy might actually be made?

Candidly, they are not bright—at least for the moment. Whether we look at situations abroad more or less similar to our own, or at the predominant trends at home, it is apparent that the underlying premises of the bureaucratized welfare state are still widely accepted and that the thrust of its expansionism is far from spent.

The nations of Western Europe, the most similar to the United States in structure, traditions, and attitudes, have travelled down the path to the welfare state somewhat sooner and somewhat farther than we. There as elsewhere attitudes toward private philanthropy are a sensitive indicator of popular feelings about such fundamental matters as the proper social role of the state, the responsibility of individuals for the general welfare, and the significance—or insignificance—of preserving private "mediating structures" to stand protectively between government and the sphere of private life. In Europe, according to the most recent accounts, private charity has quite gone out of favor. As a leftover of the past, the number of charitable funds and organizations is impressive enough: 120,000 in Britain, 32,000 in the Netherlands, 19,500 in Switzerland, 15,000 in Sweden, and 4,000 in West Germany. But the vast majority exist in name only, making only minimal outlays. Nor are new funds and foundations being created in significant numbers, because the European governments offer few inducements and many impediments to would-be donors.

On the political left, private philanthropy has acquired a bad name, and even among the political moderates and centrists it is disapproved of. The left charges that it delays the expansion of government-controlled social benefits and softens popular attitudes toward private wealth. The moderates disapprove of what they call the elitism of philanthropists who dispense large amounts of money without the controls of electoral mandates or the accountability of government agencies, themes which have become familiar enough in the United States.

Jonathan Kandell of the *New York Times* in a special analysis of the situation in mid 1978 reported the case of a gift of an indoor swimming pool to the town of Beauvais in France by Marcel Dassault, a wealthy aircraft manufacturer. In inaugurating the pool, the Socialist mayor, with Mr. Dassault standing by, made these pointed comments:

"To give ourselves over to patronage, consigning our fate to the powerful and rich, seems to us contrary to the spirit of the republic and of democracy. We should have preferred action by the nation, the fruits of efforts by the whole community, eliminating charitable practices that degrade those who benefit from them."

In Sweden, where according to Mr. Kandell popular feeling against private philanthropy probably runs highest, there have been few recent cases of large private donations. He quoted an official of the Budget Ministry to the effect that "that sort of philanthropy is suspect nowadays. . . . In the past philanthropy was an important substitute for social benefits for the poor. But we've had such a fast buildup of public welfare services since the end of the war that all political parties now believe that philanthropy should be the function of the state and of local communities."[1]

In the United States, antagonism toward philanthropy seems somewhat less vehement and widespread, although it is not inconsequential. The erosion of inducements for private giving to charity continues and the expansion of government activity in almost all the fields once considered the area of action for private nonprofit institutions continues. The policies and proposals of the

Carter Administration, consistent with those of previous Democratic and Republican presidents in the postwar era, are clearly negligent of and in some respects adverse to the interests of the Third Sector while strongly supportive of larger and more comprehensive government-administered social programs.

So preponderant is the presumption of government responsibility and competence that the possibility of relying to a greater degree on private institutions and voluntary efforts, if only as providers of social services, is rarely even considered as an alternative. Any study of Congressional proceedings, for example, will show that the only issues that are seriously contested in considering the endless flow of proposals for the elaboration of government programs and the extension of governmental responsibility for "the general welfare" are how, and how much: How much additional budgetary deficit can be justified? How should the benefits be allocated? How should the structures for their direct administration be designed? And how should their costs (other than those concealed in inflation) be allocated among various income groups?

To the limited extent that Third Sector institutions are given any attention in such debates it is almost never because they are regarded as having special merits and qualities to be utilized and protected. Rather, they are regarded simply as another clamoring interest group—to be ignored if possible and to be accommodated if necessary, but then only in proportion to the power of their constituencies. It would appear that here as in Europe the underlying premise that government should be the means of providing an ever-wider range of services is unchallenged—least of all by the multitude of eager petitioners from business, labor, agriculture, the poor, the educators and scientists, and all the others that now swarm around its door.

Moreover, in the view of influential prognosticators of both the political right and left, the still further growth of state power and the diminution of diversity and of private autonomy throughout the remaining democratic nations is—for differing reasons depending on the particular author—inevitable. Those on the right perceive a coming "crisis of governability" for the Western countries: Their political systems are overloaded with participants and demands and are unable to cope with the complexity confronting them, which sets in motion a vicious cycle of consequences. Government credibility declines, citizen alienation develops, the effectiveness of implementation of decisions taken decreases, and all this feeds back into progressive ineffectiveness and further vulnerability. According to this view, with political terrorism loose in the world and with the constant threat of Soviet imperialism hanging over them, the democracies if they are to survive must tighten their control and given new emphasis to cohesion and social unity. Above all they must not give strength and encouragement to diversity and thereby to what are seen as disintegrative tendencies. In the Harvardian words of Professor Samuel Huntington, one of the most prominent of these spokesmen for the claims of authority over liberty, "A value which is normally good in itself is not necessarily optimized when it is maximized. We have come to recognize that there are potentially desirable limits to economic growth. There are likewise potentially desirable limits to the indefinite extension of political democracy."[2]

By a different route, Robert Heilbroner, the widely read and respected economist of a left-liberal orientation, comes to essentially the same conclusion, namely that global and historical circumstances will force the greater and greater extension of state control in the democratic nations. In his view, progressively more severe resource shortages, environmental pollution, and international tensions will force the replacement of the present "business civilization" of the West, with its looseness and pluralism, by more totally planned and controlled systems. This new statism is virtually inescapable; and its central element will be the "elevation of the collective and communal destiny of man to the forefront of public consciousness and the absolute subordination of private interests to public requirements."[3]

Counterindications and Contradictions

Such present trends and future expectations can hardly lift the hearts and spirits of those who are concerned that reliance on government to serve human needs may have gone too far and that the possibilities of greater reliance on private initiative and responsibility are unduly ignored. But they need not necessarily despair, for there are discernible counterindications that suggest their day may be coming, and possibly quite soon.

The democratic welfare states, for all their great achievements and contributions to human benefit, are everywhere beyond their depth and in trouble—not in worse trouble than that of the dictatorships of the communist and the underdeveloped worlds, but in different and still dangerous trouble. Inflation, an inability to balance the growth of their social programs with economic and productivity growth, and general political malaise is their common predicament.

That malaise is a most curious and interesting mixture of contradictions. To take the United States as a particular case in point, the most obvious feature of current political thinking is the coexistence of two dominant and antithetical ideas—a general and swelling desire for the services provided by a modern welfare state and a broad and deep discontent with big government and big bureaucracy.

These conflicting attitudes are not on the whole held by separate groups of the population; indeed, most citizens hold both of them. And though they may seem inconsistent they are not irrational because both are rooted in the nation's recent political experience. The faith in government has strong foundations. Beginning with the Great Depression, its capacity as an instrument for achieving broad national objectives was impressively demonstrated. The New Deal proved the positive possibilities of government action in dealing with social needs. World War II provided equally powerful evidence of the ability of government to mobilize national energies in fields as diverse as scientific research and new techniques of industrial production in support of a military effort. In the postwar years, the Marshall Plan was a brilliant instance of the potentialities of combining idealism, international cooperation, and organized government action in support of a peacetime task of economic reconstruction. These were major achievements. Together they created the firm base of public support based on practical experience for a broad range of ambitious subsequent undertakings at home and abroad, from Point Four to Medicare to Head Start.

This base has been further reinforced by the experience in recent years of large elements of the population—including the elderly, the handicapped, the poor, and the racially disadvantaged—who have in fact found government to be their best if not their only available source of relief and redress. There is consequently no general popular disposition whatever to wish to dismantle the American welfare state.

On the other hand, the growing concern of a great many of these same citizens about the costs and dangers of unlimited reliance on government and of the unlimited growth of government is equally rooted in their own direct experience. Along with some successes, they have now witnessed and in some instances been victimized by major fiascoes in government social programs— from urban renewal to low income housing to care of the elderly to jobs programs for ghetto youth. Established services, from the post office to public transportation, have seriously deteriorated. Other programs, from social security to health care, have turned out to involve immense costs that were unanticipated and are seemingly uncontrollable. Still others, such as environmental protection and job safety, have entailed regulatory burdens and nuisances that are widely resented. At the overall level of economic and fiscal policy, perhaps the most monumental failure of all has occurred—where despite the efforts of a succession of Presidents, ruinous inflation combined with persistent stagnation in the form of high unemployment and slow economic growth has prevailed.

Politicians and bureaucrats have kept up a brave front, but these failures and the increasing incapacity of government to cope have not gone unnoticed. The opinion polls show that the American people feel that they are now both overgoverned and badly governed. They have repeatedly registered their feeling that government programs are wasteful and ineffective and their belief that they are paying more and getting less in social services, especially in the cities—where 70 percent of Americans now live.

Such feelings appear to be spreading and growing more intense. They are reflected in the changing editorial positions of even some of the nation's most staunchly liberal publications. The *Washington Post*, for example, after the mid-term Democratic Party conference held in Memphis, Tennessee, in late 1978, criticized those at the meeting who attacked the President's new antagonism to inflationary expenditures as "illiberal" in these sharp words: ". . . we will state it as a certainty that it is a misdefinition of liberalism to suggest that it is somehow in favor of any and all federal government expenditures on social programs and extensions of authority into people's lives and indifferent to efforts to modernize the nation's military or to get a long overdue grip on inflation and its effects on the average householder."[4]

The new public mood was reflected also in political explosions such as the passage of Proposition 13 in California, which slashed the allowable level of property taxes in the state. Still more significant was the success of a movement for a constitutional amendment requiring that Congress balance the federal budget; by mid 1979, more than four-fifths of the required 34 resolutions by state legislatures to force Congressional action had already been passed.

These trends were consistent with what was happening in Europe, where there were mounting signs that after a quarter century or more of rapid increases in public spending, the economic and political limits were being reached. Figures published by the Organization for Economic Cooperation and Development in Paris, whose members are the main industrialized countries, showed that their public spending spurted from 28 percent of national output in 1955–57 to 34 percent by 1967 to 41 percent by the mid 1970s. But now there is reliable evidence that this rapid rise is tapering off. Sweden, Austria, Norway, and Finland, for example, had substantially lower government outlays in 1977 and 1978. In the Netherlands the government is planning to cut spending by $5 billion during the next three years. In France fierce taxpayer resistance has developed to increases in local taxes, and in Denmark the antitax Progress Party has within a few years become the second biggest in Parliament. In Great Britain, in the spring of 1979, the voters elected a new conservative government, headed by Margaret Thatcher, with a clear majority. The outcome was generally interpreted as solid evidence of a shift in public sentiment against further increase of governmental expenditures and social programs.

In the United States, not only has deep and pervasive doubt about the fiscal and administrative competence of government been generated, but the faith of the public in the basic decency and responsibility of government had also been dealt a series of heavy blows, of which the war in Vietnam and Watergate were the most shattering.

This combination of operational and moral failures has produced a general decline of confidence and trust in national institutions of almost every kind and of national leadership in almost every field. It has also produced a huge decline in participation in the political process. The number of voters who now say they are unwilling to associate themselves with either political party is greater than the number of avowed Republicans or Democrats. Some 70 million voting-age Americans were so turned off and embittered by election day of 1976 that they would not vote for either presidential candidate. According to a report of the Committee for the Study of the American Electorate published in August 1976, nearly 9 million of the 70 million nonvoters voted frequently up to 1968, but have since become estranged from such political participation.

The parallel existence of great hope in—and hopelessness about—government is the central political fact of American democracy today. To dismiss it as mere illogicality or whimsicality on the part of the citizenry would be to fail to grasp what may be the great reshaping force of the next phase of the evolution of the American welfare state.

Ideological Disarray and Displacements

The changes and confusion in public attitudes are now visibly reflected in the ideological migrations of the intellectual vanguard. For the past thirty years, thinking about public policy in the United States has been characterized by a frozen polarity between pro-government liberals and anti-government conservatives. The disputes between the two were typically a sterile con-

frontation of smug aggressiveness on the one side and fearful
negativism on the other. But rather recently, indeed almost suddenly, that dreary scene has come to life, and a good many of the
country's leading social thinkers—including academics, political
activists, and social-service professionals—are now visibly in the
process of reexamining basic issues and even changing their positions.

The exponents of the New Criticism are a mixed and motley
group, impossible to classify according to the traditional left-right,
liberal-conservative spectrum. They are themselves diverse and
ideologically in transition. Irving Kristol and Daniel Bell, two of
the most prominent and influential "neoconservatives," began as
socialists. Ben Wattenberg and Daniel Patrick Moynihan, two of
the most vigorous and influential members of the Coalition for a
Democratic Majority, which is strongly challenging the liberal
wing of the Democratic party on many issues, were once stalwart
New Dealers. Through a series of often brilliantly written attacks
on the premises and results of governmental economic and social
policies, they have thrown what remains of the old liberal intellectual establishment on the defensive and have begun to attract
the affiliation of a good number of bright, young writers and
scholars.

Moving in the opposite direction politically is Richard Cornuelle, author of one of the holy texts of American conservatism,
Reclaiming the American Dream, and until 1969 a vice-president
of the National Association of Manufacturers. In his most recent
book, *De-Managing America,* he has gone a good way toward radical populism by arguing that "modern management is failing because it is authoritarian, and authority simply doesn't work any
more. It is built on the idea of subordination" while Americans
"are everywhere becoming insubordinate, and unmanageable."
Which is all right, in his view, since the country is really divided
into two Americas: "front office America," which comprises all the
entities that presume to manage the country and its organizations,
and "unmanaged America"—the people who do the work and
make things run. The country works in spite of management.
"People are self-propelling" and they are now propelling a new
revolution in behalf of diversity and self-expression which the

agencies of management and authority are going to have to submit to if they hope to stay around.[5]

The social-action movements represent another kind of break from the old liberalism. A singular characteristic of many of their leaders is their rejection of the assumption of the inherent beneficence of government and their readiness to attack what they see as the excesses and evils of government as well as of the corporations. Their approach has been pragmatic and tactical, not ideological in any conventional or coherent sense. But in their general assault on "institutional" faults and failures, in both the private and public sector, they have in effect adopted an unformulated philosophical position in behalf of decentralization, citizen responsibility, and other values emphasized by both the New Left, the neoconservatives, and the "libertarians"—the bright, irreverent, and aggressive conservative youth movement whose program is radically liberal in the nineteenth-century meaning of the term.

These activists on the whole have been the amateurs in reformism. But among the professionals too—including the sociologists and social workers, the political scientists, penologists and the lawyers—a similar attitude toward government and bureaucracy has begun to develop. David Rothman, the distinguished social historian of Columbia University, has described the rise of this new generation with its new aims and orientation. The old Progressives, he writes (carefully avoiding use of the now sensitive and ambiguous label "Liberals"), "were certain that the state and its clients enjoyed a nonadversarial relationship, that relief and even correctional programs could simultaneously serve everyone's best interest. What promoted the safety of society promoted the welfare of its members. Social order and individual betterment went hand in hand. . . . It was unnecessary—counterproductive actually—to limit or to circumscribe officials' discretionary powers." But now, according to Rothman, a post-Progressive generation is committed not to promote paternalistic state intervention in the name of equality but "to restrict intervention in the name of liberty. Our predecessors were determined to test the maximum limits of the exercise of state power in order to corect imbalances. We are about to test the minimum limits of the exercise of state power in order to enhance autonomy."[6]

Sheldon Wolin, the Princeton sociologist, sums up the disenchantment of many liberals and radicals with the results of the explosive expansion of governmental programs in behalf of egalitarian objectives in these words:

> One sign that our society is undergoing a transformation of its identity is the way that programs and policies produce the opposite of their original intentions. Democracy is gradually undercut by programs designed to strengthen it. Social legislation is introduced with the avowed aim of improving the health and well being of citizens; it brings instead a system of dependence and powerlessness which enables the bureaucracy to discipline and control the poor. The same effects could not be accomplished if the rulers of our society had decided to institute dictatorial control. The same phenomenon, of democratic intentions recoiling to produce antidemocratic results, has occurred in education.[7]

A prominent private commission in Britain appointed in late 1977 to review the probable role of private voluntary organizations in the future in that country has come to precisely the same conclusion. The "Wolfenden Report," named after the commission's chairman, Lord Wolfenden, contained this key passage: "As we look forward over the next 25 years, we cannot see any likelihood that public expenditure on the social and environmental services will continue to grow as fast as it has done during the last quarter of a century. Nor can we see any likelihood of a diminution in the rate at which additional services will be expected and demanded. In the past, there has been a tendency to think and act as though the answer to social problems is for the state to assume direct responsibility and provide resources for the extension or intensification of statutory services. We believe this assumption is only partially valid and that there is an urgent need to look afresh at the whole present pattern of social and environmental services and their organization. We are not thinking simply of a redistribution of activities between the statutory and voluntary sectors. What we are proposing is the development of a new long-term strategy, by a new examination of the potential contributions of the statutory, voluntary and informal sectors, and their interrelationship. In our view, this examination is likely to point to the need for a substantial extension of the last two sectors."[8]*

What is common to all these diverse perspectives is that they proceed from a recognition that modern democratic government must extensively administer to the public welfare but also from a concern that in so doing it has become intrusive, wasteful, ineffective, and corruptive of the capacity of citizenry for self-government. This is precisely the mixed sentiment of many ordinary citizens, who by and large are still committed to the achievement of a more just and compassionate society but who also have growing reservations about attempting to achieve those objectives essentially through turning to the state as parent and benefactor. If this discontent is still inchoate, a malaise more than a program, it is nonetheless deep, broad, and strong. Combined with what is going on among the intellectuals, the activists, and the social-service professionals a considerable new political force may be developing for the replacement of the governmental-bureaucratic model of the welfare state with some kind of new private-public model for meeting human and social needs.

From Criticism to Construction

If we are now to move from criticism to construction—to the development of a modified and more satisfactory successor to the present form of the welfare state—three of its central dilemmas must be resolved:

First, the dilemma of unlimited demands and limited resources; second, the dilemma of the need to improve the efficiency and effectiveness of government programs and at the same time to reduce governmental oppressiveness; third, the dilemma of pursuing egalitarian democratic objectives without at the same time producing a condition of civic abjectness and inertia.

As regards the first of these potentially explosive dilemmas, a

---

* In British usage, the statutory sector corresponds to what is here called the governmental sector and the voluntary sector to what is here called the Third Sector. The "informal sector" represents the help and support family, friends and neighbors give to each other.

"revolution of rising expectations," or entitlements as some have designated it, has erupted in recent years, which has set off a spiral of increase in the cost of social services and transfer payments, which in turn has created severe budgetary strains for state and local governments as well as the Federal government. The tide of demand for still more comprehensive social services continues to rise even as the United States enters what is likely to be a prolonged period of slower economic growth, balance of payment problems, resource shortages, continuing inflationary pressures, and heavy governmental budgetary deficits. If the course of public policy is to continue to attempt to meet these massive demands essentially through the expansion of government funded and administered programs, the consequences in terms of major tax increases, increases in government deficits, accelerated inflation, greater impediments to economic growth, and intensifying political competition for the available budgetary resources of government can become dangerously divisive. Alternatively, if government, caught in this cruel bind between unlimited demands and increasingly limited resources, should seek to resolve the problem by drastic cutbacks of services, equally dangerous and divisive consequences could follow.

The Third Sector provides no ready and complete answer to this formidable and looming collision of forces. But it does offer the possibility of deflecting some of these demands from government, reducing their cost, and improving their delivery by greater reliance on voluntarism and voluntary organizations. Governor Edmund G. (Jerry) Brown, Jr., of California, in an extemporaneous speech to citizens of the city of San Jose in mid 1977, described the need for rebuilding a giving, caring, sharing society in unusually plain and human terms:

> "Why is it that despite the public philosophy of those in key positions, government gets bigger and bigger, more complex, more involved, and your taxes keep going up?"
>
> The very simple reason is that it takes more than words to put some limit on that growth. There are certain needs and obligations in the community that just have to be taken care of, and if you don't do it through some volunteer movement, some other arrangement

outside of the public sector, then inevitably government will take on the task and assume those obligations.

If you take, let it be the mentally ill, the narcotic-abuse program, the alcohol programs, child-care, nursing homes, hospitals, training activities, and you meet every need that can be identified, you would have to double and possibly even triple the existing government activity that we now have at the state, local, and Federal level.

Something as straightforward as police activity—how many police can you hire and how many are patrolling the streets? The ratio will never be high enough unless people assume a greater degree of responsibility for their own defense and protection. That's not to say that we don't need police—sure we have to have them—but unless the public sector in its manifestation of security by police activity will link itself with the citizens, then all the money in the world will not make the streets safe. . . .

There is no substitute for neighborhoods, for mutual-support systems in the private sector. Whether it be neighbors who know each other, who have some responsibility for someone other than themselves and their family—you can't get away from it. The idea that you can put it on government, if you want to, is going to triple your taxes because then you have to hire a full-time person who doesn't have the commitment involved in it that you would to do that kind of work. . . .

That's my simple message: that voluntarism is not a luxury, it is a necessity for a civilized society that wants to truly meet its human needs. And we have to expand it in a dramatic way across a broad front of government and human activity. We have to find some way to re-create the spirit of neighborhoodliness and mutual self-support that existed before the mobility and the anonymity and increasing information flow that has been the product of this very prosperous society. . . .

But in order to expand the productivity, the freedom, the mobility, the prosperity, we have segregated, we have specialized, so we have nursing homes for the old, child-care for the young, mental hospitals for those who act in a rather strange way or are different from the rest of us. And schools that start early and keep going till one's mid-20's, longer if possible. . . . We're institutionalizing everybody.

The myth of specialization and division of labor is creating a soli-

tary society of dependent people who have to go to a paid professional to tell them how to make basic human decisions. Yes, you
need a lot of these professions: I'm not saying you don't. But a lot of
what goes on is something you, your friends, your neighbors, those
in coalitions—whether they be religious, political, labor, or voluntary—can do to look after yourselves.[9]

Brown is an enigmatic figure to both conventional liberals and
conservatives, but in his warning about institutionalizing everyone and professionalizing every social service, his views have
evoked response from both.

The second of the central dilemmas of the American welfare
state—how to increase the efficiency and effectiveness of its programs without increasing its oppressiveness—could if it goes
unresolved also have major and damaging political repercussions.
The waste, corruption, and sheer failure of many of the social programs of government is now a fact of American political life so
large and so resented that it can no longer be ignored. Proposals
for civil service reform and for the delegation of administration of
programs to lower levels of government, though they may have
some useful results, must be regarded in relation to the total
problem as mere palliatives. One more fundamental way of trying
to deal with it would be to impose much greater centralization
and control over Federal programs and over private institutions,
profit-making and nonprofit, which are now being regulated to
achieve various social objectives—from environmental protection
to equal employment opportunity. Such an approach offers the attraction of logic, order, and forceful action, but it also is certain to
worsen, not improve, the problems of governmental gigantism,
unresponsiveness, and bureaucratic waste. It also contains the
possibility of producing vehement public reaction because of its
threat of destruction to those "mediating structures" which in a
pluralistic society served to protect vital areas of private life from
governmental power. Again, both from the left and right have
come demands for a fundamentally different kind of solution.

Amitai Etzioni, a prominent sociologist of Columbia University,
argues from a liberal perspective that new vehicles must be invented for serving public needs which can combine efficiency and
expertise from the private business sector and accountability and

social responsibility from the nonprofit and government sector. He believes that "the most promising solutions to our domestic problems are among the third sector approaches now evolving." Instances of the experimentation with new forms now going on include, among many others, the public–private mix of elements developed under NASA for Project Apollo, Amtrak, Comsat, and the Corporation for Public Broadcasting.

In Etzioni's view, the possibilities of doing more of the government's business through such hybrid agencies—including such functions as the administration of welfare programs, food and drug testing, and the provision of legal services—are tremendous. He concludes that "enough is already known for us to be able to state now that greater reliance on the third sector, both as a way of reducing government on all levels and as a way of involving the private sector in the service of domestic missions, would be significantly more effective than either expanding the federal or other levels of government or dropping them on a private sector."[10]

From the other end of the political spectrum, the American Enterprise Institute, comes a similar viewpoint. Its recent publication, *To Empower the People,* opens forthrightly with the statement: "We aim at rethinking the institutional means by which government exercises its responsibilities. The idea is not to revoke the New Deal but to pursue its vision in ways more compatible with democratic governance."

The authors, Peter Berger and Richard Neuhaus, as an alternative to greater centralization and resort to the command-and-control approach, urge much greater reliance on private "voluntary associations" to carry out governmentally funded social welfare programs. This will improve their effectiveness and will help break public and professional monopolies over social services in such areas as education, child care, law enforcement, housing, and health care. At the same time, "empowering the people" to control and take responsibility for those activities which are closest to their lives and aspirations will help avoid, in their view, even more fundamental dangers to American society—dangers which relate to the third of the problems confronting the welfare state.[11]

John Stuart Mill, in a classic statement of the nineteenth-century liberal view, once wrote that "there is scarcely anything really important to the general interest, which it may not be desirable or even necessary that the government should take on itself." But he warned that "the mode in which the government can most surely demonstrate the sincerity with which it intends the greatest good of its subjects is by doing the things that are made incumbent upon it by the helplessness of the public, in such a manner as shall tend not to increase and perpetuate, but to correct that helplessness." [12]

Today, as in Mill's time, the indispensable element in a free, just, and responsible society is free, just, and responsible individuals. If we seek to have such a society we must exert ourselves to create situations and incentives which encourage and develop these qualities in the citizenry, not stifle them. At present they are in fact under assault by a number of forces. The most obvious of these, as Berger and Neuhaus have stressed, is a widespread, almost universal, sense of anonymity, powerlessness, and rootlessness; of a lack of credible opportunities to participate in decision-making processes; and of being at the mercy of large-scale, impersonal organizations generally. This is a consequence not of particular political ideologies but rather of the sheer size and complexity of modern society and of the rapidity of change.

Adding to the effects of gigantism and the baffling interlocking patterns of modern social, economic, and political arrangements has been a sense of dependency engendered by the well-intentioned efforts of government to promote egalitarianism and provide human services. Responsibility for a multitude of matters formerly the direct local concern of families, neighborhoods, and communities has been transferred to distant centers of planning and administration. By the means which have been chosen to carry out desirable ends, individuals and various natural social groupings have been incapacitated, feeding a deadening sense, in Mill's term, of helplessness.

The general result of these tendencies is that individual development is stunted and the individual sense of self-reliance and civic responsibility is eroded. Meaningful and effective democracy to that extent is dying at the roots.

The Third Sector, if it can be revitalized and be more fully utilized, can help check that rot and strengthen the very foundations of American pluralism and democracy. It does not offer a substitute for the social and humanitarian programs of the modern welfare state. But it does offer a means of supplementing and stimulating them and of lessening some of the most dangerous fiscal, psychological, and political side-effects of excessive bureaucratization, centralization, and depersonalization of governmentally administered programs. The benefits which would result would come from activating and involving the population, not simply "servicing" it. These could be immense, both for the population and the programs. But they would not be without some cost, whether in coordination, central control, or "efficiency" as measured in purely monetary terms. Whether such costs are considered worth incurring depends on the kind of democracy we wish to have and the kinds of citizens and citizenship we want to produce.

Opinions will vary greatly about the precise balance to be struck in the future between government and private responsibility, centralization and decentralization, freedom and control, or efficiency and participation. But there is no longer much doubt, as the American welfare state sinks deeper and deeper into difficulties, that these are relevant issues which must be addressed. The unlimited and indiscriminate assumptions of the old liberalism about government role and responsibility, and flat rejection of such assumptions by the old conservatism, have lost all meaning and usefulness. It may be therefore that an important watershed in the evolution of the American welfare state is being approached and that the United States is on the verge of a period of great political innovation and creativity as it seeks to achieve its purposes of social justice, individual freedom, and responsible government in some fundamentally new combinations of private and public initiative and capabilities. If this is so, and there are many and increasing indications that it could well be, then the Third Sector and the values it embodies become crucially important both as a touchstone by which to judge new policy courses and as an instrumentality for their execution. From the near desperation of its present predicament, it could emerge in new and modernized form as an idea and a set of institutions which could arouse the hopes and enthusiasm of many disparate and now divided kinds of Americans, the young and old, black and white, liberal and conservative, Democratic and Republican. The Third Sector could thus be a key to the outcome of the American Republic's third century.

Notes

1. THE SECTOR NOBODY KNOWS

[1]The term is not original, having previously been used by a number of writers. Conservative Richard Cornuelle in his volume *Reclaiming the American Dream* (New York: Random House, 1965), employed it as a basic concept in his attack on the pro-government bias of the liberals. Amitai Etzioni of the Center for Policy Research at Columbia University discusses it, from a liberal perspective, as an underutilized means of improving the execution of government programs. See his article, "The Untapped Potential of the Third Sector," *Business and Society Review* (Spring 1972) no. 1, pp. 39–44. Theodore Levitt of the Harvard Business School, in his book *The Third Sector* (New York: AMACOM, 1973), focuses on the social-action movements—which on the whole he deplores for having created "a national pathology of brooding discontent and unrelieved suspicion." John D. Rockefeller 3d, the distinguished philanthropist, in a *Reader's Digest* article in April 1978 entitled "America's Threatened Third Sector," argued that the common thread that runs through the diverse elements of the Third Sector is "a belief in being of service to one's community and other people, without relying on government and without any expectation of personal profit. At the heart of the Third Sector is individual initiative and a sense of caring."

[2]Gabriel G. Rudney, "Scope of the Private Voluntary Charitable Sector," *Research Papers*, Sponsored by the Commission on Private Philanthropy and Public Needs (Department of the Treasury, 1977), pp. 135–41.

[3]David Horton Smith, "Values, Voluntary Action, and Philanthropy: The Appropriate Relationship of Private Philanthropy to Public Needs," *Research Papers*, Sponsored by the Commission on Private Philanthropy and Public Needs (Department of the Treasury, 1977), pp. 1102–8.

[4]*Ibid.*

[5]Eli Ginzberg, "The Pluralistic Economy of the U.S.," *Scientific American* (December 1976), 235(6):25–29.

[6] Arthur M. Okun, *Equality and Efficiency: The Big Tradeoff* (Washington: The Brookings Institution, 1975), p. 120.

[7] Speech by Kenneth E. Boulding to a Conference on Foundations, Sponsored by The Charles F. Kettering Foundation, Dayton, Ohio, November 11–13, 1970.

[8] Letter from John Gardner to Waldemar Nielsen, March 28, 1977, quoted with permission.

[9] William J. Baumol and William G. Bowen, *Performing Arts: The Economic Dilemma* (Cambridge, Mass.: MIT Press, 1968), p. 321.

[10] *Giving in America: Toward a Stronger Voluntary Sector,* A Report of the Commission on Private Philanthropy and Public Needs (Commission on Private Philanthropy and Public Needs, 1975), p. 14.

[11] John W. Gardner, *The Voluntary Sector and the Tax System,* A Report Delivered to the United Way of America Biennial Staff Conference, New Orleans, February 28, 1978, p. 12.

[12] Kirkpatrick Sale, *Power Shift: The Rise of the Southern Rim and Its Challenge to the Eastern Establishment* (New York: Random House, 1975).

[13] W. John Minter and Howard R. Bowen, *Private Higher Education, Third Annual Report on Financial and Educational Trends in the Private Sector of American Higher Education,* Association of American Colleges, Washington, D.C., pp. 58–59.

[14] Figures from the Office of Federal Procurement Policy, Office of Management and Budget, Executive Office of the President, Washington, D.C.

[15] *Ibid.*

[16] *Giving in America,* p. 35.

[17] Alan Pifer, "Quasi Non-Governmental Organizations," An Introduction to the Carnegie Corporation Annual Report, 1967.

[18] Kingman Brewster, Jr., in *The Report of the President, Yale University, 1974–75,* An Address at the Annual Dinner of the Fellows of the American Bar Foundation (New Haven: Yale University, 1975), pp. 17–24.

[19] Derek Bok, "The President's Report to the members of the Board of Overseers, 1974–1975," *Harvard Today* (January 19, 1976), p. 10.

[20] Daniel Yankelovich, *The New Morality: A Profile of American Youth in the 70's* (New York: McGraw-Hill, 1974), pp. 9–11.

2. THE FOLKLORE OF AMERICAN PLURALISM

[1] William Bradford, *Of Plymouth Plantation, 1620–1647* (New York: Knopf, 1952), pp. 120–21.

[2] Brooke Hindle, *The Pursuit of Science in Revolutionary America, 1735–1789* (Chapel Hill: University of North Carolina Press, 1956), p. 140.

[3] Samuel Eliot Morison, *Harvard College in the Seventeenth Century* (Cambridge: Harvard University Press, 1936), 1:26–27.

[4] Frederick Rudolph, *The American College and University: A History* (New York: Vintage Books, 1962), pp. 14–15.

[5] Louis Hartz, "Laissez-Faire Thought in Pennsylvania, 1776–1860," *The Tasks of Economic History* (December 1943), no. 3, pp. 69–70.

[6] Frederick K. Heinrich, "The Development of American Laissez-Faire: A General View of the Age of Washington," *The Tasks of Economic History* (December 1943), no. 3, pp. 53–54.

[7] *Hospitals: Journal of the American Hospital Association* (January 1, 1976), vol. 1, no. 1.

[8] George H. Daniels, *Science in American Society: A Social History* (New York: Knopf, 1971), p. 176.

[9] Allan Nevins, *The State Universities and Democracy* (Urbana: University of Illinois Press, 1962), p. 14.

[10] Morison, *Harvard College*, p. 30.

[11] Alexis de Tocqueville, *Democracy in America* (New York: The Colonial Press, 1900), 1:191–92.

[12] Oscar Handlin, "Laissez-Faire Thought in Massachusetts, 1790–1880," *The Tasks of Economic History*, (December 1943), no. 3, p. 55.

[13] Hartz, "Laissez-Faire Thought," p. 75.

[14] Rudolph, *American College*, pp. 254–55.

[15] Daniels, *Science in American Society* p. 283.

[16] Calvin Tomkins, *Merchants and Masterpieces: The Story of the Metropolitan Museum of Art* (New York: Dutton, 1970), pp. 22–23.

[17] *Ibid.*, p. 77. For a good review of recent controversies over art, money, and ethics involving American museums see also Karl Meyer, *The Art Museum* (New York: Morrow, 1979).

[18] Nevins, *State Universities*, p. 6.

[19] Mary Risley, *House of Healing: The Story of the Hospital* (Garden City, N.Y.: Doubleday, 1961), p. 215.

[20] Abraham Flexner, *Medical Education in the United States and Canada*, A Report to the Carnegie Foundation for the Advancement of Teaching (New York: Carnegie Foundation, 1910).

[21] *Ibid.*

3. HIGHER EDUCATION

[1] Samuel Bowles and Herbert Gintis, *Schooling in Capitalist America: Educational Reform and the Contradictions of Economic Life* (New York: Basic Books, 1976).

[2] *The States and Higher Education: A Proud Past and a Vital Future*, A Commentary of the Carnegie Foundation for the Advancement of Teaching (San Francisco: Carnegie Foundation, 1976).

[3] Frank Newman, *National Policy and Higher Education*, A Report Produced

by a Special Task Force to the Secretary of HEW (Washington, D.C.: Office of Education, 1973), p. 48.

[4] *The New York Times,* April 11, 1977, p. 26.

[5] Donald M. Stewart, "The Not So Steady State of Governance in Higher Education," paper prepared for the Aspen Institute for Humanistic Studies in 1976.

[6] Kenneth M. Deitch, *Financial Aid: A Resource for Improving Educational Opportunities,* a paper prepared for the Sloan Commission on Government and Higher Education, March 24, 1978, p. 63.

[7] Larry L. Leslie, *Higher Education Opportunity, Decade of Progress* (Washington, D.C.: The American Association for Higher Education, 1977). See also Deitch, *Financial Aid,* pp. 22ff.

[8] Jacques Barzun, *House of Intellect* (New York: Harper & Row, 1959), p. 191.

[9] *Ibid.,* p. 130.

[10] *The New York Times,* October 9, 1977.

[11] Waldemar A. Nielsen, *The Big Foundations* (New York: Columbia University Press, 1972), pp. 392–93.

[12] Bruce L. Smith, ed., *The New Political Economy: The Public Use of the Private Sector* (New York: Halsted, 1975), p. 121.

[13] *Ibid.,* p. 122.

[14] Earl F. Cheit, "What Price Accountability?" *Change* (November 1975), pp. 30, 32.

[15] *Ibid.,* p. 32.

[16] *A National Policy for Private Higher Education,* A Report of the Task Force of the National Council on Independent Colleges and Universities (Washington, D.C.: Association of American Colleges, 1974).

[17] "Government and the Ruin of Private Education," *Harper's,* April, 1978. (For a fuller discussion of the rigging of "the educational marketplace" by Federal policy, see also "Public Policy and Private Higher Education," eds. David W. Breneman and Chester E. Finn, Jr. (Washington, D.C.: The Brookings Institution, 1978), 468 pp.

[18] *Ibid.*

4. PURE SCIENCE AND THE PUBLIC

[1] Michael Polanyi, *The Logic of Liberty: Reflections and Rejoinders* (Chicago: University of Chicago Press, 1951), pp. 89–90.

[2] Daniel Greenberg, *The Politics of Pure Science: An Inquiry Into the Relationship Between Science and Government in the United States* (New York: The New American Library, 1971), p. 266.

[3] For detailed and updated information, see: *Surveys of Science Resources Series: Federal Funds for Research, Development, and Other Scientific Activities,* issued annually by the National Science Foundation.

[4] Greenberg, *Politics of Pure Science,* p. 298.

[5] *Ibid.*, p. 58.
[6] Quoted in Geoffrey White, "Federal Support to Academic Research," paper prepared for the Sloan Commission on Government and Higher Education, April 17, 1978, p. 78.
[7] Vannevar Bush, *Pieces of the Action* (New York: Morrow, 1972).
[8] Greenberg, *Politics of Pure Science*, p. 121.
[9] Ivan L. Bennett, Address Delivered at Conference on Science in the Services of Man (Oklahoma City: October 1966), quoted in Greenberg, *ibid.*, p. 283.
[10] Don Price, *The Scientific Estate* (Cambridge, Mass.: The Belknap Press of Harvard University Press, 1965), p. 179.
[11] *Ibid.*, p. 51.
[12] Robert M. Hutchins, *Science, Scientists, and Politics*, An Occasional Paper on the Role of Science and Technology in the Free Society (Center for the Study of Democratic Institutions, 1963), quoted in Greenberg, *Politics of Pure Science*, p. xii.
[13] Philip Boffey, *The Brain Bank of America: An Inquiry Into the Politics of Science* (New York: McGraw-Hill, 1975), p. 248.
[14] Stephen Jay Gould, Review of *The Brain Bank of America* by Philip Boffey, *The New York Times Book Review* (May 4, 1975), p. 8.
[15] Dorothy Nelkin, "The Science-Textbook Controversies," *Scientific American*, April 1976, pp. 33–39.
[16] *The New York Times*, September 14, 1976, p. 39.
[17] *The New York Times Magazine*, November 7, 1976, p. 59.

5. THE HEALTH SYSTEM

[1] Department of Health, Education and Welfare, *Annual Hospital Survey* and *Master Inventory Survey*, Reports prepared by HEW (Washington, D.C.: HEW, 1976).
[2] U.S. Bureau of the Census, *Historical Statistics of the United States: Colonial Times to 1957* (Washington, D.C., 1960), p. 34.
[3] *New England Journal of Medicine*, June 20, 1974, pp. 1408 ff.
[4] Ruth Mulvey Harmer, *American Medical Avarice* (New York: Abelard-Schuman, 1975), p. 253.
[5] "Editorial, The American Foundation Proposals for Medical Care," *Jama* (October 16, 1937) 109:1281.
[6] Julius B. Richmond, *Currents in American Medicine* (Cambridge, Mass.: Harvard University Press, 1969), p. 16.
[7] Arthur M. Schlesinger, Jr., *The Coming of the New Deal* (Boston: Houghton Mifflin, 1959).
[8] Harmer, *Medical Avarice*, pp. 205–7.
[9] *Ibid.*, p. 18.
[10] *The New York Times*, August 30, 1976, p. 1.

[11] See his "Lead Agency Memorandum on National Health Insurance" sent to the President and members of the Cabinet on April 3, 1978.

[12] *The Wall Street Journal,* July 19, 1978.

[13] Aaron Wildavsky, "Doing Better and Feeling Worse: The Political Pathology of Health Policy," *Daedalus,* Winter 1977, p. 122.

6. CULTURE AND THE ARTS

[1] Dick Netzer, *The Subsidized Muse* (New York: Cambridge University Press, 1978), p. 12.

[2] For a more detailed review of French and British developments, see: *The Arts, Economics, and Politics,* especially the chapters by Gérard Bonnot, Claude Menard, and Sir Hugh Willatt (New York: Aspen Institute for Humanistic Studies, 1975).

[3] Personal correspondence with author, quoted by permission.

[4] Report of Commission des Affaires Culturelles, Sixth Plan, Commissariat du Plan, Paris, 1969.

[5] *New Cultural Policy in Sweden* (Stockholm: Swedish National Council for Cultural Affairs and the Swedish Institute, 1973), pp. 20–23.

[6] Russell Lynes, *Confessions of a Dilettante* (New York: Harper and Row, 1966), pp. 18–19.

[7] *The Performing Arts, Problems and Prospects,* A Rockefeller Panel Report on the Future of Theatre, Dance and Music in America (New York: McGraw-Hill, 1965), p. 207.

[8] See, for example: *National Endowment for the Arts—Guide to Programs, 1975–76.*

[9] Netzer, *Subsidized Muse,* p. 3.

[10] *Report of the Joint Committee on the Arts* (California: California State Legislature, February, 1975).

[11] *The Finances of the Performing Arts,* A Report Prepared by The Ford Foundation (New York: The Ford Foundation, 1974).

[12] For a knowledgeable discussion of some of these problems, see: the paper prepared for the Aspen Institute by Eric Larrabee, former head of the New York Arts Council, "The Public Funding Agency," October 8, 1975. For the most interesting and realistic effort being made to develop a theoretical basis for more precise economic criteria by which subsidy allocations might be made, see: "Large-Scale Public Support for the Arts," by Dick Netzer, *New York Affairs* (Fall 1974), 2(1):76–82, and his more recent book, *The Subsidized Muse,* cited above.

[13] Emmet John Hughes, *The Ordeal of Power* (New York: Atheneum, 1963), pp. 88–91.

[14] *The New York Times,* December 26, 1976, sec. II, p. 5.

[15] *Ibid.*

[16] W. McNeil Lowry, "Grant Makers, the Arts and Public Policy," *Foundation News*, March/April 1978, pp. 14–15.

[17] *The New York Times*, February 24, 1979, summaries the documents which have now become available under the Freedom of Information Act and which detail this program to purge public television and make it serve Administration aims.

[18] *The New York Times*, October 16, 1977, sec. II, p. 1.

[19] *Ibid.*, sec. II, p. 36.

[20] *Ibid.*, October 12, 1977, p. C19.

[21] *Ibid.*, December 18, 1977, p. 35.

[22] *Ibid.*, October 16, 1977, sec. II, pp. 1, 34.

7. SOCIAL-ACTION MOVEMENTS

[1] Hans Kohn, "Youth Movements," *Encyclopedia of the Social Sciences* (New York: The Macmillan Co., 1957), 15:517.

[2] Jean-François Revel, *Without Marx or Jesus* (New York: Doubleday, 1971).

[3] *The New York Times*, March 9, 1976, p. 33.

[4] Clem L. Zinger, Richard Dalsemer, and Helen Magayle, *Environmental Volunteers in America: Findings and Recommendations of the Steering Committee of the National Center for Voluntary Actions Environmental Project* (Washington, D.C.: National Center for Voluntary Action, 1973), p. 13.

[5] David Horton Smith, "The Role of the United Way in Philanthropy," *Research Papers*, Sponsored by the Commission on Private Philanthropy and Public Needs (Department of the Treasury, 1977), pp. 1353–80.

[6] *The New York Times*, January 11, 1976, sec. IV, p. 9.

[7] Milton Moskowitz, "Corporate Charitable Contributions and Corporate Social Responsibility," *Research Papers*, pp. 1827–38.

[8] Sarah Carey, "Foundations and the Powerless," *Research Papers*, pp. 1093–1107.

[9] *New York Times*, April 29, 1978, p. 23.

[10] Samuel M. Loescher, "New Incentives for Middle Class Philanthropy: Radical Funding for the Public Good," *IUSTITIA* (Fall/Winter 1974), 2(2):80.

[11] Tim Saasta, "Ralph Nader on Future Support for the Public Interest Movement," *Foundation News*, November/December, 1978, p. 5.

[12] *Newsweek*, May 31, 1965, p. 22.

[13] Martin Luther King, Jr., "Letter from a Birmingham Jail," *Aspen Institute Readings* (New York: Aspen Institute for Humanistic Studies, 1977).

[14] Final Report of the Select Committee to Study Governmental Relations With Respect to Intelligence Activities, United States Senate; Supplementary Detailed Staff Reports on Intelligence Activities and the Rights of Americans, Book III. *Dr. Martin Luther King, Jr., Case Study* (Washington, D.C.: U.S. Government Printing Office, 1976), p. 160, quoted in Morton H. Halperin et

al., *The Lawless State: The Crimes of the U.S. Intelligence Agencies* (New York: Penguin Books, 1976), pp. 78–80.

[15] *The New York Times*, April 27, 1976, p. 25.

[16] *Ibid.*, July 21, 1975, p. 54.

[17] David Ginsburg, Lee R. Marks, and Ronald P. Wertheim, "Federal Oversight of Private Philanthropy," *Research Papers*, 5:2575–2668.

[18] Halperin et al., *Lawless State*, p. 87.

[19] Harlan Cleveland and Stuart Gerry Brown, "The Limits of Obsession: Fencing in the National Security Claim," *Administrative Law Review* (Summer 1976), 27(3):327–46.

[20] Philip Moore, "Foundation Grants to Corporate Activist Groups: The Donee Perspective," *Research Papers*, pp. 1343–51.

[21] From *Balancing the Scales of Justice–Financing Public Interest Law in America*, Council for Public Interest Law (Washington, D.C.: 1976), p. 280.

8. THE NEW POLITICS OF PLURALISM

[1] Speech delivered to the NCVA/ACTION Information Institute at the Ambassador West Hotel, Chicago, October 17, 1975.

[2] J. Bronowski, "Disestablishing Science," *Encounter*, July 1971, pp. 8–16.

[3] Anthony Wedgwood Benn, "Towards a New Dictatorship?" *Encounter*, September 1971, p. 94.

[4] Edward Shils, "The Disestablishment of Science: On Dr. Bronowski's Proposal," *Encounter*, November 1975, p. 93.

[5] Charles L. Schultze, *The Public Use of Private Interests* (Washington, D.C.: The Brookings Institution, 1977).

[6] Theodore J. Lowi, *The End of Liberalism* (New York: Norton, 1969), ch. 10, "Toward Juridical Democracy," pp. 287ff.

9. PROPOSALS FOR PUBLIC POLICY

[1] Peter Petkas, *The New Federalism, Government Accountability and Philanthropy*, A Paper Prepared for the Commission on Private Philanthropy and Public Needs, 1975.

[2] On the general subject of accountability and the relationship between government and private organizations, see Bruce L. R. Smith, ed., *The New Political Economy: The Public Use of The Private Sector* (London: Macmillan, 1975); and *idem*, ed., *The Dilemma of Accountability in Modern Government* (New York: St. Martin's Press, 1971). These studies resulted from an initiative of the Carnegie Corporation in 1968.

[3] "Government: Wrong Kind of Competition," *Government Executive*, May 1976, p. 16.

[4] Peter F. Drucker, *The Age of Discontinuity* (New York: Harper and Row, 1968), p. 234.

[5] Amitai Etzioni, "The Third Sector and Domestic Missions," *Public Administration Review*, July/August 1973, pp. 314–22.

[6] *The New York Times*, February 13, 1978, p. A20.

[7] *Ibid.*, August 9, 1977, Op Ed page.

10. PROSPECTS AND POSSIBILITIES

[1] *The New York Times*, June 29, 1978.

[2] See *The Crisis of Democracy, a Report on the Governability of Democracies to the Trilateral Commission* for a fuller presentation of Huntington's views as well as an excellent analysis, from this perspective, of the situation in Europe by a French sociologist, Michel Crozier (New York: New York University Press, 1975).

[3] Robert L. Heilbroner, *Business Civilization in Decline* (New York: Norton, 1976).

[4] *The Washington Post*, December 12, 1978.

[5] Richard Cornuelle, *De-managing America* (New York: Random House, 1975).

[6] For a brief statement of this theme, on which Rothman has published extensively, see *The New York Times*, March 7, 1978, p. 35.

[7] Sheldon Wolin, "Carter and the New Constitution," *New York Review of Books*, June 1, 1978.

[8] *The Future of Voluntary Organizations—Report of the Wolfenden Committee* (London: Croom & Helm, 1978).

[9] From a transcript made available by Governor Brown's office.

[10] Amitai Etzioni, "The Third Sector and Domestic Missions," *Public Administration Review* (July/August 1973), pp. 314–22.

[11] Peter L. Berger and Richard John Neuhaus, *To Empower People*, American Enterprise Institute for Public Policy Research, Washington, D.C., 1977.

[12] Sir W. J. Ashley, ed., *Principles of Political Economy, with Some Applications to Social Philosophy* (New York: Augustus M. Kelley, 1961), p. 978.

Index

Academic excellence, 74
Accountability, 39, 192-93, 212; in government, 23-24, 189, 205; in higher education, 32-33, 66-67; in science, 83, 85, 86, 89, 96, 194-96; in health field, 117; of institutions, 157, 160, 199; plane of, 197; of Third Sector, 207, 215-17
ACE. *See* American Council on Education
ACTION, 185, 211
Activists, 5
Adams, John, 33
Adams, John Quincy, 31
Advisory Council on the Arts, 136
Advocacy groups. *See* Social-action movements
AEC. *See* American Medical Association
Aeronautics and Space Engineering Board, 93
Affirmative Action, 66
Agassiz, Louis, 31
Age Discrimination in Employment Act (1967), 66
Agriculture: research in, 80
Alaska pipeline case, 167
Alexander, Donald, 173
Alienation, 24, 230
AMA. *See* American Medical Association

American Academy of Medicine, 44
American Association for the Advancement of Science, 31, 94, 97
American Association of Community and Junior Colleges, 68n
American Association of Fund Raising Counsel, 10-11
American Association of State Colleges and Universities, 68n
American Association of University Professors, 70
American Chemical Society, 81
American Civil Liberties Union, 166, 177
American Council on Education (ACE), 19, 55, 64, 67, 68n
American Federation of State, County, and Municipal Employees, 221-22n
American Federation of Teachers, 70
American Historical Society, 10
American Hospital Association, 112
American Medical Association, 102, 105-16, 118, 204; Board of Trustees, 107; House of Delegates, 107; as political instrument, 108; *Journal*, 108, 110, 112, 113, 114; breakup of monopoly of, 125
American Philosophical Society, 27
American Public Health Association, 116
American Revolution, 157